KARMAPA
The Politics of Reincarnation

Lea Terhune

WISDOM PUBLICATIONS | BOSTON

WISDOM PUBLICATIONS
199 Elm Street
Somerville MA 02144 USA
www.wisdompubs.org

Library of Congress Cataloging-in-Publication Data
Terhune, Lea.
    Karmapa : the politics of reincarnation / Lea Terhune.
        p.   cm.
    ISBN 0-86171-180-7 (pbk. : alk. paper)
    1. Ogyen Trinley Dorje, Karma-pa XVII, 1985– 2. Kar-ma-pa lamas—China—Tibet—Biography. 3. Kar-ma-pa (Sect)—History—20th century. I. Title.
BQ7682.9.A2 O397 2003
294.3´923—dc22

                                                        2003023096

Cover photo of Karmapa by Dieter Ludwig; photo of prayer flags by Robin Bath.

Cover design by Bob Aulicino
Interior design by Jane Gossett. Set in Garamond MT 11/13.

Printed in the United States of America.

KARMAPA

Table of Contents

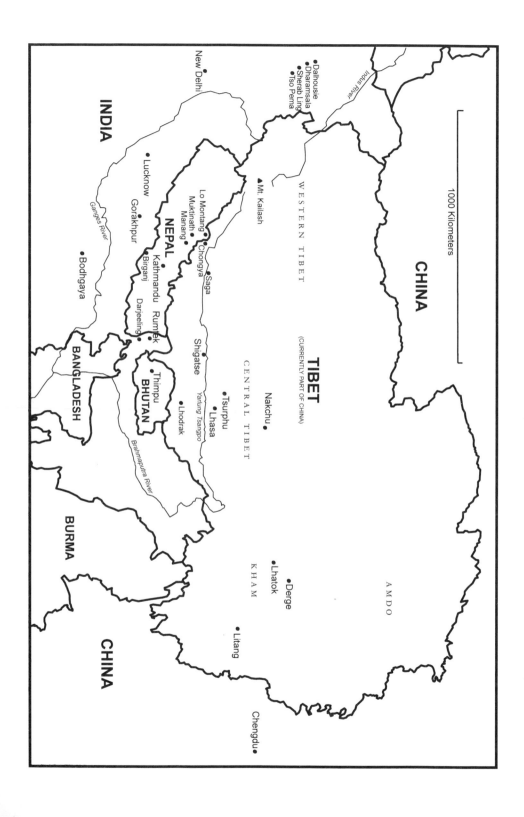

CHINA

1000 Kilometers

INDIA

New Delhi •

Indus River

• Dalhousie
• Dharamsala
• Sherab Ling
• Tso Pema

• Lucknow

Gorakhpur •

Ganges River

• Bodhgaya

NEPAL

Lo Montang
Muktinath
Manang

Kathmandu
Birganj

Darjeeling

Rumtek

Chongya
• Saga

▲ Mt. Kailash

WESTERN TIBET

TIBET
(CURRENTLY PART OF CHINA)

Shigatse

CENTRAL TIBET

Yarlung Tsangpo

Nakchu •

Tsurphu
• Lhasa

BANGLADESH

Thimpu
BHUTAN

• Lhodrak

Brahmaputra River

KHAM

• Lhatok
• Derge

AMDO

BURMA

• Litang

CHINA

Chengdu •

Cast of Characters

Karmapa (A.K.A. Gyalwa Rinpoche)—The Karmapa is the name given to the head of the Karma Kagyu lineage of Tibetan Buddhism. The first incarnation was born in 1110, and successive incarnations are believed to be emanations of the bodhisattva of compassion, Chenrezig. The current, seventeenth Karmapa, Orgyen Trinley Dorje, was born in 1985. His monastic seats are Tsurphu Monastery in Tibet and, in exile, Rumtek Monastery in Sikkim, India.

Shamarpa (A.K.A. Shamar Rinpoche)—An important Karma Kagyu incarnate lama, his current incarnation is usually listed as the thirteenth. The Tibetan government banned his incarnation for 250 years because of the political intrigues of the Tenth Shamarpa. One of the four main disciples, or heart sons, of the Sixteenth Karmapa, he is also a nephew.

Tai Situpa (A.K.A. Situ Rinpoche)—The twelfth and current Tai Situpa is one of the four heart sons of the Sixteenth Karmapa. His monastic seat was Palpung Monastery in Derge, eastern Tibet, and his seat in exile is Sherab Ling Monastery in Himachal Pradesh, India.

Jamgon Kongtrul (A.K.A. Kongtrul Rinpoche)—The Third Jamgon Kongtrul was another of the four heart sons of the Sixteenth Karmapa and an important incarnate lama of Palpung Monastery. He was very close to the Karmapa, having lived with him at Rumtek most of his life. His seat in exile is at Pullahari near Kathmandu, Nepal.

Goshir Gyaltsapa (A.K.A. Gyaltsap Rinpoche)—The traditional regent of Tsurphu Monastery, the Gyaltsapas are one of the chief incarnate lamas of the Karma Kagyu. The Twelfth Gyaltsapa traveled with the Sixteenth Karmapa from Tibet as a child of six and lived most of his life at Rumtek with him.

Amdo Palden—A holy man in Lhatok, Tibet, who advised the parents of the Seventeenth Karmapa and looked after his well-being in the years between the boy's birth and his recognition.

Damchoe Yongdu—The late chandzo, or chief administrator, for the Sixteenth Karmapa, first in Tsurphu. He came out of Tibet with the Karmapa in 1959 and served as chandzo at Rumtek.

Topga Yugyal—A nephew of the Sixteenth Karmapa, he was a scholarly monk at Tsurphu and Rumtek who held the post of Master of Studies until he left the monkhood to marry a Bhutanese princess. He became chandzo of Rumtek after the death of Damchoe Yongdu.

Prologue

At least they didn't have to travel in winter. The way was remarkably smooth under the clear, azure skies of May, with summer just ahead. The sun shone bright in the daytime, with a nip in the air in the shade, a chill in the evening. Snow still lay on mountains above them. The small group of monks were on an unusual mission, yet one that, by necessity, was accomplished time and again over the centuries. They have traveled a thousand miles, guided by a cryptic message:

From here to the north, in the east of the land of snow,
is a country where divine thunder spontaneously blazes.
In a beautiful nomad's place with the sign of a cow
the method is Dondrup and the wisdom is Logala.
Born in the year of the one used for the earth
with the miraculous, far-reaching sound of the white one.
This is the one known as Karmapa.

There was more to the message, but the main concern of the monks grasping this guide in their hands was to find the beautiful nomad's place and locate the boy. Then the rest would explain itself. They had traveled a thousand miles, from Central Tibet to the east, to find him. Asking questions along the way, the monks came to a place called Bakor, the Cow Pasture. In this peaceful nomad's rest in a stony valley greened by flowing streams, they asked more questions. Was there a Mr. Loga here? They had letters for him. No, there was no man named Loga, but there was a woman. One detail of the message confirmed, each said to the other, nodding, encouraged: the mother, the "wisdom," is Loga. What is her husband's name? A natural question. His name is Dondrup. The "method" is Dondrup. The party, containing their excitement, went to meet the couple, who, it was said, had a young son of the right age.

They found a nomad family camped in a meadow where spring flowers were beginning to bloom. The family tended their livestock as they did every year in Bakor, their spring pasture. Only this year the herds were driven there early because of their seven-year-old son. For months he had been saying he was going away. He even went so far as to pack up his belongings and put them on his favorite goat, calling it his mule. He insisted on coming a month early to Bakor, and he became so upset when his parents told him it was too soon that they finally acquiesced. They were puzzled, but there had been signs that this boy was different since his birth. People had heard a conch blown, the sound echoing from the mountains, about the time he was born in their tent in this same spring pasture. He often knew surprising things, sometimes before they happened. Lately he had been saying special prayers and doing other things that made them wonder.

So the family went to Bakor early, and so were there at the appointed place when the search party arrived. The small boy was the one the monks were looking for. This red-cheeked child in scruffy nomad dress, born in the Wood Ox year, was the Seventeenth Karmapa.

Introduction

IT WAS THE LATE 1970S. The fine weather enticed a few lamas, unmistakable in their maroon robes, into the small garden for a stroll. The garden was part of a park that included an aviary near the Karmapa's "summer house," an airy getaway a hundred or so feet up the hill above Rumtek Monastery. There was a view of surrounding green hillsides, which were dotted with the distinctive whitewashed, slate-roofed houses typical of the place. Enjoying a break from their normally rigorous routine, the four young lamas gathered informally around the Karmapa. It was a perfect opportunity for film director Ramesh Sharma, who was there shooting a documentary. The scene was Sikkim, an exquisite Himalayan state in northeast India. The filmmaker captured blithe moments between the guru—the Karmapa—and his four "heart sons,"[1] the young Shamarpa, Tai Situpa, Jamgon Kongtrul, and Gyaltsapa, as they chatted and joked with one another. The film, like amber, preserved the transitory nature of the event.

When I saw this film, *Monastery Wreathed in a Thousand Rainbows,* a few years later at a Buddhist retreat center far away from India, in New York's Catskill Mountains, the world of these lamas seemed like a charmed Shangri-la. It depicted an exalted, exotic family of playful living buddhas. The Karmapa himself was captivating, in his joviality, in his seriousness, in the graceful way he moved his hands, gesturing with ritual implements, reiterating ancient patterns in timeless rhythm. No one knew, of course, that within five years the Karmapa would be dead, at age fifty-nine, with the heart sons embarking upon their own separate enterprises, thereby seeding a new story.

The film wasn't my first contact with the Karmapa. That happened on a dinner date in 1978. For many years before that I had been attracted to Buddhism, particularly that eminently practical and down-to-earth doctrine: "Do not simply believe whatever you are told, or whatever has been handed down from past generations, or what is common opinion, or whatever the scriptures say." The Buddha cautions against accepting something as true "until you, yourselves, directly know" that the principles are wholesome and wise. "Then you should accept and practice them."[2]

Test it and accept only what you know, from your own experience, to be true. This, probably more than anything, awakened my interest in Buddhism. It also guided the evolution of this book, which is an account of the Karmapa, a unique Tibetan proponent of Buddhism. Even before I actually met the Sixteenth Karmapa in person, there was a strong, invisible pull, difficult to describe in practical, nonmystical terms, that drew me inexorably to him and to Tibetan Buddhism. At a Manhattan restaurant one evening, over the tinkle of wine glasses and cutlery, the friend I was dining with mentioned the Karmapa. He described something called the Black Crown Ceremony that he had witnessed some years before. It utterly fascinated me.

Then a chain of coincidences led me to the Karmapa's American center, Karma Triyana Dharmachakra, in Woodstock, New York. This quaint Catskill retreat in 1979 consisted only of an old Victorian hotel that was called in its heyday the Meads Mountain House. After my visit, during which I met the abbot,

Khenpo Karthar, I began attending lectures that Khenpo Karthar regularly gave at the Manhattan Karma Kagyu Center. *Kagyu* is the name of one of the four surviving schools of Tibetan Buddhism, the other three being Sakya, Nyingma, and Gelug. The Karma Kagyu is one of its most important Kagyu subdivisions. Khenpo Karthar was reserved, yet warm, with a no-nonsense manner. He obviously took his vocation as a Buddhist teacher seriously. He was disciplined by many years of study and solitary meditation retreat, a hallmark practice of the Karma Kagyu tradition. It was my first glimpse of a very different world.

New York was alive with eminent Tibetan lamas in those days: the great Sakya scholar Dezhung Rinpoche lived in Seattle and frequently made extended visits to the Sakya center on 125th Street; Dudjom Rinpoche, head of the Nyingma sect, the oldest of the four Tibetan Buddhist schools, stayed with his entourage at the Yeshe Nyingpo center in Manhattan; the Kagyu yogi Kalu Rinpoche had established centers across the United States and periodically came from India to teach at this center in a loft near Union Square; even Tulku Urgyen, who rarely left his meditation retreat in Nepal, came with his son Chokyi Nyima Rinpoche. Geshe Wangyal taught pristine Gelug tenets in nearby New Jersey. There were great opportunities to learn about Tibetan Buddhism from genuine masters who had fled Tibet and who are all now gone.

I had been investigating Buddhism for more than a year when the Sixteenth Karmapa made his third, and last, U.S. visit in May of 1980. The effect was galvanizing. The Karmapa cast a spell of a very high order. It affected everyone he encountered, and was felt and interpreted in just as many individual ways. He insisted on making the tour despite grave illness: a large part of his stomach had been removed to rid him of the cancer that was discovered the year before. Though his face was drawn, his personal power had not diminished a bit. Everybody who could, from the curious off the street to Peter Max and David Bowie, came to see the Karmapa at some point during his last tour of the United States.

Of the many memorable incidents of his visit, one stays in

mind in particular. It was a hot afternoon. A room full of Buddhists and interested bystanders sat quietly crowded together on the polished wood floors of the Karma Thegsum Choling center on 86th and West End listening to him speak. His stay in New York was nearly over. He surveyed the room and said, in the course of his talk, "Your minds are like boiling pots." His delivery was serene, matter-of-fact. It was a hectic time and he was quite right, my mind was—and probably still is—like a boiling pot. His aim seemed so accurate, cutting straight to the heart of the matter. He dispensed gems of insight as easily as he breathed. Such simple wisdom that slices through nonsense, the remarkable individual who offered it, and the fabulous story surrounding his life are what inspires this book.

This book is also a response to the many people who have asked for succinct definitions of Tibetan Buddhism or explanations of the reincarnate lama phenomenon. Meeting this request is a challenge because of the complexity of the subject and because of its paradoxes: the most basic truths of Tibetan Buddhism are simple and crystal clear, but its history and manifestations can be baffling, even contradictory. Most people have heard of the Dalai Lama, but unless they are particularly interested, their knowledge of Tibetan religion and culture stops about there: an occasional news item or an article in *National Geographic*. Others may be informed by fanciful accounts of Tibetan Buddhism provided by movies or by the writings of T. Lobsang Rampa, whom Tibetan scholar Donald S. Lopez calls "the greatest hoaxer in the history of Tibetan Studies."[3] Still others may have attended teachings by Tibetan lamas or spent time exploring the copious literature now available on the subject. The history of the interface between Tibetans and Westerners has been a complex one, and cultural assumptions on either side have led to misunderstandings. Any intelligent assessment of Tibetan Buddhism requires awareness of these cultural contexts.[4]

It was through lamas such as the Sixteenth Karmapa that Westerners first became directly involved with Tibetan Buddhism. After the Sixteenth Karmapa left Tibet for Sikkim in 1959, he gained new audiences in the East and West. His introduction to the West meant that he, his history, and his lineage were perceived by thousands of people who had no accurate frame of reference, who assessed him according to very different criteria, but who also recognized the innate qualities of an extraordinary individual. His story has interested people everywhere, Tibetans and non-Tibetans—perhaps for very different reasons. Though this version is intended for a non-Tibetan audience, it is well to remember that it is, in the end, a Tibetan story.

The story involves Tibetan politics, a subject that at best has been imperfectly understood by outsiders. This leads to another rationale for writing a book about the Karmapa: to rectify, as well as I am able as a non-Tibetan casual scholar, misconceptions about the Karmapa and his lineage. Controversy that erupted during the process of finding and recognizing the Seventeenth Karmapa has muddied the waters about who and what he is. The life of this controversy has flagged, particularly since the Karmapa escaped to India and demonstrated his unique qualities to a broader public. But that a debate over who the real Karmapa is continues at all, even among a small faction, has something to do with the intersection of Tibet and the West, the gap in understanding between two cultures, their differing expectations and worldviews. The highest lamas are never far from politics, even when they do not indulge in them personally. Tibetan religious and political imbroglios typically have roots in incidents hundreds of years past, and are suffused with subtleties beyond the grasp of outsiders. One of the biggest challenges for a Westerner studying Buddhism is coming to terms with these paradoxes, learning to separate the liberating teachings and genuine teachers from the rigid conventions and petty politics that are not necessarily enlightened.

This is not easy. The zap of recognition one experiences when a truth is spoken and heard, or when a person of integrity is met, can be so powerful that it is hard to reconcile subsequently upon learning more of the political context. It is like that with the Karmapa. I feel quite fortunate to have met two of them. During an audience with the Sixteenth Karmapa on his last visit to the United States, he told me, "You should go to India." Not having any great interest in going to India, I asked why. He said simply, "It's a holy place. It would be good for you to go." The Karmapa died the following year, and I did not see him again, as I had hoped to. But I did go to India in 1982, partly because he had touched me so deeply, and by some quirk of fate I have lived there ever since.

Another reason I decided to go was that I met the Twelfth Tai Situpa, one of the Karmapa's four heart sons, whose lucid presentation of Buddhism convinced me he should write a book aimed at Western students. I wanted to work on it with him, and we eventually did two books.[5] Thus I was drawn into the circle of the Karma Kamtsang—a name for the Karmapa's branch of the Kagyu lineage. Resources and circumstances came together so that I could go to India in October 1982 on a pilgrimage of sorts in memory of the Sixteenth Karmapa who had moved me so unaccountably. The Rumtek chief administrator, Damchoe Yongdu, invited me to come see the Karmapa's projects and perhaps write a few fundraising brochures. I did not intend to stay longer than a three or four months.

My close association with the Karma Kagyu lineage has offered me an unusual view of the inner workings of Tibetan monastic and lay life over time. It allowed me to witness first-hand much of the story that is the subject of this book. It is the result of research, interviews, personal experiences, and many years of study of Tibetan Buddhist philosophy, culture, and history. Every effort has been made to accurately reflect the events related to the Karmapa and the aspects of Tibetan culture and religion that are relevant to the story.

The current, seventeenth Karmapa, Orgyen Trinley Dorje, was born in 1985. He was recognized and enthroned in Tibet in 1992. He made good a harrowing escape over the mountains to Nepal and from there to India in January 2000. This book is about him. As the seventeenth in a lineage of adepts, he is believed to represent the sum total of the Karmapas' cumulative experience and attainment. He is revered as the same entity, in fact, one who incarnates again and again to help others.

6

To understand this reincarnate lama business, one needs some grounding in Tibetan religion, history, and politics. It is necessary to look at how the tradition of *tulkus,* or incarnate lamas, began. Who were the first ones, and how did they behave? The story of the progenitors of the Kagyu school is a good place to find out. With the Karmapas came the Tibetan practice of "recognizing" incarnate lamas. Their line of incarnations has spanned a millennium, and each Karmapa played a significant role in his time. After the death of the Sixteenth Karmapa in 1981, something unprecedented took place. His heart sons had to find the next Karmapa while living in exile. From the time of his death, through the recognition of the Seventeenth Karmapa in 1992, until today, a medieval drama has played itself out that involved the chief tulkus of the Karma Kagyu in both sacred and political pursuits. Now the young Seventeenth Karmapa, frustrated at limitations on his spiritual aspirations in Tibet, having made his dramatic escape at the age of fourteen, studies and grows to adulthood under virtual house arrest in India, thanks to the convergence of both internal Tibetan politics and geopolitics. To quote a Tibetan proverb, *cho chenpo du chenpo,* "In the place where great truth spreads, great evil does also." Difficult for key players, but a colorful tale nonetheless, it is a drama that will continue to play.

While researching for this book, I mentioned to the Seventeenth Karmapa the challenge of presenting all sides of such a complicated story, hoping for some guidance. He offered this advice: "Some people will be pleased, some people will not, but as long as the Dharma [truth] is the overall message, it will be balanced. It should be an impartial account, not partisan." Such is my goal. However, Tai Situ Rinpoche, one of the key figures in this account, is an old, dear friend and teacher, as was the late Jamgon Kongtrul Rinpoche and others. So I cannot claim to have achieved a perfectly neutral perspective. Yet I offer what knowledge that I have acquired through my close proximity to events as they unfolded over two decades to shed some light on a history that has been much distorted in more superficial accounts. I believe that Orgyen Trinley Dorje is indeed the real

Karmapa, and I feel the claims in support of the Shamarpa's candidate are seriously flawed. My assessment is backed up by my longterm experience of the Karma Kagyu lamas, what I see as the balance of the evidence available, and of course the opinion of His Holiness the Dalai Lama.

By recording these events as I have seen them, I hope to clear up misconceptions and present an accurate picture that ultimately will be beneficial.

Lea Terhune
New Delhi, 2003

Informal portrait taken at Gyuto Monastery, 2001
(Photo by Angus MacDonald)

1. Against All Odds

"The possibility of study and practice of Buddhism in Tibet was limited and could not satisfy what I wanted. As a Tibetan I must study the literature of Tibet and I must study the philosophy of Buddhism. To do that I came to India."
— *Orgyen Trinley Dorje*[6]

CLEARLY, SOMETHING WAS UP. Usually spare and serene, today the Gyuto Monastery shrine room was festooned with microphones. Sheet-swathed tables fanned out before the large, gilt statue of the Buddha. Chairs had been rented for the occasion from the local "tent wallah" who supplied the booming marriage trade in Sidhabari, a village seven kilometers from Dharamsala. Seated or milling about were an uncharacteristically subdued group of about a hundred journalists. It was a safe bet that none of them had ever been to a press conference quite like this before. Enormous *tangkas*—Tibetan scroll paintings—had been hung up for the event, creating an odd mix of the secular and religious. Tibetan flute music trilled over the sound system provided by the Tibetan Institute of Performing Arts. Beneath a large portrait of the Dalai Lama propped upon a six-foot-high, brocade-bedecked throne was a regular chair, also draped with bright red and gold brocade. As soon as the tall young man walked in from a side door and seated himself, there was a rush forward by photographers to get pictures and producers to position their mikes on the carved, gaily painted Tibetan table in front of him. Security guards discreetly moved to quell the commotion. Unruffled, he surveyed the crowd with large, dark, and penetrating eyes.

The Seventeenth Karmapa Orgyen Trinley Dorje had been in India for fifteen months, having fled Tibet in the closing days of 1999. He had appeared in Dharamsala on January 5, 2000, to the cheers of some and the immense consternation of others. The escape had come to light within days: a high lama, a mere adolescent, had made his way with five companions over a difficult route from Tibet to India. It was an ordeal of mythic proportions. A few days after word of his arrival in Dharamsala had leaked out, journalists were camped outside his hotel. Details were sketchy. Both the Indian government and the Tibetan administration forbade press access to the lama or any of his party. It was known that he was fourteen years old, one of the three most important lamas in Tibet, and that he had made the difficult journey with his companions overland from his monastery near Lhasa into Nepal. From there they came to India.

This boy, Orgyen Trinley Dorje, was the Karmapa, head of an important order of Tibetan Buddhism, the Karma Kagyu. Who was he, what was the nature of his relationship to the Dalai Lama, what was his importance in the Sino-Tibetan picture, and how had he managed such a daring escape were only a few of the questions that arose. In the eyes of the Indian government, his escape was a serious development that called for the keenest diplomacy. This young man was the only incarnate lama selected through the traditional process whose recognition was both confirmed by the Dalai Lama and sanctioned by the Chinese. He was no ordinary refugee. He was a potential international incident. Furthermore, the Karmapa has a large following of non-Tibetan Buddhists scattered around the world, in Europe, North America, Australia, and Southeast Asia. As if this were not enough, there was a faction within his own religious order trying to lay claim to the Karmapa's property in the name of a rival candidate introduced by the Shamarpa, a dissenting lama. Such considerations ensured that the story of his escape hit the front pages across the globe.

The months following his defection found him virtually a prisoner at Gyuto Monastery. The monks there offered him their hospitality after his escape. This turned into a kind of incarceration, partly because of Indian government fears of political ramifications, and partly out of concern for the Karmapa's welfare. To his surprise, not only was he denied access to Rumtek, his own monastery in Sikkim, but he was also prevented from even visiting nearby Sherab Ling, the monastery of one of his most important teachers, the Twelfth Tai Situpa. At last, in February 2001, the Karmapa was officially granted refuge by the Indian government. Shortly thereafter, he was allowed to make a pilgrimage to sacred Buddhist sites, which was one of his stated goals for fleeing Tibet. But he had not officially spoken to the media. This was his first press conference, more than a year after his escape.

The Karmapa had the full attention of the journalists. After reading a statement describing his escape and his reasons for it, he coolly fielded questions with deftness stunning in one so young. Mid-meeting a thunderstorm broke. Sheets of rain curtained the view outside. A bolt of lightening struck the roof and the power went out. Thunderclaps resounded through the hall. A generator fired up and kept the mikes going. Then the sun came out and produced a rainbow nearby. The electricity was restored and everything returned to normal. If it had been during a village birth in Tibet, residents might have started talking about the powerful omens and what they portended. The teenage Karmapa sat through it all, including a few mildly hostile questions from the press corps, unmoved.

The Karmapa's escape from Tibet had always been contemplated. A lot of people wondered why he hadn't been smuggled out right away, before the Chinese knew of his recognition. Others, like most of the chief lamas of his Karma Kagyu lineage, felt that he was born in Tibet for a reason, and that perhaps he should stay there until he chose to leave. The will of a Karmapa is said to be a mystical thing, associated with the belief that he is an enlightened being, proven again and again over the centuries. Even a Karmapa in the years of his minority is credited with wisdom beyond the average child. A *bodhisattva,* which is what he is believed to be, takes birth wherever he chooses and consciously knows his own destiny as a spiritual leader. Disciples believe his actions, including his birth in Tibet, may be for reasons beyond their ken. At the time he appeared, the Chinese were undergoing a dramatic liberalization process, which appeared to include a policy of religious freedom. Perhaps the Karmapa planned to restore Buddhism in Tibet, a dearly held dream of many Tibetans.

Less than a year after the Seventeenth Karmapa's enthronement, and years before his defection, the Dalai Lama expressed his doubts about the young lama's situation in an interview in Dharamsala.[7] "My real worry is that now the Chinese will try to manipulate him," he said, adding that he didn't feel the Chinese would allow the Karmapa to leave so easily as the Kagyu lamas hoped. "They will use every means to brainwash him and then occasionally let him go to the outside world to tell people that inside Tibet religion is completely free, that the situation there is very good, that the Dalai Lama is a splittist, and some such things. I think this would not be of much benefit to the Chinese, but it would be very harmful to the Karmapa." The way the Chinese are handling it, he said, "clearly shows their attitude certainly comes not out of respect but out of some political motivation." He warned Tai Situpa about this, he said, and added, "Now Karmapa Rinpoche must be brought outside [to India]." Eight years later, the Karmapa echoed the Dalai Lama's words during his first press conference on that warm April day in Sidhabari. "I heard it said that in a sense the government of China would make use of me. I was certainly treated very well on a tour I made of China. But I suspected there might be a plan to separate the Tibetan people from the Dalai Lama through me," he told journalists.

Now that the Karmapa was in India, those concerned about his welfare and his education could rest more easily. He could receive teachings from the appropriate teachers of his lineage and be looked after properly. Fears had grown, with the passage of time, that he was in danger in Tibet. Once in India, he immediately resumed his studies. But although his teachers, including Tai Situpa, visited frequently, staying with him for extended periods, his own travel was severely restricted by the Indian government. Not being allowed to go to his monastery Rumtek, or even Sherab Ling, "is confusing to me," the Karmapa admitted. It ironically replicated his circumstances in Tibet.

The reason given for these strictures is "security," and indeed, the Indian government has cause to be cautious. People alleged to be Chinese agents are apprehended from time to time. It is easy for them to cross the border into India posing as Tibetan refugees. Relations with China have thawed only since the Soviet Bloc disintegrated. India was an ally of the U.S.S.R., often at odds with the Chinese. There were disputes with China over Himalayan borders: China did not formally acknowledge the northeastern state of Sikkim as part of India, and the fact that China issued maps showing parts of India belonging to China helped spark the Sino-Indian war in 1962. Tensions have eased greatly since then, but troops are still posted along the Indo-Chinese border on both sides. The Chinese government was not pleased about the Karmapa's escape. Allied with the Dalai Lama the Karmapa becomes a potential weapon turned against them in the Sino-Tibetan propaganda war. If India wanted to retain both good relations with China and their reputation as a refugee haven for Tibetans, including their Nobel Peace Prize–winning leader, the Dalai Lama, they had to tread carefully.

Alongside the international concerns are the more internal, Kagyu politics. Within the Kagyu order a faction led by one of its chief tulkus, the Shamarpa, opposed the Karmapa's recognition, selecting a rival Karmapa candidate of his own. He has relatively few supporters among Tibetans and holds court mainly in Europe, particularly in Denmark, Germany, and France. This group has made no secret of its animosity, circulating books promoting their view and planting stories in the media antagonistic to the Karmapa. In Sikkim and other parts of India, associates of the Shamarpa have filed court cases to gain control of the Karmapa's assets in Sikkim and New Delhi. The group, years ago, took over the Karmapa's International Buddhist Institute (KIBI) in New Delhi. The Shamarpa's faction has the ear of some bureaucrats in the Indian Home and External Affairs ministries, and over the years they have sown sufficient doubt in the halls of already nervous ministries to keep the Karmapa, for all intents and purposes, under house arrest. Feeding suspicions about how and why the Karmapa escaped, they characterized him and his close associates, particularly Tai Situpa, as treacherous. The group likes to portray Tai Situpa and others involved in the Karmapa's recognition as Chinese agents—including, oddly, the Dalai Lama himself. When asked by a journalist if it was true that Tai Situpa is a Chinese agent, the Karmapa responded, "I repeatedly asked the Chinese government to invite him so I could receive teachings, but they refused to allow it because Situ Rinpoche had too close a connection to the Dalai Lama. Now if he was such as you say, I would think they would have been delighted to let him in."

Early in the summer of 1998 the Karmapa insisted on going to his summer house some distance away from the main monastery at Tsurphu. Like his predecessor, he is strong willed, and although his monk attendants respect his whims, they still try to dissuade him if they feel there is a good reason. In this case, they told the young lama to wait another week or so because the road was washed out. Let the repair work be done first, they said. The Karmapa set off anyway, on foot, determined to do a week of meditation retreat, which he did. A few days after his departure, one of his attendants went into the room next to the Karmapa's bedroom on an errand. Books and baggage were kept there, and as he was looking around, he stumbled upon more than he bargained for. Amid some stored bedding he saw the hair on the top of a human head. Three sleeping men, apparently Chinese, were hidden among the boxes. The monk raised an alarm and other monks ran to his aid. They detained the men and found some suspicious items upon their persons—wires, wire-cutters, some "black dough" wrapped in plastic bags, and small electronic devices. The local police were informed and quickly came to the scene. The men were taken away, along with their paraphernalia. The worried monks were told the intruders were thieves. The police added a warning that the monks were not to say a word about the incident to anyone or there would be trouble. The head of the Lhasa police reportedly said the culprits were later sent to Beijing.

Details of the story came out when two monks who had been at Tsurphu at the time left Tibet. The general suspicion at Tsurphu was that it was an attempt to assassinate the Karmapa, because the men were literally lying in wait for the Karmapa's return from his retreat.[8] Who was behind the intrusion is anyone's guess, whether an element of the Chinese government unhappy with the Karmapa or otherwise. But, together with stepped-up religious suppression in Tibet, the incident fueled anxieties for the Karmapa and his monks and gave impetus to an escape plan.

By 1999 Tai Situpa knew that the Karmapa wished to escape, however he says he did not think it would be so soon. According to Tai Situpa, he sent a message to the Karmapa in the summer of 1999 in which he expressed concern for the Karmapa's safety. The older lama cautioned him that escape was dangerous and he should not try it unless he felt it was his only option and was convinced it could be accomplished safely. If he did decide on that course, he should do it only after verifying through prayer, meditation, and divination that nothing would go wrong.

When two monks from Tsurphu requested permission to make a routine business trip that would take them near the Nepal border in the autumn of 1999, their unremarkable request was granted. It was perfectly normal to travel for monastery business, be it for fundraising or for purchasing supplies. What the Chinese authorities did not know was that Nenang Lama and Tsultrim Gyaltsen were on a reconnaissance mission for a perilous enterprise: the escape of the Karmapa.[9] The route for their journey was determined after several weeks of deliberation. Only a few people besides the Karmapa knew about the planned escape beforehand. The Karmapa's tutor Lama Nyima and his attendant knew of his desire to escape. Lama Nyima suggested Nenang Lama as a reliable person to effect a plan, since he had experience managing Nenang Monastery affairs and was loyal to the Karmapa. The Karmapa commissioned Nenang Lama to make the arrangements, and Nenang Lama enlisted the help of two trusted associates, Tsultrim Gyaltsen and Gelek Konchok. According to Nenang Lama, they swore an oath not to disclose the plan to anyone until it had been executed and the Karmapa was safe. The Karmapa had given them only two months to conceive and execute the task. He wanted to be in India by Tibetan New Year in early February. They knew full well that odds were against success, but their faith in the Karmapa inspired them, Nenang Lama said afterward.

The reconnaissance trip had shown them it could take at least ten days, if not longer, even in the newly purchased Mitsubishi land cruiser. The route to the Nepal border at Mustang was longer than other possible routes, but it was safer. There were fewer checkposts, and those that were there often went unmanned, perhaps because the road was poorly maintained.

The Karmapa poses in his travel disguise on a road in Tibet.

Their trip took them as far as Lo Montang, just across the border in Nepal, where they found that an ordinary business travel permit was all that was necessary to give them entree. Passports were not required. The two monks made careful notes and photographed all installations that could pose a threat to their enterprise. They reported back to the Karmapa.

Tsultrim Gyaltsen and Nenang Lama bought provisions for the trip in Lhasa. As far as the authorities were concerned, it was to be a routine fundraising trip. Nenang Lama let it be known that he had to go to Nakchu for business, and told his driver Tsewang Tashi it might take fifteen days. The appointed day for departure was December 28th. The Karmapa repaired to his rooms for an eight-day meditation retreat, during which only Tupten his cook and Lama Nyima his tutor could meet him. This was also routine. The Karmapa frequently went into short retreats, so his absence from view would not raise suspicion.

Darkness falls late in Tibet. All territories in the People's Republic of China observe Beijing time. So the sun set on Tsurphu at 9:30 P.M. on December 28th. At 10:30 P.M., when the Karmapa and his elderly attendant Gelek Konchok dropped down the eight feet from the window of his room to the roof below, it was still light. The night was clear and cold. They had changed from their maroon monk's robes to civilian clothes. The Karmapa wore a navy down jacket, running shoes, a hat, scarf, and spectacles. The Mitsubishi was parked behind the monastery, the driver and Tsultrim Gyaltsen waiting inside. The Karmapa and his attendant made their way across the roof of a shrine room that slopes down to the back of the monastery. While they were on the roof of the shrine, a sentry monk was on rounds below. To warn the Karmapa of this peril and to distract the sentry, Lama Tsultrim shouted to the monk, "Have you seen my driver?" The Karmapa and his attendant crouched on the roof until the guard had gone. At last they reached the lower roof, where a short jump brought them to the land cruiser. Though the Chinese posted guards at the monastery, they did not work around the clock. The party avoided any confrontation by exiting by a side road. They were to rendezvous with Nenang

Lama and another driver at Tolong, some fifty kilometers down the road.

"We were worried and tense as we waited," said Nenang Lama, "asking ourselves, could they get out of the room? As far as the car? Once in the car, would anyone follow? Each moment was drawn out endlessly with worry." Nenang Lama had come with the provisions and his driver in a taxi to the rendezvous point, which was just a stretch of open road. It was on this lonely highway where Tsewang Tashi, the driver, who until now had been kept in the dark about the real destination, was told what was going on. Fortunately, he readily agreed to go along with the plan. "He was my man. I knew we could trust him," Nenang Lama said. The Mitsubishi bearing the Karmapa, Nenang Lama, Lama Tsultrim Gyaltsen, Gelek Konchok, the drivers Dhargye and Tsewang Tashi, arrived on schedule. The provisions were hurriedly loaded and the six took off, driving all night and the next day until almost midnight. They took back roads to avoid notice. Luckily, they were not stopped by patrols checking identification. The checkposts were all unmanned.

They were particularly cautious near the two big military posts along their route. When they came to the first post at Saga, they waited until 1:30 A.M. before going past the camp to minimize the danger of discovery. Four of them, including the Karmapa, got out of the car and walked toward the mountain in the darkness. Night in the Tibetan countryside, where there is no electric light pollution, is about as dark as it can get. Tsewang Tashi and Lama Tsultrim Gyaltsen drove past the camp, which was about a kilometer from the road, with the vehicle headlights turned off. The cold was extreme. In this high Himalayan desert, at night, in the dead of winter, their breath formed wispy clouds in front of their faces. The four on foot faced a climb over a steep, trackless mountain full of thorny bushes. They all got cuts on their hands as they clawed their way through the thick shrubbery. It took four hours to walk the seven kilometers across the valley and more than an hour for them to find the car. "It was a scary few hours. Dawn was coming soon. We thought we had missed each other, or else that the others had been caught," Nenang Lama recalls. He said the Karmapa looked worried, "but he told us 'don't worry, we'll meet the car.'" As far as they were concerned, there was no turning back, and they were "determined to go for it" on foot, if necessary. They followed the main road, and once they reached it, they looked for the land cruiser. It wasn't there. But after another seeming eternity they finally saw the land cruiser coming slowly toward them in the dark. It had passed them in the blackness and come back to look for them along the road. "It was a big relief," Nenang Lama continued. "I personally thought the driver and Lama Tsultrim Gyaltsen had been caught." But they were reunited and continued cautiously on their way.

They reached the second army camp, Chongya, two hours later. It was farther from the road than the Saga camp, and so less risky. It was still early morning, no one was about, so they took a chance and drove on through. No one stopped them. The border to Mustang was at Nyichung, and they reached it and crossed without incident. Again, no one was there to check their papers. They sailed across the border. It was the morning of December 30, 1999.

Once they were safely on the Nepal side, they decided it was best to abandon the car. The road was bad and quickly got worse as it became a track into the mountains. Also, they had no permits. The monks left the land cruiser with a family, asking them to keep it for a few days while they went on some business. They then hired horses for their journey to Lo Montang. It is arid, high country, its stony trails well above 10,000 feet elevation. After a two-hour ride on mountain paths, they arrived at the house of a Kagyu follower in Lo Montang who put them up for the night. The group had a few hours to relax for the first time since they left Tsurphu.

The next morning they started out again on horseback but ended up making most of the trip on foot. The terrain was steep for the horses, so the party dismounted and went on foot, leading the horses. The travelers clambered over swaths of scree. They passed occasional villages along the trail. The most important on the route was the pilgrimage town Muktinath, where

The rugged trail to Manang, traversed on pony and foot.

Hindus and Buddhists throng to worship the temple's sacred fire, which is fueled by gases coming out of the rocks. But the escape party bypassed this town, not wanting to draw any attention to themselves.

The highest pass the Karmapa and his companions crossed was Torang-la at 17,650 feet, resting in the shadow of the great peaks of the Annapurna range. Providentially, there was no snow on the pass. Locals told them that for several years previous the weather had been very bad. It is a place known for sudden snowstorms that claim the lives of the unwary. They were lucky. The top of the pass is marked, as is the custom, by a large cairn. Travelers add stones to the pile or tie scarves for a lucky journey, and to placate the nature spirits who rule the high places. "This part was extremely difficult and exhausting," the Karmapa later said, "due to the poor and often dangerous condition of the paths and the freezing cold weather. During this time, I was tired and not very well physically." The high altitude took its toll on him. He added, "Despite the difficulties, I was completely determined to reach my goal." They trekked through the alpine ter-

On horseback, the
Karmapa leads the
monks past a stupa in
Mustang, Nepal.

rain, dry because it is shielded from rain by the "monsoon shadow" provided by the towering mountains. They passed cave-perforated ancient cliffs. Scree spilled over the track between clumps of scrub. The party reached Manang at 7:30 in the evening and checked into a travelers' lodge. They might have been an ordinary group of trekkers but for their unseasonable appearance there.

In Manang were friends. A five-hundred-year-old Kagyu monastery is one of several in the vicinity. An acquaintance of Nenang Lama's had arranged for a helicopter "taxi" to pick them up, a standard form of transport in this area for those who can afford it. The only other way out is on foot or pack animal. Five days after they set out, on January 2, 2000, a Fishtail Air helicopter arrived to fly them to Nagarkot, near Kathmandu. It was a small helicopter so two trips were necessary. Once in Nepal, they made two significant phone calls. One was to Tsurphu, where they found to their dismay that their escape had been discovered.

The Karmapa
and one of his
attendants
board the
Fishtail Air
helicopter taxi
in Manang.

They also notified their contact in India that the Karmapa would soon be there.

From Nepal the way was comparatively easy. The Karmapa was eager to reach India, so they did not tarry in Nepal. They traveled by taxi to the border at Birganj, where they paid the customary bribes that ease the way for those without proper documents and crossed to Raxaul in India. Then they, like many travelers before them, hailed another taxi to take them to the railhead at Gorakhpur. From there they boarded the train to Lucknow. It was 1:00 A.M. when they emerged onto the platform under the dim, orange lights of the Lucknow train station, where nimble tea vendors shouted, inevitably, "Chai! Chai garam!" But the Karmapa and his monks looked for something other than tea at that moment. Their arrival was expected. Somewhere among the swarm of bobbing heads and luggage hefted on shoulders were those who would take them to their final destination, the hill station of Dharamsala, where the Dalai Lama lives and maintains his government-in-exile. The two parties missed each other on the crowded platform, but eventually met. Hiring two taxis, the exhausted group drove with only a few tea stops from Lucknow to Delhi,

The Dalai
Lama greets
the
Seventeenth
Karmapa in
India.

a trip of twenty-four hours through the vast state of Uttar
Pradesh.

The Karmapa, impatient to get to his goal, did not want to
stop. So in Delhi they hired new taxis for the final leg of the
journey to Dharamsala, about twelve hours, which took them
through the fertile plains of the Punjab and up into the hills and
hairpin turns of Himachal Pradesh. The only mishap of the
entire journey came on the winding road to Dharamsala. The
Karmapa's taxi drove into a ditch in the fog. It was a minor incident, however, and no one was injured. They made it to McLeod
Ganj, the Tibetan settlement above the town of Dharamsala, at
10:00 A.M. It was January 5th.

After traveling nearly nonstop for eight days, rarely stopping
even to sleep, they were exhausted but happy. They had reached
their once improbable goal. They first checked into the Bhagsu
Hotel. But before resting, and with untreated abrasions on his
hands and feet, the Karmapa and his party went to meet the
Dalai Lama. "Immediately after arriving," the Karmapa said, "I
went straight to meet His Holiness the Dalai Lama," adding,
"He is the very embodiment of compassion. He received me
with extraordinary love and affection. My joy knew no bounds."

The Dalai Lama knew that the Karmapa was going to escape. He was not told the exact details beforehand, he says, but he was expecting the young lama because Tai Situpa had come to Dharamsala a day or so previously to inform him that he had received news that the Karmapa had escaped. Nenang Lama recounts that when the two eminent lamas met, a common understanding and natural affection was evident. "The Karmapa has great respect for the Dalai Lama, and when they met the Dalai Lama stood up and they held hands for a long time. The Dalai Lama welcomed him wholeheartedly and said, 'Well done.'"

After the meeting the party was moved from the Bhagsu Hotel to Chonor House, the official guesthouse of the Tibetan government-in-exile. It is a pleasant place, done up in colorful Tibetan style, and is a short walk from the Dalai Lama's own residence on a neighboring hill. The Karmapa was examined by a doctor and found to be fit, except for cuts and bruises, exhaustion, and insufficient nourishment. Tai Situpa was contacted and immediately came over from Sherab Ling, about seventy kilometers away—a two-hour drive on country roads. After meeting Tai Situpa, it was time for the Karmapa to rest. He was at last able to sleep in safety, which he did, for a good twelve hours. He had made it against all odds. The third most important incarnate lama of Tibet was now a refugee in India.

The Karmapa and the Dalai Lama with other refugees. On the far right is the Karmapa's sister, Ngodup Palzom, who had arrived separately. Nenang Lama is on the Karmapa's right.

2. Tibet, China, and Politics

"The Living Buddha has simply gone abroad."
—China Daily, *January 2000*

SETTLEMENTS WERE SMALL and remote from each other. The vast open spaces separating these sparse knots of civilization encompassed thousands of square miles of harsh terrain: plains, impassable deserts, and the highest mountains in the world. Nevertheless, a surprising amount of political interaction was sustained over the centuries between Mongolia, China, and Tibet. History tells of warfare, treaties, marriages, and tributes— and the entwined political relationships of the region had much to do with high lamas and their monasteries.

The Karmapas, in the course of their successive incarnations, did their share of low-key political intervention to quell hot tempers of warlords, although they remained principally religious leaders. They were politically important because the Karmapa was an influential figure in an emphatically theocratic state. When outsiders dealt with Tibet, they had to deal with incarnate lamas like the Karmapa if they wanted to get anywhere. While the Karmapa himself might have a purely spiritual function, his

Karma Kagyu lineage was politically powerful. And although the Karmapas generally strove to avert sectarian conflicts, there were those of his adherents, high lamas among them, who sought to politicize the lineage in bitter rivalries against other orders. The Gelug order and the Dalai Lama, which eventually came to rule Central Tibet, became a particular target. Of course, the Kagyupas were not alone in this. Every sect had its politicians along with its saints, and it was not always easy to distinguish between the two.

The four main schools of Tibetan Buddhism, also referred to as lineages, orders, or sects,[10] have already been mentioned: Nyingma, Sakya, Kagyu, and Gelug. The Kagyupas[11] predated the Gelugpas, and so did their power. Kagyu hierarchs were not rulers of Tibet, as were the Sakyapas and Gelugpas, but they had powerful kings as patrons. The Pagmodrupa, Rimpungpa, and Tsangpa dynasties, whose combined tenure dominated Central Tibet for nearly three hundred years between 1350 and 1623, were staunch Kagyu supporters. Even after the Gelug government was well established in central Tibet, eastern Tibet remained a Kagyu and Nyingma stronghold. In the old days, "Tibet" referred to the provinces of U and Tsang—central Tibet. It was there, after the ascent of the Dalai Lamas, where the Gelug government could really call the shots. Outside that sphere, in outlying areas like Kham, Amdo, Golok, and Lhatok, kings and tribal chieftains ruled autonomously, in ways not so different from the old Scottish clans, with analogous incidences of interclan warfare. They pledged deep-rooted allegiance to lamas and monasteries, and the religious order that retained the greatest power outside of central Tibet, generally, was the Kagyu.

In the relations between China and Tibet, use of lamas as conduits of political influence was a late development. There are indications that belligerent Tibetan tribes worked away at the borders of China as early as the second century B.C., but Tibet only emerges as a political entity in the seventh century A.D. By then the tribes achieved enough cohesion to mount successful military operations against the Chinese under one leader.

Tibetans were sufficiently forceful that the Tang emperor acceded to their demand that his daughter be given in marriage to the Tibetan king Songtsen Gampo. On one hand it looked like a coup for the Tibetans, and no doubt it was. On the other hand, it put Tibet in a relationship to China that—as always in the Chinese universe vis-à-vis outsiders—could be construed as inferior. To the Chinese emperor, Songtsen Gampo was merely a royal son-in-law. The complexities of Sino-Tibetan relations began in those obscure times, but as Hugh Richardson points out, "Tibet and China, it is clear, were then two powers on an equal footing," something borne out in Tang dynasty records. The communist Chinese later deliberately recast some of that history in their attempts to justify their hold on Tibet."[12]

During all eras the Chinese faced a quirky and sometimes fiercely isolationist Tibetan system, which developed partly as a result of Tibet's extreme geographical features. Tibetan racial origins are vague but are thought to stem from two main strains, one perhaps related to the ancient Turks and Mongols, the other a "proto-Chinese" stock, whose descendants include Chinese, Burmese, and Thais. Tibetan language, in spite of its Sanskrit-based script, is Tibeto-Burman. Their land was thinly populated, and much of that population was nomadic. Tibetans engaged in farming, herding animals, and trade. Besides its military excursions against its neighbors, trade was Tibet's main link to the outer world. Astute business minds built up vigorous trading houses that sold wool, skins, yak tails, salt, and borax to India in exchange for cotton textiles, household goods, and staple foods. From China they obtained the black brick tea they favored, brocade silk, porcelain, and china.

Society in Tibet remained pretty much the same until the mid-twentieth century, so we have a good idea of how it functioned from the highest government official to the lowliest peasant. Serf may be a more accurate designation for this lower rung of a society that resembled, in some ways, the medieval feudal societies of Europe. Although there was, at least in modern times, a middle class of traders, managers, and bureaucrats, Tibet was dominated by landed gentry. Whether these were lay or religious, their estates were worked by people bound to the land. These laborers, who were bonded for life, tilled the fields of the land-lord who customarily provided seed and plow animals. They were allotted a patch of land rent free, but they were paid no wages for the considerable services they performed on the rest of the estate. On the contrary, they were usually taxed, their payments most often rendered in kind. They were expected to serve the landlord according to need. But there were, theoretically, legal agreements that prevented exploitation and, with luck and good management, serfs could become wealthy in their own right. If the feudal lord was just and generous, they could build upon their rightful share of the yield. These landlord-tenant arrangements were not necessarily oppressive, and there was an easy openness between the servant class and nobility. A bad landlord could abuse his power, of course. The state, perhaps, placed the greatest burden upon the serving class: the obligation to provide food and transport animals for traveling aristocrats or others who passed through their neighborhood bearing the proper credentials. From the government's point of view, it was an efficient system for administrating huge expanses of mountain and desert with the least monetary outlay. The onus was on the peasants.[13]

Landlords were often lay aristocrats, but the landlords of largest dominion were the monasteries and incarnate lamas. These religious landlords were significant forces in a country where something like 13 percent of the population—26 percent of the males—adopted the monastic life.[14] Major monasteries were like small towns, housing thousands of inhabitants. They even boasted their own priestly security forces, known as *dobdobs,* or fighting monks, who had their own form of martial arts, occasionally employing the fearsome-looking Tibetan keys they carried as weapons.

There were several reasons to join a monastery. One was religious: obviously, young men drawn to the spiritual life gravitated there. The other was practical. Parents often offered one of their sons to the monastery as a matter of course. They knew that in a monastery their son would be educated and, if he distinguished himself, could rise in position, bringing the family greater influence and status.

There were plenty who joined the monastery for this reason alone because, at least in central Tibet after the Dalai Lama was established as king, the monks had most of the clout. The government was run by parallel administrations comprised of lay nobility on one track and monks from the three most important Gelug monasteries—Ganden, Sera, and Drepung—on the other. The two sets of officials were ultimately supervised by the Dalai Lama, who discharged his role as spiritual and temporal authority with the assistance of this dual bureaucracy. After the death of a Dalai Lama and before a new incarnation reached majority, the government was ruled by a monk regent. Usually a lay chief minister presided over the *kashag,* or council of ministers. The kashag consisted of four members: three laymen and one monk, who had automatic seniority. These individuals, called *zhabpe* or *kalon,* were counselors to the Dalai Lama. From the kalon radiated the various levels of administration that handled the necessary aspects of governmental management, both lay and religious. A more recent development, dating from the nineteenth century, was the National Assembly, which met only occasionally and consisted of lay and monk officials and abbots of monasteries. Sometimes a larger assembly was called that involved district representatives. Lay and religious officials were recruited, ideally, according to ability, but frequently family connections and bribery played a role.

Economically, the government depended on estates for taxes and fulfillment of service obligations. The monasteries relied for income upon their estates, government grants, and donations from patrons and devotees. Some monasteries were very rich. Melvyn C. Goldstein notes, "Drepung monastery was reputed to have held 185 estates, 20,000 serfs, 300 pastures and 16,000 nomads."[15] Powerful, wealthy families typically were affiliated with particular religious sects and supported them, donating money to colleges that existed within the monasteries. While the role of the lay nobility was to render taxes and join the civil service, the role of the monks and monasteries was to pray for the greater good.

Central to the monastery setup was the institution of incarnate lamas. Each lama had a *labrang,* a group of administrators and adherents, who insured the continuity of the lama's property and wealth and line of incarnations. The labrang kept the incarnate lama's estates intact so that they could be passed on to successive generations of the same incarnation.

The nature of Sino-Tibetan relations is much too complex to discuss adequately here, and it has been further complicated by communist Chinese attempts to rewrite and reinterpret history to suit their own claims upon Tibet. But a brief discussion will be useful for our narrative. The foreign entanglements that began to siphon power away from the Tibetan rulers began with the Mongols. The Mongol rulers traditionally patronized Tibetan lamas of various sects, beginning with the Sakyapas in the mid-thirteenth century. But the Gelugpas eventually cornered this patrimony during several generations of charismatic preachers who traveled to the court of the Mongol Khans. The Gelugpas gained such ascendancy that successive Mongol Khans gave the Dalai Lama his name[16] and appointed him spiritual, and later temporal, ruler of Tibet. Although the suzerainty of the Mongols in China had declined by the time of the Dalai Lama's appointment as supreme ruler, and the Ming emperors had replaced the Yuan dynasty (1279–1368) founded by Kublai Khan, Mongols remained a significant force in their own territories and in Tibet. The Ming dynasty in China was threatened by Manchu tribes consolidated under capable leadership and was eventually overcome by them. The Qing dynasty was established by the Manchus in 1644. Palpable Chinese influence began to be felt in Tibet after the second Qing emperor, Kangxi, sent military aid to Lhasa, which was under attack by the Dzungar Mongols in 1720. It was at this point that influence in Tibet shifted from Mongol to Chinese hands.

A credible commentator of this period is the Jesuit priest Ippolito Desideri, who lived for five years in Lhasa between 1716 and 1721, spoke and read Tibetan fluently, and was at Sera Monastery when the Dzungar Mongols attacked and sacked the city. He recounts the betrayal and downfall of the king, the royal family, and their retainers in detail. Desideri is particularly reliable because of his even-handed assessment of the Tibetans, of whom he was an intimate observer. Throughout his account of their society, customs, and religion, he makes it clear he admired them for their ethics, their religious devotion, and their good works, however much he deplored their penchant for intrigue. He reports that Lhasa was taken by the Mongols "owing to the treachery of a certain number of laymen and lamas who let down ladders and opened the city gates to them."[17] The king's assassination was facilitated by a nobleman who was a relation of the former ruler, killed earlier by the incumbent.

Desideri witnessed the subsequent Chinese military expedition in 1720 and reported that troops were not the only instruments deployed. The Chinese emperor made use of a young boy, who was said to be the reincarnation of "the Grand Lama," (the young Seventh Dalai Lama, Losang Kalsang Gyatso) to gain leverage with the Tibetans and dislodge the Mongols from their influential role in Tibet. The boy was being held captive by the emperor, and Tibetans tried without success to gain access to him. The Tibetans revered the young incarnate lama and feared for his safety. It would be a very ill omen, if not a catastrophe, were anything to happen to him. "Proclamations were addressed to monks, governors and people saying if they wished to fight him they were to join with the treacherous Giongars (Dzungars), but if in this youth they recognized their venerated Grand Lama, they must obey all the commands of the leaders of this army."[18] In case this was not sufficient inducement, the Chinese pressed all men from age twelve into military service. Contrary to Tibetan practice, monks were not excluded, and Desideri himself narrowly escaped forcible conscription.

An imperial edict memorializing these events was inscribed upon a stone pillar at the Jokhang Temple in Lhasa, where it still stands. It was the first in a series of subtle distortions of history that led to the Tibetans being regarded as vassals of the emperors of China, at least by the Chinese themselves. There were at least two ways Sino-Tibetan interactions could be viewed, and the Chinese invariably saw themselves as the overlords; however in the centuries before the twentieth this was more delicately expressed. For the most part Tibetans, while sometimes calling upon the Chinese for military aid, saw them as meddlers and intruders. The generals who arrived from China in 1720 took it upon themselves to revamp the Tibetan government and put a garrison of Chinese soldiers in Lhasa. The troops were withdrawn after Tibetan protests. Instead, civilian ambassadors, or *ambans,* were installed as representatives of the emperor. Shortly thereafter the Chinese attempted to subvert the Dalai Lama's power by inviting him to China, taking him as far as Litang, and preventing his return for seven years. His absence resulted in increased power for the lay officials. It was also around this time that the Chinese began to pit the Panchen Lama—deemed the second most powerful lama in Tibet—against the Dalai Lama by offering the former greater power. This divisive strategy is one the Chinese returned to again and again, long after the emperor had been replaced by the communist politburo.

More than one hundred years after Desideri's stay in Tibet, two Lazarist priests, Abbe Huc and M. Joseph Gabet, visited Tartary, China, and Tibet. Their *Reminisces of Travel* relating their exploits between 1844 and 1846 are entertaining, almost rollicking at times, as they describe some of the characters they meet en route. They give special insight into the politicking of the Chinese ambans in Lhasa because they became embroiled with a supercilious mandarin by the name of Ki-Chan. Ki-Chan disliked exotic foreigners preaching strange religion on what he considered the emperor's turf. He manipulated the priests and the Dalai Lama's regent who had befriended them, forcing them to leave Tibet under Chinese escort. As if that were not enough, Ki-Chan denied them their chosen, shortest route—a trip of about twenty-five days to India—compelling them to go to the far end of China, a journey of eight months. Their appeals to the Tibetan regent were fruitless. Like Desideri, Huc and Gabet are shrewd observers, not given to judgmental analysis of Tibetan ways. They are less prone than the earnest Desideri to refutation of the Tibetans' pagan beliefs, though they too cherished hopes of conversions.

About sixty years before the visit of Huc and Gabet, Englishman George Bogle had visited Shigatse, Tibet's second largest city, as envoy of the East India Company. There he established a rapport with the Panchen Lama and acquired a Tibetan wife. By Huc's time the British had a reputation in Tibet. Huc quotes the head of the affluent Kashmiri community in Lhasa, with whom he was friendly: "He told us the that the Pelings (English) of Calcutta were now the real masters of Kashmir. 'The Pelings' said he, 'are the most cunning people in the world. Little by little they are acquiring possession of all the countries of India, but it is always rather by stratagem than by open force. Instead of overthrowing the authorities, they cleverly manage to get them on their side, to enlist them in their interest. Hence it is that, in Cashmere, the saying is: The world is Allah's, the land the Pasha's; it is the Company that rules.'"[19]

The British, their power already consolidated in India, extended their attention to Tibet by way of self-interest. They were initially attracted to trade in Tibet, since that was the *raison d'etre* of the Calcutta-based East India Company. It was the beginning of what was to be called the "Great Game," a rivalry with Russia, that lasted most of the nineteenth century. To the British, Tibet was an effective buffer zone between India and any foes coming through Central Asia. The Great Game was a long, drawn-out power play between Britain and Russia for dominance in the regions peripheral to India. All the while the ambans remained in Lhasa, continuing to exert their influence on a government that was afraid to alienate the Chinese.

Though there was a constant flow of outsiders through Tibetan territory in the trade caravans traversing the Silk Route, interference from China or anyone else was irksome to the Tibetans and contributed to their xenophobia. But as the Great Game between Russia and Britain intensified, Tibet was less able to escape the attention of foreigners. Russians made overtures to the Tibetan government. The pundit-spies—native Indians employed in espionage by Britain—roamed Tibet, and the British worried about a Buryiat Mongol from Baikal by the name of Agvan Dorjieff who had settled in Lhasa for religious studies and was influential with the Dalai Lama. The British suspected that Dorjieff was a Russian agent. The "pundits" were an interesting breed, most of whom remain unsung. They risked their lives gathering information for their British employers and ranged about Tibet and other parts of central Asia often posing as pilgrims. Tibetan prayer beads and portable prayer wheels concealed their surveying tools. The most famous of these pundits is Tibetan scholar Sarat Chandra Das, who is thought to be the model for Huree Chunder Mookerjee in Kipling's Great Game–inspired *Kim*.

The ins and outs of this drama are complex, but British fears coupled with a changing political climate finally led to its denouement in Colonel Francis Younghusband's mission to Tibet in 1904. Lord Curzon, who was viceroy of India, convinced London that an expedition must be sent to discover Russian intentions and bring the Tibetans into a relationship with Britain. An earlier attempt at this, in 1903, was rebuffed by Tibetans, who wanted to maintain their insularity. The British asked the Tibetan government to send negotiators to Gyantse for talks a second time. Younghusband was sent to negotiate an Anglo-Tibetan agreement in Gyantse, not to kill Tibetans— although Lord Curzon sent soldiers in case military persuasion was required. Gyantse is a town not far from the Sikkim-Tibet border. No Tibetan negotiators turned up, so Younghusband forged ahead to Lhasa. The 1904 Younghusband expedition was disastrous. Hundreds of primitively armed Tibetans attacked the British forces along the way and were killed by the superior army. But the expedition did at least result in dialogue. Hugh Richardson, later British resident[20] in Lhasa, said, "...it must remain a source of great regret that it should ever have come to the use of force against Tibetans,"[21] though he defends Younghusband's actions in the circumstances. Younghusband himself called it "a ghastly business."

In any event, it took a push to Lhasa through charging bands of Tibetan fighters for Younghusband to locate any Tibetan with the power to negotiate. The Dalai Lama and the suspect Dorjieff had fled Lhasa, but the high lama of Ganden Monastery, Ganden Tri Rinpoche, who was acting regent, obtained the authority to sign an Anglo-Tibetan Convention of 1904. This agreement provided for trade mechanisms to be administered by resident British agents at Gyantse, Gartok, and Yatung; it delineated the Sikkim-Tibet border; and it denied other foreign powers political leverage in Tibet. It was a landmark agreement, a culmination of British efforts during the Great Game years. Because of disagreements within the British government, however, much of the positive force of the agreement to promote Tibet as an independent nation was dissipated as subsequent conventions were signed by the British with China in 1906 and Russia in 1907. Although the Tibetans were not consulted in either case, the latter agreements made certain concessions to China that placed the Chinese in a position of power in Tibet that they never, in actuality, held. In the Anglo-Russian agreement the British even agreed to only negotiate with Tibet through the Chinese government. Britain effectively sacrificed most of the hard-won advantages achieved by the 1904 Anglo-Tibetan Convention. Nevertheless, the British gained the confidence of many in Tibet. Wealthy Tibetans began to send their children to the British-run schools in Darjeeling for a Western education. The British lobby achieved a higher profile against the Chinese and Russian contenders for Tibet's hand. The Great Game drew to a close, but an alert China was watching, considering its next move.

Fierce debates continued among the kalons and other officials in Lhasa about whether to interact politically with foreign countries. There were those who wished to relax the restrictions on the entry of foreigners. Sometimes these disputes boiled over into violence. As the Younghusband expedition discovered, the anti-Russian sentiment was as strong as the anti-British in Tibet. And there was, of course, long-term resentment of Chinese interference. It was one thing for Tibetans to ask for help of the larger neighbor in times of war, but another thing altogether when the Chinese tried to usurp power internally and feign control to the world outside. Forward-thinking people who saw change as inevitable and wanted to prepare for it by opening up to new influences were in the minority. They were more likely to be murdered by adamant conservative isolationists than thanked for their liberal views. Tsering Shakya observes in his comprehensive study of Tibet in the latter half of the twentieth century, *Dragon in the Land of Snows,* "Resistance to change came mainly from the religious community, which was opposed to any kind of reform that appeared to diminish its power. High lamas and the monasteries used their enormous influence to obstruct reforms that were desperately needed to transform Tibetan society."[22]

This was no doubt exacerbated by the lack of real consensus among those governing central Tibet. As Goldstein notes, although Tibet "espoused a religious ideology" the Dalai Lama, his three chief abbots, monasteries, and monk officials were often at odds. One of the main officials and a former regent, Demo Rinpoche, went so far at to attempt to assassinate the Thirteenth Dalai Lama through black magic. The Dalai Lama was one of those who favored change. And while there was plenty of infighting among the religious, the lay officials contributed their mite by regularly opposing the monasteries politically while being involved with them on some level as patrons. "In fact, the Tibetan political process was typified by a network of crosscutting interests and alliances," Goldstein writes, with considerable understatement.[23]

Rinchen Dolma Taring, in her autobiography *Daughter of Tibet,* tells of the life of nobility during the early years of the twentieth century, describing some of its darker convolutions as a matter of course. Her own father, Tsarong, was murdered partly because of his openness to foreigners, though the main instigators were apparently jealous colleagues who fell from grace as he gained eminence. Her brother was murdered along with him, presumably to prevent revenge. The irony of the murder is that, had there been more openmindedness like Tsarong's and less petty intrigue, Tibet might have established its independence in time enough to stay out of China's grasp. As it was, progressives like Tsarong were silenced by those fearing loss of money, power, and influence.

The first decade of the twentieth century saw increasing Chinese intrusions into the affairs of Tibet. They tried to

38

manipulate the thirteenth Dalai Lama, declared him to be no more than a vice-regent of the sovereign emperor, and broached Tibet's borders. Chinese military activity in eastern Tibet intimidated the Dalai Lama enough to move him to appeal to Britain for aid against them. Amid a flurry of diplomatic correspondence between Britain, China, and the amban in Lhasa, in 1910 the Chinese general Chung Ying successfully marched into Lhasa in with 2,000 troops. The Dalai Lama fled to India, and the Chinese took over the Tibetan government. On the four previous occasions when Chinese troops entered Tibet, it was with the consent of the Tibetans. For the first time they came as invaders. Although the Chinese tried to enlist the Panchen Lama, inviting him to stay in Lhasa during the Dalai Lama's absence and preside over official functions, the Tibetans were intractable. The Chinese were unsuccessful in controlling things without the Dalai Lama and his ministers, who were all in exile in Darjeeling. The Chinese were expelled by 1912, distracted by revolution in their own territory, as the Qing Manchu dynasty was overthrown and a civil war erupted between revolutionary factions. The Chinese garrisons in Lhasa fell apart through mutiny, desertion, and combat with Tibetans, who objected to Chinese mutineers looting the town. The Thirteenth Dalai Lama returned.

Internal strife occupied the attention of the Chinese for several decades, but they didn't forget about Tibet. In 1949 they turned their eyes westward again and began resolutely to annex Tibetan territory. Unfortunately, Tibet was ill-equipped to meet the threat, and the only powers in a position to help—Britain and the United States—were unwilling, in the end, to support its nationhood.

After ten years of escalating Chinese encroachment, beginning with the imposition of "reforms" by a communist Chinese bureaucracy in "cooperation" with the Tibetan government, and the importation of large numbers of the Peoples Liberation Army—so many that the always meager natural resources of Tibet were severely strained—China held Tibet in a stranglehold. The Thirteenth Dalai Lama had died in 1933, and the young Fourteenth Dalai Lama, born in 1935, occupied the throne. He and his government strove to counter the Chinese moves, but in vain. As early as 1950 the PLA began attacking outposts in eastern Tibet, later destroying monasteries and killing monks and civilians. Khampas—the inhabitants of Kham, or eastern Tibet—sent alarming messages, but an indecisive cabinet in Lhasa failed to respond. As the Chinese became more aggressive, more people fled across the border to India, Nepal, and Bhutan. The excruciating process of occupation culminated in March of 1959, in what Tibetans call the Uprising, when the people of Lhasa rebelled, not only against the Chinese, but perhaps equally against the Tibetan officials they felt had betrayed them.[24] The Chinese shelled Lhasa. The Dalai Lama fled to India.

In the years following the Dalai Lama's arrival in India, Chinese and Tibetan attitudes toward each other became entrenched in a propaganda war. The Dalai Lama reconstituted his government in exile. He re-appointed his cabinet, the kashag. He expanded the kashag and endeavored to make it more democratic. Now the members of the kashag are elected. The role that has evolved for the Tibetan exile government in India is to look after Tibetan refugees, who still straggle in from Tibet. And it maintains the polemic against China. The Dalai Lama himself is a dual emissary: he represents Buddhism and peace, but he also keeps the issue of Tibet alive on the world stage. China, for its part, keeps up the propaganda against the Dalai Lama and the Tibetan freedom movement, while it continues to manipulate the institutions in Tibet—incarnate lamas and monasteries—in which Tibetans have confidence. In many ways the Tibetan and Chinese propaganda are two sides of the same coin, the coin of mythology, as Tsering Shakya cogently points out: "Neither the Tibetans nor the Chinese want to allow any complexities to intrude on their firmly held beliefs. This has resulted in what I have called 'denial of history,' in which responsibility is abdicated." He continues, "It is difficult for the Tibetans to admit that they were not merely a passive agent in their recent history or that there was a much more complex issue surrounding the relationship between Tibet and China." In the same way, China denies that the Tibetans have any perspectives of their own, because that would be admitting they might have had a separate identity from China.[25]

The closing decades of the twentieth century have seen the Chinese liberalize and then clamp down on religious freedom in Tibet. The Dalai Lama at last renounced his call for Tibetan independence in favor of a plea for genuine Tibetan autonomy, much to the dismay of independence activists. That his plea has altered things in Tibet is doubtful. China continues to import its surplus population into Tibet; it continues to obliterate landmarks of Tibetan history and culture. After a brief respite, it has cracked down on religious practice once more. To be fair, there is prosperity in Tibet in many places which were formerly desperately poor. Education is generally available, where previously it was a luxury restricted mostly to the affluent and religious. The Cultural Revolution has long been seen as a shaming mistake, and Chinese still apologize for it today. But religion is suspect, and China's diatribe against the Dalai Lama rarely lets up. Whether the exchange of visits between the Chinese officials and the Dalai Lama's representatives in 2002 and 2003 signals a significant attitude change remains to be seen. The wished-for autonomy in the so-called Tibetan Autonomous Region still has limits. If nothing else, the escape of the Seventeenth Karmapa dramatized the plight of Tibetans who want to be free to practice their Buddhist religion, so precious to them, and choose their own incarnate lamas in the traditional way, which is for them a sacred duty.

Milarepa
(tangka from the Rubin Collection)

3. High Mountain Crossings

WHEN THE SEVENTEENTH KARMAPA stole past the Tsurphu Monastery guards and the People's Liberation Army posts in his bid for freedom during the last days of 1999, he trod in the footsteps of a tradition more than two thousand years old. The modern story is founded on a rich past, and a look at that past helps in understanding who, exactly, the Karmapa is. The Seventeenth Karmapa's place within the Tibetan Buddhist system, his religious importance and the politics that surround him today, are concomitant with the history of all the Karmapas. The story starts even before the Karmapas with a series of fascinating religious heroes. Their lives, and those of the Karmapas, are recounted here as they are given in the Tibetan annals, miracles and all.

The biography of a Tibetan incarnate lama is never just a simple life story. It spans centuries of lifetimes. The Karmapa's story begins with mountain crossings made much earlier, by similarly hearty individuals who had a single-pointed commitment to obtain or share knowledge about a relatively new philosophy, Buddhism. They often came, like the Seventeenth Karmapa, over the mountains from Tibet into Nepal. For Tibetans, Nepal was a convenient place to acclimatize to the harshly hot weather awaiting them in India. For the Indian teachers, it was a haven: from the ninth century, tantric Buddhist teachers fled there when wars made things difficult in India. Nepal became a center of tantric Buddhism. Nepalese Buddhist teachers taught Sanskrit to Buddhist monks, and skilled Nepalese craftsmen and artists were in demand to build Buddhist temples in Tibet. Even today, some of the finest statues of Buddhist figures are cast in Nepal.

Another route taken by such wanderers was through Western Tibet, either via Gilgit, into what is now Pakistan, or through Ladakh to Kashmir. The traveler can still experience the change-less atmosphere in these remote places. On the journey to Ladakh by road along one of these old routes, the verdant alpine meadows of the Kashmir Valley fall behind and the landscape becomes increasingly elemental. After crossing the Zoji-la Pass, the stark, gem-toned mountains seem almost to speak. Mountain dwellers believe the high snow mountains have a mysterious, inherent force; they see these rocky Himalayan giants as entities with terrible power and personality. It is an animism that is thousands, if not millions, of years old. Around a hair-raising bend, Lama Yuru Monastery rises up in the dun-colored distance, fused with the landscape, an ancient fortress of Buddhism that sits in harmony with the mighty mountains around it. This integration with the environment that characterizes Tibetan monasteries is somehow symbolic of the blend of sophisticated Buddhist philosophy with the adamant forces of nature—so unyielding on the Tibetan plateau—that is Tibetan Buddhism.

For at least a thousand years Tibet has been influenced by a doctrine that began six centuries before the birth of Jesus Christ, when a young Indian prince renounced the life of a householder and king for one of a mendicant. After spending many years wandering, in asceticism and meditation, he arrived at a place now located in India's Bihar state, Bodhgaya. There he meditated under a pipal tree and reached the final goal of his spiritual quest: complete enlightenment. He became the Buddha, a Sanskrit term for "wise" or "awakened one." It is a term for one who is fully aware of all dimensions of reality, who is possessed of understanding so transcendent that he or she is purified of all tendencies that lead to automatic rebirth and suffering. In the Buddhist cosmology, this can only take place after lifetimes of experience on the "wheel of life," where one is born repeatedly into various realms. These range from multilevel hells, unfortunate spirit realms of "hungry ghosts," and the animal realm, to the realms of gods and demigods. At the midpoint of these realms comes the balanced—and most fortunate—birth, the realm of the humans. Here an individual has the opportunity to make conscious choices and achieve liberation when a "precious human birth" is achieved, that is, a birth conducive to the spiritual quest. There is another realm of existence that is not on the wheel of life. That is the realm of bodhisattvas, those individuals nearing complete enlightenment. They are not buddhas yet, but they no longer create the negative karma that compels them to uncontrolled rebirth.

Karma, as taught in Buddhism, is not a predetermined fate. The term describes the consequences of our actions. Harmful actions lead to lower births, just as positive actions lead, eventually, to liberation from suffering. Karma is essentially cause and effect. A farmer plants good seed in optimal conditions, and it grows into a healthy plant. If the farmer is careless or lazy—as in the biblical parable of the farmer who sowed good seed among thorns or on rocky ground—the results will be less satisfactory. Ideally, the individual learns from mistakes and refines his or her consciousness over lifetimes.

There are stories about the Buddha's many lives called the *Jataka Tales,* familiar to children in India. In these the Buddha incarnates as monkeys and princes, jackals and nature spirits, lizards and lions, queens and gods, to name a few in the vast multiplicity of lives. These are morality tales that pit right-doing against wrong-doing or demonstrate the consequences of certain actions. For instance, a gluttonous jackal devours an elephant by gnawing into a carcass and crawling inside. He stays so long feasting and sleeping there that the seasons change, the elephant's hide shrinks and hardens in the sun, the hole the jackal gnawed to get in closes up, and he is imprisoned in darkness, "cut off from the world and confined to the interspace between the worlds."[26] The jackal hurls himself against the enclosure, but he is trapped until a rainstorm softens the hide and the entrance hole opens up again. The law of impermanence and change affords an unexpected opportunity. The jackal barely escapes, losing all his hair in the process. It is a highly symbolic tale, but the lesson, simply put, is that he realizes his problems resulted from his own greed, and he vows never to be greedy or get into a carcass of an elephant again.

At last the future Buddha learned the necessary lessons as he progressed from life to life and through positive deeds created the opportunity to take his final birth, as a human. During this lifetime he would be liberated once and for all. He became enlightened sitting beneath the Bodhi Tree in what is now called Bodhgaya in Bihar. Afterward, he shared his insights with others, giving his first teaching at Saranath, near Varanasi in Uttar Pradesh. The Buddha continued to teach into old age, traveling with a band of his disciples. He died not far from where it is thought he was born, near what is now the border of India and Nepal. Buddhists call this event his *parinirvana,* the end of the stream of rebirths. His teachings spread.

For nearly a thousand years the Buddha's Dharma, or teachings, flourished in India, where great monastic universities were built near sacred Buddhist sites. Buddhism radiated south, where evidence still remains in the caves at Ellora and Ajanta. It moved north to Kashmir, which was a center of Buddhist learning prior to the introduction of Islam. From India the philosophy was carried abroad, along trading routes by land and sea. By the time Buddhism was obliterated in India—a process helped by successive Muslim invasions, though Hindu kings contributed their energies, as well—it had migrated to countries throughout Asia where it was preserved. Sri Lanka, China, Japan, and Southeast Asia all maintained vibrant Buddhist traditions into modern times.

46

Buddhism came late to Tibet, but the form of Buddhism that flourished there in Tibet's isolation remained pretty much intact, thanks to the way knowledge was preserved and transmitted both orally and in writing from generation to generation. But in the beginning, it wasn't at all certain that Buddhism would survive there. So cut off was Tibet by geography that it took hundreds of years for Buddhism to penetrate its near impervious borders in any significant form. Buddhism spread rapidly throughout India and beyond within a few hundred years of the death of the Buddha. The first signs of it in Tibet came in the fourth or fifth century, but these were only inklings, shrouded in myth. Some Buddhist texts and ritual implements came there from India. Oral tradition has them falling from the sky. Modern historians, of course, credit traveling scholars. Nobody knew what the artifacts signified, however, and the king of the day was said to be awaiting further elucidation of the strange writings from on high.

It is hard to know exactly when Buddhism did enter Tibet, particularly in the absence of archeological evidence, put out of reach by Chinese government restrictions on exploration. Although parts of the story have lately been challenged by scholars, tradition has the first significant ingress of Buddhism coinciding with two Buddhist wives of the seventh-century warrior-king Songtsen Gampo. His Chinese queen, Kongjo (Wei Chen), and his Nepalese queen, Bhrikuti Devi, converted him to Buddhism. Because of King Songtsen Gampo, Buddhism gained its first toehold in Tibet. His interest in translating Buddhist texts into the Tibetan language caused him to send Tonmi Sambhota to India to study the languages there. At the time, it is said, there was no script for the Tibetan language; knowledge was retained in memory and passed on orally. Sambhota is usually credited with inventing Tibetan writing after studying Gupta Devanagari script at Nalanda University, though Gendun Choephel, among others, contends that Tibet had its own written language that was lost.[27] In any case, there is historical certainty about the role of Songtsen Gampo in casting modern Tibetan script. Besides text translation, he

adopted Buddhist principles and reigned by them, spreading
the doctrine through his acts and edicts.

It was only a beginning. Tibetans were not a peaceful people.
They were raider nomads who fought with considerable success
against all of their neighbors at one time or another. They were
also devout animists, followers of a religion known as *Bon* that
was replete with gods, nature spirits, and sorcerers who could
effectively invoke the netherworld. Tibetan sorcerers were so
good at it that Tibet gained a reputation in India as a land of
strange magic. When Songtsen Gampo tried to introduce
Buddhism, the Bonpos, as believers are called, strenuously
opposed him. Their stiff resistance continued for several hundred years.

Buddhism achieved no firm foundations in Tibet until the
eighth century, during the reign of King Trisong Detsen. The
king's ministers were at odds about Buddhism. Most of them
favored it, but one was against it. That lone dissenter was buried
alive, and the Buddhist ministers proceeded to found monasteries and bring the Indian pandit Shantarakshita to teach in them.
Shantarakshita was a brilliant scholar who had studied at
Nalanda, but his erudite philosophy could not win the hearts of
Tibetans, steeped as they were in shamanism. They were also put
off when a devastating thunderstorm damaged crops and livestock all around shortly after Shantarakshita delivered a sermon.
Bad omens, said the Bon priests.

Not all Buddhist teachers were scholarly philosophers like
Shantarakshita. In the thousand years it took Buddhism to reach
Tibet, it had transformed from an austere path of ascetic sim-
plicity into the more fulsome Mahayana or "great vehicle" path.
And the Mahayana transformed further when elements of
Indian tantrism were incorporated into Buddhist practices and
the Vajrayana, or "diamond vehicle," took shape. Buddhist masters of tantric magic emerged. Stories about such *mahasiddhas,*
men and women who achieve miraculous powers, are still used
to inspire students to apply themselves to the humdrum work of
enlightenment. This is the sort of religion that had great appeal
to Bon believers.

48

The gurus and disciples in the following stories are only a few of the many who shaped Buddhism in Tibet. Those chosen are the direct forerunners of the Karma Kagyu lineage. Yet each of the four lineages of Tibetan Buddhism, and indeed each monastery, has its own particular patron saints, some famous only in the region. A commonly quoted proverb is "Every valley a different lama, every lama a different Dharma." The Nyingma, or "Old Order," was founded by the Indian tantric master Padmasambhava in the earliest days of Buddhism in Tibet. It is the first teaching lineage. Despite the difficult years after its genesis, the lineage persists to the present day. Two hundred years after Padmasambhava, two more lineages emerged. Concurrent with the development of the Kagyu lineage was that of the Sakya, or "Grey Earth" order, named after the place where its first monastery was built on the Upper Tsangpo River, northwest of Lhasa. Like the other two orders, the Sakya tradition also originated with an Indian Buddhist teacher, Virupa, who is believed to have visited Sakya. Sachen Kunga Nyingpo, a descendant of King Trisong Detsen, became Virupa's student. He excelled as a scholar and practitioner of Buddhism and was the progenitor of an order that would have both secular and religious importance. Unlike other lineages, the responsibility to head the Sakya lineage is passed along blood lines. The Sakyapas are renowned for their scholarship. Sakya Pandita, who lived in the first half of the thirteenth century, is probably the most famous Sakya scholar. He began a line of rulers patronized by the Mongols. After they were deposed as political figures, the Sakya lineage continued to produce notable broad-minded scholars, and the library at Sakya remained unsurpassed, but their time as rulers of Tibet was over.

The fourth and youngest of the schools was created by the scholar and tantric adept Tsongkhapa, who was disturbed by the corruption of the Buddhist priesthood of his time. Born in eastern Tibet in 1357, Tsongkhapa found his teachers in different lineages, and he was even ordained by the Fourth Karmapa, Rolpe Dorje. Following the lead of the earlier reformer Atisha, he believed the *vinaya,* the monastic code laid down by the Buddha, was the key to correcting the errors of his day, and the Gelug order to this day retains a strong emphasis on monasticism. In 1409 he founded the first Gelug monastery, Ganden. As did the Sakyapas, the Gelugpas placed a strong emphasis on reasoning and philosophical analysis in addition to their tantric practices. Gelug monasteries were established throughout Tibet and in Mongolia, but their strongest presence was in central Tibet. The Ganden Tripa is the seniormost cleric of the lineage. The First Dalai Lama, Gendun Drub, was a nephew and disciple of Tsongkhapa whose charisma and drive helped the Gelug sect take firm root. He founded the great Tashilhunpo Monastery in Shigatse, which later became the seat of the Panchen Lamas. Gendun Gyatso was identified as Gendun Drub's successor, and after him, Sonam Gyatso. Sonam Gyatso, another firebrand teacher of great attainment, converted the Mongol Altan Khan. Altan Khan bestowed the title "Dalai" upon him, a title that was later applied retroactively to Sonam Gyatso's two predecessors, so that Sonam Gyatso is known as the Third Dalai Lama. Dalai means "ocean" in the Mongolian language and salutes the lama's depth of wisdom. Subsequent Dalai Lamas maintained a relationship with the Khans. The Mongol Khans once again played kingmakers in Tibet when Gushri Khan appointed the Fifth Dalai Lama secular and religious ruler.

OTHER DIMENSIONS

Now to explore a bit of the mystical history of Tibet, which inevitably intersects with the mundane and the political. The biographies of Buddhist masters, including the Karmapas, are filled with the supernatural. The subjects walk through walls, leave footprints in stone, cause flowers to fall from the sky, and at death they dissolve into rainbows of light. The lives of Tibetan Buddhist saints have been recorded and embellished for centuries. They are individuals who, like the yogi Milarepa, show the way to realization with an adamant, almost crazy commitment. Woven in with solid, documentable history, such accounts of marvels are not regarded as flights of imagination by the devout. On the contrary. Such phenomena were explained by the late Kagyu master Drupon Dechen Rinpoche as the fruit of a highly developed consciousness that perceives the truth that appearances do not really exist: "A person who has learned to experience phenomena as only a product of spirit knows the material has no objective existence." That understanding can enable the adept to perform extraordinary feats, like leaving impressions in stone.

In some ways, such convictions throw the dichotomy between Eastern- and Western-style thinking into deep relief. On some levels Buddhist philosophy "makes sense" to the Western mind because it is so well and rationally organized. But the centuries-old rational orientation of occidental thought, which is the basis for modern society in the developed world, can also be an obstacle, blocking one's ability to grasp the significance of certain aspects of Buddhism when it moves into the otherworldly. For years Westerners have been taught that anything supernatural is unscientific and therefore impossible, and the attitude of looking askance at such phenomena is deeply rooted. But with recent developments in the study of the mind, many Westerners are also beginning to recognize the pragmatic power of thoughts and beliefs. Tibetans are a pragmatic people, too, and like Western pragmatism, theirs also is based on experience.

Tibetans can be notoriously stubborn in their beliefs, as scores of Christian missionaries can attest. After a short time in Tibet, Shantarakshita could see he was not getting through to people. He recommended another Nalanda scholar who was an adept in tantric magic, Padmasambhava, the "lotus-born." Padmasambhava was invited to Tibet by King Trisong Detsen. He accepted the invitation and presented himself in 747 A.D. Meanwhile, Shanta-rakshita withdrew to Nepal. Padmasambhava dazzled the Tibetans with tantric fireworks, with taming demons and working miracles. If the Bon deities and their sorcerer priests were angered at the new religion, Padmasambhava was capable of taking on priest and goblin alike, and beat them at their own game. He was born in Uddiyana, what is now Swat in Pakistan. His father Indrabhuti was also a famous tantric adept. Like the Bon priests, Padmasambhava was not celibate. In fact, one of the secrets of his yogic power stemmed from his ability to transmute ordinary sexual energy into enlightened wisdom and compassion. He had two renowned consorts who were themselves adepts, the Tibetan Yeshe Tsogyal and the Indian princess Mandarava.

In his early career, when he was mastering yoga tantras in the ancient Himalayan kingdom of Zahor, he got involved with the king's daughter, Mandarava. He found her as a young nun meditating in a cave. The story goes that he took her as his consort and they meditated and practiced tantra together. When the king discovered this, he was enraged. He seized Padmasambhava and meant to execute him. He had him tied to a pyre, intending to burn him alive, but when the wood was set alight, the flames could not harm the adept. Padmasambhava transformed the burning pyre into a lake with lotus blossoms. Tradition has it that Rewalsar, called Tso Pema in Tibetan, located near Mandi in Himachal Pradesh in India, is believed to be this same lotus lake. Mandarava is said to be an ancestress of the rajas of Mandi.

On his trip to Tibet, there was no water at one of the campsites along the way. Padmasambhava struck a rock with his staff and water began to flow. When he reached the court of King Trisong Detsen, he refused to prostrate, saying the king could not handle it. To demonstrate what he meant, he gestured to a rock, which exploded. Then he saw some royal trappings and gestured toward those. They burst into flames. The king got the idea and prostrated to Padmasambhava instead. Such tales of his exploits are found in collections attributed to himself or to his consort Yeshe Tsogyal, among others. In straight reckoning, Padmasambhava spent no more than eighteen months in Tibet.

The real miracle is that he drove the stake of Buddhism so firmly into Tibetan soil. He inducted vanquished Bon gods and demons into what would become a distinctive Tibetan Buddhist hierarchy of protectors, helpful spirits, super-yogis, and bodhisattvas. The highest Bon divinity, for instance, became the ultimate yogi Kuntu Zangpo, the focal point of core Buddhist meditation practices. Padmasambhava adopted Bon rituals and made them Buddhist. As with the king, who prostrated to him when he recognized his power, malignant spirits reformed and offered to serve him and the Buddhadharma. He established Samye Monastery near the Tsangpo River, the first important Buddhist college in Tibet and the seat of the Nyingma school. Padmasambhava, called Guru Rinpoche, or "precious teacher," remains at the center of Nyingma practice today, as do some of the formerly Bon deities he turned into Buddhist figures. After his whirlwind of activity, Shantarakshita was called back and put in charge of Samye, where he remained until his death thirteen years later.

Padmasambhava made two trips to Tibet. He is thought to have died on his second trip back to India, but some traditions conclude that it was only a magical emanation that left Tibet. One version relates that some of the king's troublesome ministers insisted that the king expel Padmasambhava. Padmasambhava obliged by a magical deception, dispatching a look-alike emanation into exile, while he actually stayed on for another fifty years or so. Much of the literature of the Nyingma tradition consists of the *terma,* or "hidden treasures," that are attributed to Padmasambhava, teachings he concealed in miraculous ways that can only be discovered at just the right moment in the future. Often they turn up in some dank cave. Those who discover such texts are incarnate lamas called *tertons,* or "treasure finders," who had a particular relationship with Padmasambhava in previous lifetimes.

The dynamic relationship between these two diverse teachers— the thundering tantric Padmasambhava and the erudite sage Shantarakshita—made an indelible impression, giving a form to Tibetan Buddhism that endures until today. But the story doesn't end with them. Buddhism was on shaky ground for years to come, thanks not only to Bon kings and politicians but to divisiveness among Buddhists. Other noted Indian pandits came to foster Buddhism along with Chinese Buddhist teachers, who set themselves up as rivals to the Indians. The Chinese were also Mahayanist, but they preached the doctrine of nonexistence, which suggests that beneficial actions get you nowhere, that nirvana and enlightenment is obtained by complete, contemplative inaction. Not surprisingly, this school achieved a following. There were arguments between adherents of this quietist Chan philosophy and the Indian school, which held that good works and right conduct reaped the highest reward. It led to a famous debate.

Kamalashila was a celebrated disciple of Shantarakshita who was asked to come from India to debate the Chinese priest Hashang Mahayana in the presence of the king, probably at Samye Monastery in 792–94. Legend has it that Kamalashila won, and the king ordered his people to follow the interpretation propounded by Kamalashila, while the Chinese teacher's views were banned and he was banished. Kamalashila stayed in Tibet and taught for many years. But the defeated Hashang had a long memory. Years later he sent four Chinese butchers to kill Kamalashila, which they did, by "pinching his kidneys with their hands."[28] His body was preserved, and the mummy was seen by British diplomat and scholar Charles Bell in the 1920s.

A grandson of Trisong Detsen, Ralpachen, evidently achieved peace between China and Tibet by using Buddhist priests as mediators on both sides. He had many successes, military and diplomatic. He became an arbiter of Buddhist teachings and created guidelines for the kinds of texts, out of the many available, that should be translated. His leanings were toward the Hinayana school of thought, and he frowned on tantric mysticism. His promotion of this stricter, intellectual form of Buddhism may have been his undoing. It also may have worked against the growth of Buddhism at the time. Despite his achievements, he was assassinated at a fairly young age. His elder brother Langdarma, who was passed over for some reason in favor of his bright younger brother, now gained the throne. Anti-Buddhist to the core, he mounted a campaign against Buddhists that became so severe that he, too, was finally murdered—by a Buddhist monk.

It is a romantic story that is often replayed in Tibetan dance performances. The monk Palgyi Dorje came specially prepared for his audience with Langdarma. He rode a white horse that had been blackened with soot and wore a robe that was black on the outside and white on the inside. In its roomy sleeves he carried a bow and some arrows. As he made obeisance to the king, he withdrew the bow and arrows from his sleeves and shot Langdarma through the chest. He galloped away on his horse, making for the nearest river. He washed the soot from the horse's coat, turned his reversible cloak inside out and escaped. It was about the year 900 A.D. Though persecution of Buddhists persisted for nearly one hundred years and the religion all but died out in Tibet, a resurgence was about to begin.

The next significant players in the evolution of Tibetan Buddhism, who actually gave impetus to the development of powerful monasteries headed by lamas like the Karmapa, emerged in Western Tibet at the turn of the first millennium. A king named Yeshe O and a monk-translator named Rinchen Zangpo were instrumental in bringing this about. Rinchen Zangpo was born in 982 in Amdo. As a young man he was sent to India to pursue Buddhist studies by Yeshe O, who was king of Guge. Rinchen Zangpo survived the hardships of a trip that took the lives of about twenty traveling companions. He studied and brought back Buddhist texts. He later founded monasteries in Western Tibet, notably Toling, and he is thought to have founded Tabo and Nako monasteries in Spiti, Himachal Pradesh, now part of India.

The growing tolerance toward Buddhism in Tibet coincided with Muslim invasions in India, which began in earnest in the late tenth century, led by Mahmud, the "Lion of Ghazni." His incursions paved the way for various sultanates during the twelfth to fourteenth century. Indian masters still crossed the Himalayas. Of those who came at this period, Atisha set Tibetan Buddhism back on a firm footing. One of the most respected Buddhist teachers in India, he was famous for his extensive travels in pursuit of knowledge, and it is thought he got as far as what is now Indonesia. His most significant contribution was to elucidate the Kadampa tradition. It set down clear principles for incorporating Buddhist ideals into ordinary life. The Kadampa teachings became a part of the Kagyu teachings and would later inspire Tsongkhapa, founder of the Gelug lineage, as well. The

Kadampas emphasized monastic discipline and study linked with compassion.

Buddhism began to thrive in Tibet. Students were drawn to India for instruction. Among these was an irascible yet remarkable character who would become the source of a new lineage of Tibetan Buddhism: Marpa the translator. Even the representations of Marpa in Tibetan art set him apart, with his crew cut and rather pained expression. He was born in 1021 into a wealthy farming family in Southern Tibet, in an area called Lhotrak, adjoining Bhutan. According to biographers, Marpa was an unmanageable child whose parents sent him off to the monastery to be disciplined. This did not work out as well as they hoped, although he was good at his studies in spite of being unruly and willful. One of his teachers who had studied in India taught him Indian languages, including Sanskrit. When he decided to go to India, his strong will helped him survive the rigors in store for him.

On the way to India, in Nepal, Marpa encountered two Nepalese disciples of the yogi Naropa. "By just hearing the name of Lord Naropa, a connection from a former life was reawakened in Marpa and he felt immeasurable yearning."[29] The two disciples urged Marpa to go to Naropa for teachings, but advised him to first adjust to the heat in Nepal. He stayed three years at Swayambhu, on the western edge of Kathmandu across the Vishnumati river. After his studies there, Marpa made the difficult trip to Nalanda in India and on to Pullahari, where he at last met Naropa.

Now Naropa was a great scholar, or *mahapandita*. He distinguished himself at Nalanda and Vikramashila, where he achieved the highest academic posts. But he forsook his sheltered university life after a vision in which a horrible-looking woman convinced him that he had not understood the depth of the teachings. His tantric guru was Tilopa, a wandering yogi who got his name from the years he spent pounding sesame seeds (*til*, in Sanskrit) for a living. To supplement his income while perfecting his realization, Tilopa also worked a night shift as a pimp in the market town of Pensalna, in Bengal. As with Naropa, an old

woman—who was actually a dakini, or female bodhisattva—
came to him in visions early in life and directed his course, from
boyhood study and ordination as a monk, through his town life,
to his life as a mad yogi. She directed him to Pensalna, and
according to some accounts, Bamina, the prostitute who was his
employer, was also was a highly evolved dakini.

Dakinis figure often in Tibetan religious stories, so it might be
useful to describe these interesting female "celestial beings."
Often simplistically characterized as goddesses or female deities,
they are much more than that in the Vajrayana view. Deity is a
confusing misnomer, because Buddhism is nontheistic. Dakinis
and *dakas,* the male counterparts, are entities who personify profound depths of consciousness. They can be human beings of
high spiritual advancement or beings who are beyond human
and exist in a "pure realm." In Tibetan the word for dakini is
khandro, or "sky goer," which more faithfully indicates her nature
as purveyor of wisdom, compassion, and emptiness. Whether
human or celestial manifestations, they are essentially *yidams,* or
personal embodiments of buddha mind, and may be invoked to
stimulate greater awakening. They may be peaceful or wrathful,
and they often play tricks to challenge the practitioner or act as
guides, offering clues to the right path.

Dakinis are somewhat analogous to angels in the Christian
cosmology, but there are interesting parallels to such beings in
Western folk literature, as well. The Welsh Mabinogeon and
other European tales feature supernatural crones and tricksters
who play similar roles for the heroes and heroines, challenging
and helping them toward the realization of the goals of a heroic
quest. They may be beautiful women or old crones who bring
messages or predict the future. They may come in human form
or in dreams. Dakinis are essential to the yogi.

Tilopa is the source of the Kagyu tradition. Tilopa had a range
of students from yogins and philosophers to beer-sellers and
singers. But the disciple the dakini mentioned by name when she
gave Tilopa advice on teaching was Naropa. Naropa had already
completed a period of rigorous monastic training, so Tilopa's
methods of instruction involved a different kind of discipline.

He subjected Naropa to twelve major and twelve minor trials
that rival the worst of modern methods of torture: he is made
to throw himself off the roof of a three-story temple; he is set
up by his guru to be beaten within an inch of his life on several
occasions; he jumps into a fire, offers himself as a meal for
leeches, batters his own genitals, all at the order of Tilopa. After
Naropa passes each severe test of his mettle, Tilopa reveals a
new level of teaching. His last trial is to dismember and decapi-
tate himself as an offering, to be miraculously restored by his
teacher. Following this grueling series of tests came a final teaching: Tilopa slaps his student's face with a sandal. Even today, no
greater insult can be offered in India. But Naropa realized the
essence of all the teachings in a flash of enlightenment at that
moment.[30]

Marpa
(tangka from
the Rubin
Collection)

Compared to the treatment given to Naropa by Tilopa—or the
treatment Marpa would later give his own disciple Milarepa—
Marpa got off easily, though he had difficulties of his own to

endure. At each stage Naropa sent Marpa to the purest source of a particular practice before giving him the same transmission himself. One of these sources was Kukkuripa, a shape-changing adept who lived among a large pack of dogs on an island in a poisonous lake. "When Marpa arrived at the mountain island in the poison lake, the local spirits magically filled the sky with thick clouds. Lightning flashed, thunder resounded fiercely, and many thunderbolts struck the ground. There was a great tempest with rains and snow. Though it was the middle of the day, it became pitch black. Marpa experienced such anguish that he wondered whether he was dead or alive." He called out to Naropa and the storm cleared. Upon finding an odd individual covered with feathers sitting under a tree with his head tucked under his arm, Marpa asked him if he had seen Kukkuripa. The answer was a glare and some abuse: "Well, well, you flat-nosed Tibetans! Even a route as difficult as this doesn't keep you away. Where do you come from? Where are you going?"[31] This, of course, was Kukkuripa, whose name reflects the tradition that he became enlightened through his compassion for a starving puppy that later revealed itself to be a dakini. After a dialogue that recalls Carlos Castaneda's tales of the Yaqui Indian sorcerer Don Juan in its zaniness, Kukkuripa gives Marpa the requested initiation and teaching.[32]

Marpa had another teacher, Maitripa, who taught Marpa in the singing of *dohas,* inspirational poems that often mark the biographies of Tibetan hero-saints. Niguma, Naropa's accomplished yogini consort, also taught Marpa. After twelve years of study and practice in India he ran low on funds—not only for travel and living expenses, but for offering to his teachers—so he decided to return to Tibet. He was reunited with an old traveling companion who, in jealousy of Marpa's success, had a servant throw all Marpa's precious Buddhist texts into a river along the route. Marpa made the best of this mishap, taking it as a sign that he had adequately assimilated the teachings. He returned home and began to share them. He married, and his wife Dagmema became an important foil for his own development and that of his disciples.

Eventually Marpa gathered more gold and returned to India a second time to learn from Naropa. After that trip Marpa accepted Milarepa as his disciple. When Marpa returned to India on his third and final trip, along the way he is said to have met Atisha, who had also studied with Naropa. Naropa was not easy to find, having entered a stage of Vajrayana practice that had little to do with ordinary reality, where he was no longer meeting human beings but only spiritual ones. After months of wandering and prayerful supplications in the company of various other gurus, he finally met Naropa. Naropa threw away Marpa's offerings of gold and "touched the earth, which became gold. And he said, 'If I needed it, all this land is gold,'"[33] transmitting a profound realization in a mystical reunion. Then Naropa enjoined Marpa to give the most precious teachings only to Milarepa.

Marpa took leave of his guru and departed India for the last time. He was in his fifties. When he returned to Tibet, the son he envisioned as his spiritual heir was killed in a riding accident, and his chief disciple became Milarepa. Unlike most of the key gurus in the Kagyu lineage, Marpa lived the life of a layman, hard-drinking and scrappy. Rather than going into long retreats, he combined his spiritual practice and his ordinary life. He is among the most important figures in the translation of Indian Buddhism to Tibet. Seekers of Buddhist wisdom gradually stopped going to India after Marpa's time, as Buddhism virtually disappeared from there, monasteries, statues, and texts destroyed by the waves of Muslim invaders. The learning brought to Tibet was cherished there and preserved in its own way. The unbroken oral transmission of the Kagyu lineage became even more precious because the fountainhead had dried up.

Marpa's disciple Milarepa, who lived and wandered in the area of Southern Tibet on the other side of the mountains from Nepal and Bhutan, was just as colorful as Marpa, though in a different way. He was born in 1040 to an affluent farmer. But Milarepa began his career by erecting enormous obstacles to his future spiritual progress. He became a sorcerer at the behest of his mother, who wanted him to wreak vengeance on relatives who shamelessly cheated his family of their property and used them as servants after the death of his father. Milarepa was a brilliant student of sorcery and learned his craft so well that he demolished his uncle's house from afar while a wedding feast was in progress, killing thirty-five people. Later he destroyed all the crops in the fertile valley cultivated by his uncle's family by conjuring a tremendous hailstorm. Eventually he came to regret his evil deeds. He was an all-or-nothing sort of person. "I was filled with remorse for the evil I had done by magic, and by hailstorms. My longing for the teaching so obsessed me that I forgot to eat," he says in his autobiography, *The Life of Milarepa*.[34] This text and *The Hundred Thousand Songs of Milarepa*[35] create a fascinating picture of Tibet's most popular saint.

Milarepa went in quest of a teacher. "Hardly had I heard the name of Marpa the Translator than I was filled with ineffable happiness. In my joy every hair on my body vibrated."[36] At the same time Marpa had a prophetic dream of his guru Naropa. Marpa's wife Dagmema also had a prescient dream. Marpa knew what the dreams meant, and the next day he went to plow a field, work usually left to his laborers. He went there deliberately to meet Milarepa on the road. The first thing he did was to make Milarepa finish plowing the field. Marpa took him into his household. Because of Milarepa's past, he had many sins to expiate before he could progress on the path that would turn him into an enlightened Buddhist master. Knowing this, Marpa set one hard test after another for him, skillfully helping Milarepa develop his unique potential. He made Milarepa use his bare hands to build and tear down a tower of stone numerous times, each seemingly on a whim. He abused Milarepa, who continued to serve him and his family devotedly.

Finally, after years of penance, Marpa gave Milarepa the teachings he yearned for, and Milarepa began solitary meditation in a cave. A dream of his sister caused him to break retreat and leave his guru in order to visit his old home. When he got there he found his dead mother's remains and the house haunted. His sister had wandered away, no one knew where. He prayed and meditated in remorse, and eventually went into a twelve-year meditation retreat in another mountain cave.

During retreat he subsisted on nettle soup, which is why he is often depicted in *tangkas*—Tibetan scroll paintings—with green-hued skin. He also had a talent for song, and much of his teaching was given in dohas.

The Hundred Thousand Songs tells of Milarepa's encounters with the elements, demons, animals, dakinis, sorcerers, logicians, and his own disciples. Everyone wants to argue with him or challenge him in some way, and they follow him to a succession of remote caves to do so. Others, like his sister Peta, try to convince him to wear clothing. Milarepa cared for nothing material, but focused entirely on inner discipline. "I am a man who cares not what may happen," he sang. "I have nothing and want nothing." The greatest—and typically earthy—teaching was given to his foremost student Gampopa. He showed him the calluses on his buttocks incurred through rigorous yogic practice.

Milarepa's students were varied. Many of them were women. He gave special teachings to women, from sixteen-year-olds to grandmothers, not neglecting demonesses, who appeared out of the blue to torment him.

Milarepa had two outstanding disciples, Rechungpa and Gampopa. Milarepa saw that Rechungpa's pride was a great obstacle, and in the end, Gampopa became the one who would flawlessly transmit the lineage.

Gampopa was a learned man, trained as a physician. After the death of his wife and children in an epidemic, he became a monk following the Kadampa tradition. When he heard about Milarepa, he made up his mind to find him. Milarepa, of course, was expecting Gampopa. Gampopa had a prophetic dream in which a green yogi in rags threw spittle at him. After being made to wait for a few weeks because of his pride, when he did meet Milarepa, the guru offered him a skull full of *chang,* Tibetan beer fermented from barley. The conscientious Kadampa monk hesitated, because drinking alcohol was against his avowed precepts. Milarepa upbraided him for thinking too much, and Gampopa promptly drained the vessel so as not to ruin the auspicious omen. By doing so, he proved himself fit for the teachings. Milarepa guided Gampopa stage by stage through the practices and levels of realization, until he had successfully transmitted to his disciple all the teachings on *mahamudra,* a tradition that had now been passed in succession from Tilopa to Naropa, Marpa, Milarepa, and Gampopa. In his songs and writings, Gampopa shows himself the worthy vessel Milarepa saw him to be. In this song after the death of his guru, Gampopa describes how awakening is achieved:

> Practice continuously, like a river.
> Rest loosely, without further fabrications.
> Rest naturally without seeking further.
> Rest easily without thinking.
>
> Experience and realization are one.
> When realization is uninterrupted, that is it.
> When it is as limitless as space, that is it.
> When one sees one's mind as Buddha, that is it.[37]

Gampopa had many disciples, and his influence shaped the Kagyu order, which subsequently developed "four great and eight lesser" branches. One disciple who would receive the entire body of teaching from Gampopa and become a chief lineage holder was the First Karmapa, the founder of the Karma Kagyu lineage.

The Karma Kagyu refuge tree, which depicts the chief teachers of
the lineage, including the Karmapas and more important tulkus. Central
is the "root guru" Dorje Chang. Represented below are the buddhas,
the protectors, the yidams, and at the foot of the tree, the faithful.

4. The Incarnations of the Black Hat Lama

THE SIXTEENTH KARMAPA, Rangjung Rigpe Dorje, portly and affable, came to the United States for the first time in 1974. He was feted in a style befitting an emperor of China at the insistence of the most important Kagyu teacher established in the United States at the time, Chogyam Trungpa. Trungpa, who invited him, wished to acknowledge the Karmapa's exalted status in this new land. To Tibetans the Karmapa is far beyond anything so mundane as a temporal ruler. The Karmapas were known for prodigious spiritual accomplishment, and the line of Karmapas outlasted dynasties of Chinese emperors. Several emperors of China have been Karmapa disciples. So even today devotees accord the Karmapa all the pomp and ceremony circumstances permit, not only as principal guru of the Karma Kagyu lineage, but as an emanation of the powerful Chenrezig, the bodhisattva of compassion, and as a future buddha. To receive the Karmapa's blessing, to be present at the unique Black Crown Ceremony that he performs, even to see him from afar is considered an auspicious circumstance by the devout. Witnessing a Black Crown Ceremony is the event of a lifetime. Devotees believe it will spare them birth in lower realms and speed up their attainment of enlightenment.

To Westerners reared on notions of egalitarianism, the grandeur associated with Tibetan religious personages and cere-monies can seem ostentatious, tacky, or exotic. Some people are put off by the grandiose trappings of high lamas such as the Karmapa—the rich brocades, incense, music, complex ritual, not to mention subservience to the lama—so out of place in the modern context. Yet others are attracted by it. Today, in the twenty-first century, high lamas eschew much of the formality of former days. But on his first visit to America, the Sixteenth Karmapa was only a few years removed from a place where time stood still, a place he had left at the mature age of thirty-six. Though living simply himself, his disciples insisted that proper respect be paid. No lama could outmatch the Karmapa in stately splendor when he was in full ceremonial mode. Disciples show-ered him with gifts, sometimes kitschy souvenirs, sometimes practical things. Besides cash to support his special projects, the rich gave very expensive offerings in the form of watches or cars. A memorable example was the eye-catching solid-gold Wheel of Dharma pin with a diamond of multiple carats at its center that the Karmapa occasionally wore on his lapel.

Lavish display honoring revered high lamas was expected on the endless, stark Tibetan Plateau. The pomp, the gilt-edged auspicious primary colors, the fabulous Chinese brocade robes, the music and chanting were doubtless savored as entertain-ment in places where there was not much going on otherwise. Today there is still pageantry. Monasteries rebuilt in exile have carried their traditions with them. At special festival times, monks don colorful costumes and masks to perform religious-themed dances. Tashijong Monastery in Himachal Pradesh has a celebration in early spring that honors Padmasambhava, and huge heads representing him and his consorts are propelled around the courtyard. Rumtek, the Karmapa's monastery in Sikkim, holds dances on a feast day in early summer and on the

Tibetan New Year. People from near and far flock to the monasteries on such days to see the wholesome entertainment and enjoy the tea and food that is provided for all.

Disciples who are donors do much to keep these events alive. They give gifts to the high lama personally as a tribute to the priceless qualities of the guru, and to help him or her continue teaching, thus upholding an ancient tradition seen earlier in the stories of Marpa and Milarepa. These sponsors also support the lama's monastery. Today charitable contributions are given to sustain the monks, often in return for special prayers to remove obstacles, bring luck, or send a departed relative on to a better rebirth. Generally, a donation to the religious is not a tithe, nor is it done in response to guru demand. It is an expression of devotion and gratitude. Naropa, Marpa, Milarepa all offered the best they could afford to their teachers as a material sign of their commitment. Since the Tibetan diaspora spread to new lands, lamas' devotee-donors have helped to build new monasteries in exile: in India and other parts of Asia, and in other countries throughout the world.

The high honorifics of Tibetan etiquette were new to the fledgling American Buddhists who met the Karmapa for the first time through his sixteenth incarnation, and it required adjustments in perception. Robin Kornman, an early Trungpa student, writes of the Sixteenth Karmapa's 1974 visit in the magazine *Garuda IV*.[38] He describes the Karmapa's monthlong tour of Trungpa's meditation centers and the preparations that began ten months beforehand. Kornman bemusedly observes, "Any place where His Holiness was received would be richly decorated with huge silk banners, thangkas, Chinese and Japanese brocade and strangely designed furniture which must have been familiar to the Tibetans." Trungpa drilled his students mercilessly on Tibetan protocol for high lamas and the significance of rituals where bells, vases filled with saffron water, and other implements are used to dispense blessings. The Karmapa, pleased with their discipline, told them that if they go on as they had begun, "The Dharma will spread in America like wildfire on a mountain." This participation in another, Eastern approach to spirituality had a profound effect upon the group. Members of Chogyam Trungpa's American Buddhist community reported a discernable shift within their group from the casual hippie style of the early 1970s to something more mature and serious. While not all Western students of Tibetan Buddhism took to wearing a suit and tie or twinset and pearls as part of their Buddhist practice, all who encountered the Karmapa experienced their own epiphany of ancient culture in this Eastern religious potentate, the Karmapa.

THE TULKU PHENOMENON AND
THE BUDDHIST SCHOOLS OF TIBET

The Seventeenth Karmapa is a *tulku,* the reincarnation of all previous Karmapas, and as such, he embodies the incarnate consciousness of all his illustrious predecessors. He is the Karmapa, past and present, the living result of their cumulative good works. Since he is perceived as the same entity inhabiting a new body, the Karmapas of the past offer clues to the Karmapa of the present. A review of the history may elucidate the phenomenon of tulkus and how they are viewed by Tibetans. As the miraculous feats are ticked off, the story may also raise more questions, even skepticism. Yet for accomplished lamas, the extraordinary becomes part of the ordinary.

The First Karmapa[39] started the practice of recognizing tulkus, a custom that spread to all lineages of Tibetan Buddhism. Reincarnation is a given in Tibetan Buddhism. It applies to every sentient being. Buddhist teachings revolve around how to free oneself from the wheel of rebirth. Once free, an individual has a choice: to rest on the laurels of liberation or turn that realization toward helping others to achieve the same state of awareness.

Tibetans believe the reincarnate lama, the tulku, is a bodhisattva. That is, he or she is an advanced being no longer bound to be reborn but who has chosen rebirth out of compassion and a desire to help others. It is a tremendous sacrifice, because it means taking birth in and experiencing all the discomforts of an unenlightened realm of existence. Though these bodhisattvas are not yet manifesting as buddhas, they are entitled to live in a buddha paradise where they are immersed in limitless meditative bliss. It is a level of attainment that is beyond ordinary understanding, because these individuals have transcended ordinary states of mind and existence. They are a realization or two away from complete enlightenment. Instead of a long life of meditation in a pristine, unobstructed place in the presence of enlightened beings, they choose to be born in benighted realms. Though they earned nirvana through their own diligence, they eschew it until all beings attain liberation along with them. Sometimes a bodhisattva reincarnates in the same area again and again to accomplish a specific work. That is how a long series of incarnations of the same name, connected to a particular teaching lineage, such as the Dalai Lama or the Karmapa, comes about. Their many recorded and remembered good works in successive incarnations endear them to their followers.

Today, a thousand years after the First Karmapa began the practice of recognizing tulkus, there are hundreds of tulkus in all four lineages of Tibetan Buddhism. Tulkus are special entities, venerated and so distinguished from others in the monastery. If it were the army, the tulkus would be generals, assisted by various officers and ADCs who had risen from the lower ranks. Not all Tibetan lamas are tulkus, and not all monks are lamas. Monks and nuns take vows to refrain from certain sinful behaviors: not to kill, lie, steal, or indulge in sexual misconduct. They often devote themselves to prayer and study, although many who have passed through the training period assume more mundane responsibilities in the monastery. Strictly speaking, a lama is one who has distinguished himself or herself in meditation practice, usually by successfully completing at least one three-year retreat, and *lama* is the Tibetan word for the Sanskrit *guru*. A tulku or a lama considered saintly may be called *rinpoche,* "precious one."

Some incarnate lamas are women, but they are far fewer than the men. Though women in Tibet enjoyed comparatively more rights than many of their counterparts in Asia, their social place meant they seldom devoted their lives to religion in the same way men did. The best known female tulku is the Dorje Pagmo incarnation, the abbess of Samding Monastery near the meandering, scorpion-shaped Yamdrok Lake in central Tibet. Dorje Pagmo is a powerful female bodhisattva who is an important protector and *yidam,* or focus of meditation. Her tulku is chosen in a manner similar to male tulkus. This traditional selection process may differ somewhat from lineage to lineage, or even tulku to tulku. But there is usually a supernatural component in the process.

Namkhai Norbu Rinpoche once recounted an incident that happened while he was still in Tibet. It relates to the recognition and the nature of incarnate lamas.[40] As a young man, in the early 1950s, Namkhai Norbu was invited to perform some ceremonies in a small province. He spent several days giving a long-life initiation, among other things. This is a frequently requested ceremony in which the blessing of the Buddha Amitabha, through his aspect Amitayus, is invoked for long life. Incense is burned, prayers and mantras said by the preceptors. At the end, participants file past the lama for a tap on the head, which physically transmits the blessing, along with a taste of consecrated saffron water and some "long-life pills," small balls of sweetened *tsampa,* roasted barley flour dough. A colored string is also given, a "blessing cord" worn as a charm imbued with the blessing of the ceremony.

Every day during that time people came to meet Namkhai Norbu in the mornings. They asked for teachings, advice, or divination of the future. Some high lamas are believed to have the gift of prescience and are asked to perform divination, or *mo.* The simplest is done using prayer beads; special dice, mirrors, or other means are also employed. An example is the dream mo, in which a combination of meditation and dreams are used over a number of days to gain insight into a serious matter. After the people paid their respects to Namkhai Norbu, the ritual to be performed that day would begin.

Rinpoche narrates, "On the last day, in the night, I had a dream. In my dream I was at that place, it was morning, and a lot of people were arriving to visit me. Someone said 'Now should we start to receive people?' and I said, 'OK, I'm ready.' So they opened the door and in came an old woman with a statue, a golden statue. She approached me and said, 'Please consecrate this statue,' and she put it down." The statue was of a monk, Namkhai Norbu recalls, "But I didn't know who it was. Then I said, 'Whose statue is this?' And she said, 'This is a statue of Lama Ngawang Gyaltsen.' I thought, 'Strange, who is this Ngawang Gyaltsen?'" Namkhai Norbu reflected that Ngawang Gyaltsen must be a Sakyapa because the name Ngawang is a typically Sakya name, but he had never heard of the lama in question. He consecrated the statue with a prayer and sprinkling of rice and gave it back. Other people came in, "And then I woke up, and I remembered this dream very clearly. I thought, 'Strange!' I told my monks, 'I had this strange dream about a Lama Ngawang Gyaltsen. Do you know who Ngawang Gyaltsen is?' They didn't know.

"Then people began to come. It is no dream now, it's real. When we start to receive people, that same lady who was in my dream comes in leading a small boy. I was very surprised." He thought to himself that it could mean the boy is some reincarnation, maybe of this mysterious Lama Ngawang Gyaltsen. "I gave him a protection cord and told this lady to keep him well because he could be someone important. And when she asked me to give him a name, I gave him the name of Gyaltsen."

Two years later, the previous Tai Situpa[41] was at the same place to perform rituals for the dead, because someone in this boy's family had died. Namkhai Norbu continues, "Someone brought this boy to Situ Rinpoche, and Situ Rinpoche recognized him as the reincarnation of a Sakya lama named Ngawang Gyaltsen. He was from a small Sakya monastery called Tashi Monastery. It once had a khenpo (master of studies) who was a very good practitioner. He spent most of his life after he became khenpo on the mountain in retreat. So people considered him very important. I never heard of that lama, but Situ Rinpoche recognized this incarnation of Tashi Monastery. The boy of my dream!" This story illustrates the subtle impressions involved in the recognition of important reborn teachers, and the metaphysical levels tapped to confirm a recognition.

The Kagyu order became one of the most developed schools of Tibetan Buddhism, with many different branches.[42] These branches, or subsects, grew up around gifted teachers whose work was later preserved at their monasteries. Sometimes these lamas reincarnated to continue teaching in the same places. Once the lama was discovered, he was brought back to his monastery. Most of these subsects no longer exist today. The teachings of some were subsumed into other, larger branches. In some cases a subsect faded entirely when the last lineage holder died. Of the eight branches of the Kagyu, only the Taglung, Drikung, Drukpa, and Karma Kagyu survive as distinct entities.

The practices that promote an individual's development to the point of complete enlightenment are common to all four orders of Tibetan Buddhism. There are no essential doctrinal differences between sects or branches within sects, although they may debate methods for achieving liberation. It is a question of different approaches to the same essential truth, using techniques that are quite similar—a matter of style and preferences, really.

The Kagyu approach is the mahamudra. *Mahamudra* is variously translated as "great seal" or "great gesture." On one level this indicates that all phenomena of the universe emanate from one source, and all are gestures of ultimate mind. Another interpretation is that ultimate essence is a seal placed upon all manifestations, akin to the monotheistic mystical concept that God inhabits all components of creation. "One can attain liberation through anything, because the essence of everything is ultimate truth. Ultimate truth is the mark all phenomena bear," Tai Situpa has said.[43] The realization of buddha nature, the true and ultimate nature of the mind, may be achieved through any manifestation of reality. So Tilopa could become enlightened pounding sesame seeds, or other adepts could become enlightened through their occupations or their character defects. In stories of the lives of the mahasiddhas, an obnoxiously garrulous man uses sound as a vehicle of realization, purifying this defect to reach enlightenment. A tailor meditates on each stitch to fashion the garment of liberation through his labor.

Gampopa drew together the original Buddhist basics, as defined by the Kadampa tenets in which he was well versed, with the Vajrayana teachings transmitted from his guru Milarepa.[44] The spiritual practices are not separate from the individual's daily life. The goal is to carry the calm, the insight, the compassionate activity developed on the meditation cushion into every task, however unspiritual it may seem.

The masters of these disciplines understand the workings of the universe so well they can perform what look like miracles to those who haven't attained their advanced perceptions—which includes most everyone. To put it more "scientifically," for Milarepa to walk through a wall was the result of his seeing reality for what it is, down to its molecular, atomic, and subatomic composition and fundamental emptiness. He understood its relative truth and its ultimate truth equally well, seeing beyond time and space limitations of past, present, and future, self and other, near and far. Thus, accomplished practitioners are believed to heal the sick, change the weather, or predict the future. Around Tibetan lamas, the best course is to maintain an open mind and see what happens.

THE FIRST KARMAPA, DUSUM KHYENPA

Tibetan high lamas are responsible for keeping records of the teachings they receive and the spiritual practices they themselves complete. They also record the teachings they pass on to others. This ensures proper transmission and preservation of the lineage. Some of the biographical material of such lamas comes from these records. Their spiritual practices and achievements are the core of each account. Accounts seem very similar from life to life, often repetitive and formulaic. Details are sketchy. Biographies are notoriously deficient in context. Little is said about social and political conditions beyond bare outlines. But the more significant incarnations left some interesting historical records in diaries and other writings. All the Karmapas have personal names, but these are not usually used until the Karmapa has died. While alive the Karmapa is called *Gyalwa Rinpoche*, meaning "victorious one," or *Yizhin Norbu*, "wish-fulfilling gem," a reference to the Karmapa as an emanation of Chenrezig, the bodhisattva of compassion, who is depicted holding a wish-fulfilling gem in his hands.

According to the Tibetan biographies, Dusum Khyenpa, the First Karmapa, was born in the mountains of Kham in 1110, of devout Buddhist parents.[45] When he was eleven he had a vision of a female protector, Mahakali. At the age of sixteen he entered a monastery to study Buddhist texts and receive tantric teachings, studying the Kadampa tradition. He was thirty years old before he met Gampopa, a pivotal event in his life. Gampopa initiated him in the Six Yogas of Naropa, which the Karmapa practiced successfully. After attaining realization in these crucial disciplines, he received the entire transmission of the Kagyu lineage from Gampopa and Rechungpa, Milarepa's other brilliant disciple, and the Kashmiri master Shakyashri. Then he began his active ministry.

The First Karmapa, Dusum Khyenpa (tangka from the Rubin Collection)

There is a prediction by the Buddha recorded in the *Samadhirajasutra* that says that about sixteen hundred years after his own death, a great master will appear by the name of the Karmapa, or "man of action," who will do much good over a series of incarnations: "Buddhism will arise in the land of the red-faced ones who will become the disciples of Avalokiteshvara (Tib. Chenrezig). During the degeneration of his teachings there will arise a Bodhisattva by the name of Sinha, called Karmapa. He will become adept in *samadhi* and will subdue living beings. Whoever sees, hears, remembers or touches him will be transported with joy."[46]

Several masters recognized Dusum Khyenpa to be the teacher prophesied, and so he was the first incarnation to be given the title Karmapa. He was also believed to be the next to become Buddha after the coming Buddha Maitreya, and would be called the Lion (Sinha) Buddha. Dusum Khyenpa's activities presaged those of his successors. He founded monasteries, the first of which was Karma Gon, later an important Kagyu monastery in eastern Tibet. It was a treasury of Tibetan religious art until the twentieth century, when much of it was destroyed by the communist Chinese. He also founded Tsurphu, in the Tolung Valley not far from Lhasa. It became his hereditary seat, where future Karmapas would return. Dusum Khyenpa negotiated peace with intractable people bent on war over a neighbor's property or revenge, healed the sick, assisted the poor, and was renowned as an accomplished teacher. Some of his students became notable scholars or adepts themselves. His biography poetically calls his ability "comparable to the sun dispelling the clouds." Because of his visions and his mastery of the highest yogas, he came to be called Dusum Khyenpa, which means "the knower of the three times—past, present and future." It is said that before he died in 1193 he left a letter with his main disciple, Drogon Rechen, describing where his next incarnation could be found. He also left Tsurphu Monastery and his texts and religious paraphernalia in his care. Drogon Rechen is an early incarnation of another tulku who would become important to the Karma Kagyu, the Tai Situpa.[47]

THE GREAT KARMA PAKSHI, THE SECOND KARMAPA

The Second Karmapa, Karma Pakshi, was born in 1206, thirteen years after Dusum Khyenpa's death. He was a descendent of the Buddhist King Trisong Detsen. It is not unusual for tulkus to be born to nobility or have illustrious ancestors. As time went on, tulkus from aristocratic families became suspiciously prevalent; in fact, this coincidence contributed to political intrigues.

Aristocratic families gained considerable leverage when they could bring pressure in both secular and religious spheres. Dusum Khyenpa's disciple Drogon Rechen had died, but he passed the entire core teachings of his lineage to his student Pomdrakpa. After a series of visions, Pomdrakpa realized the young boy descended from a king was the Karmapa, Karma Pakshi, and he formally recognized the boy as such. Presumably, Pomdrakpa also received information left with Drogon Rechen concerning the identity of Dusum Khyenpa's reincarnation. Pomdrakpa became the meditation master of this gifted child who could read, write, and comprehend Buddhist principles before he was ten years old. The boy was also an adept meditator.

Karma Pakshi was one of the most colorful of the Karmapas, and we know about his life and times through other than Tibetan sources. One of these is Marco Polo, who toured the Mongol empire in the late thirteenth century, during the latter part of Karma Pakshi's lifetime. Marco Polo vividly describes those times in his classic account of medieval Asia, *The Travels*. Polo probably did not meet Karma Pakshi, although it is possible that Polo's father, Niccolo, and uncle, Maffeo, met him on an earlier visit to Kublai Khan's winter capital.[48]

There is a lengthy account of Tibetan magicians encountered by Marco Polo at Kublai Khan's court a number of years after Karma Pakshi left it. About Tibet Polo says, "Here are to be found the most skillful enchanters and the best astrologers according to their usage that exist in any of the regions hereabouts. Among other wonders they bring on tempests and thunder-storms when they wish and stop them at any time." He is so taken with their "diabolic arts" he returns to their customs again and again, noting "a monastery of idolaters peopled with 2000 brethren" and gives a protracted report on the healing oracles.[49] He describes their lunar calendar and beliefs of reincarnation, but he always returns to useful spells cast by sorcerers. "Let me tell you of a strange thing which I had forgotten," he writes. "You must know that, when the Great Khan was staying in his palace and the weather was rainy or cloudy, he had wise astrologers and enchanters who by their skill and enchantments would dispel all the clouds and bad weather from above the palace so that, while bad weather continued all around, the weather above the palace was fine. The wise men who do this are called Tibetans and Kashmiris." While some of Polo's tales are disputed, the information about the Mongols and India is sound, and there is evidence in Chinese records that he did visit there and was even employed as a courier by Kublai Khan. The Great Khan distrusted the locals he had conquered, so for sensitive missions he shrewdly utilized "foreigners" who would be unlikely to plot against him.

Karma Pakshi may have been a "magician," but he used his skills to further the peaceful message of Buddhism. He helped to quell a war in Kham. He founded a monastery there where he completed eleven years of retreat. He became famous for his yogic feats. A dakini appeared to him in a vision and told him to chant a six-syllable mantra of Chenrezig, *om mani peme hung*, in a chorus. The practice caught on and is still done today. He did this with his monks while traveling. When Karma Pakshi was forty-four years old, in 1255, he received an invitation from Kublai Khan, who was, at that time, still emperor-in-waiting. Kublai Khan was curious about all religions that came his way, including Christianity, but he was inclined toward Buddhism. He had, years before, invited Sakya lamas to his court, continuing a tradition that was started by his cousin Godan Khan.[50]

Among his later invitees was Karma Pakshi, the Second Karmapa. When Karma Pakshi arrived at Kublai Khan's court, the Sakya lama Pakpa was already ensconced there. Kublai Khan received the Karmapa graciously and asked him for Buddhist instruction and a demonstration of yogic skills—feats similar to those that fascinated Marco Polo. Evidently some pressure was put to prove whose magic was stronger, that of Karma Pakshi or Pakpa, and Sakyapa annals indicate that a rivalry existed between the two.[51] Kublai was impressed with the Karmapa and requested him to remain as part of his entourage, but the Karmapa astutely read the political situation. Not only Sakyapas, but various other religious and political factions jostled for power in Kublai's eclectic court; and although Kublai was one of Mongke Khan's most

The Second
Karmapa,
Karma Pakshi

brilliant governors and generals, there was apparently some brotherly jealousy and, doubtless, ambition on Kublai's part. Not wishing to become embroiled in court intrigues, the Karmapa declined to extend his visit. Kublai was displeased, and it was the beginning of a rift that widened when Karma Pakshi accepted the invitation to the court of Mongke Khan, then supreme ruler of the Mongol Empire. Mongke Khan became one of Karma Pakshi's proficient students and a supporter of Buddhism.

Karma Pakshi stayed at Mongke Khan's palace in Karakorum. Mongol influence was peaking at this time. Until Kublai Khan gained control, the empire was ruled from high in the Karakorum Mountains, where business goes on at elevations of 7,000 feet or higher. People settled in oases dotted around the fearsome Takla Makan, or "desert of no return," that spreads its sands in the Tarim Basin beneath the high pinnacles of the Pamir and Tian Shen mountain ranges. This is where Karma Pakshi most certainly traveled and resided. This was a stop on the Silk Route. Caravans bearing silk, spices, jewels, tea, and other precious cargo passed through this region. So did the ideas and religions of the traders, as they traversed the perilous route from China to Kashmir or west to Persia. At this crossroads of civilization the second Karmapa Karma Pakshi taught Buddhism. He engaged in debates with Taoist masters from China, converting a number of them, according to the biographies. He accompanied Mongke Khan on a tour of the extensive Mongol lands. But when Mongke Khan asked Karma Pakshi to visit Manchuria with him, the Karmapa decided he had had enough. He returned to Tibet. Not long after, Mongke Khan died. There was a short power struggle—the son who succeeded him was summarily dispatched—and Kublai Khan assumed control as Great Khan.

Kublai, resenting Karma Pakshi's relationship with his late brother, ordered the Karmapa's assassination. After the Karmapa was apprehended by the Khan's soldiers, he was repeatedly tortured by them. Here the Karmapa's proficient sorcery was displayed to great effect. He paralyzed the horde of soldiers sent to arrest him with a special *mudra,* or gesture. But he felt sorry for them and set them free, so they took him prisoner. They tried throwing him off a cliff, but he floated lightly down to a lake, which he glided across. They poisoned him, but that backfired; he gave the soldiers a fright when intense light began to issue from his body. Burning didn't work, either, as he magically put out the flames. Then the Khan, nonplussed, exiled him to an inhospitable place without food or water, but the Karmapa survived that, too; some accounts say celestial beings brought delicacies to sustain him. Finally Kublai Khan, who by now had revealed a considerable vindictive streak regardless of any Buddhist teachings he may have received, gave up and released Karma Pakshi with an apology and a request for his blessing.

Karma Pakshi returned to Tsurphu at long last, where he ordered the casting of a massive statue of Buddha. A miscalculation caused the statue to lean too much to one side. This was hardly a problem for the adept, who righted it through the power of his meditation. Karma Pakshi did this by beginning his meditation listing to the same degree as the statue, then slowly straightened up, causing the statue to do likewise. He died in 1283, after informing his main disciple Orgyenpa, to whom he transmitted the entire lineage teachings, that the next Karmapa would be born in western Tibet.

CONTINUITY OF PURPOSE

The Third Karmapa, Rangjung Dorje, continued the vigorous activity of the previous two Karmapas. He was born in Tingri in western Tibet in 1284. Modern visitors to Tibet who take the land route from Nepal to Shigatse pass through the same, arid region below Mount Everest. The boy was intellectually precocious and entered the monastery to begin his studies at an early age. When Rangjung Dorje met his future teacher Orgyenpa, it is said that the five-year-old boy climbed up on the high throne that was the Karmapa's seat. When Orgyenpa asked him why he did this, he replied that it was because he was the Karmapa.[52]

He received the Kagyu teaching transmission from Orgyenpa and studied with masters from other lineages as well. He became a stunning scholar with a broad range of knowledge. His influence grew as he composed texts, traveled, and taught. The Mongol emperor who then ruled China, Toq Temur, invited him to his court. A gold seal that was a gift from Mongke Khan to Karma Pakshi, the second Karmapa, was included with the emperor's invitation, but the request read more like a summons.[53] The Karmapa took his time. He finally set out after a second letter from the Khan. During the Karmapa's journey there, omens of unseasonable thunder and snow indicated that Toq Temur had died. The Karmapa performed funeral prayers and continued to the imperial court in Peking. There he learned that the emperor had in fact died, just as the omens revealed. The emperor who succeeded him also died soon after.

The Karmapa presided at the coronation of the new emperor, Toghon Temur, and then returned to Tibet. Toghon Temur requested him to visit again a few years later, which he did. Tibetan accounts say that though revered by the ruler, the Karmapa irked jealous factions in the court afraid for their own political ambitions. The Yuan dynasty was decadent and failing by this time. The Karmapa offered to leave Peking, but the emperor asked him to stay, and he complied. Karmapa Rangjung Dorje died in China shortly thereafter, in 1339, but not before leaving a letter with his personal attendant predicting where his next incarnation would be found. He also told the emperor they would meet again during his next incarnation. At his death, his face was said to be visible in the moon, a phenomenon that is still depicted in religious art.

The Fourth Karmapa Rolpe Dorje was, like the others, born with distinctive signs, in 1340. As a child he told people that he was the Karmapa come back to teach his disciples. He proved to be a visionary and a poet at an early age. Emperor Toghon Temur maintained his devotion to the Karmapa, and invited him to China. Rolpe Dorje went there at the age of nineteen, fulfilling Rangjung Dorje's prophecy that they would meet again. The Karmapa refused to requisition food and animals from local people on the journey as the emperor suggested—an oppressive custom that survived in Tibet until the twentieth century. He said he did not wish to burden the people. He stayed in China from 1359 until 1383 teaching the emperor, his family, and the local people. Like his predecessors, he was reputed to combat plagues and influence the weather, along with ending droughts. He was widely respected.

On his way back to Tibet, near Lake Kokonor, Rolpe Dorje met a young boy to whom he gave lay ordination. He predicted the boy would be of great benefit to Tibet. The boy was Tsongkhapa, who later would found the Gelug lineage and inspire the master who would become the first Dalai Lama. After the Yuan dynasty fell in 1368, the first Ming emperor invited the Karmapa to visit, along with other illustrious lamas. He did not go but maintained a correspondence with the emperor thereafter.

The Karmapa and his entourage traveled like nomads in a *garchen,* which is the Tibetan term for a large nomadic camp. The Karmay Garchen[54] was a tent monastery, and in it the Karmapa maintained the same monastic discipline as he did when he was at Tsurphu. The Karmapas traveled more often than not, rarely remaining even at Tsurphu for extended periods. These encampments became a hallmark of the Karmapas. The Karmay Garchen was a stunning sight to see, by all reports, with its sumptuous tents decorated in brightly colored brocades and hung with tangkas, precious not only for the fine technique, but for paints ground from red, green, and blue gems and pure gold. The Garchen had all the accouterments of a monastery built with mortar and stone. The Karmapa may have sojourned near important monasteries, but his goal was to benefit as many people as possible through teaching, healing the sick, and other characteristic good works. A garchen was an effective way to do this in predominantly nomadic regions. All the Karmapas shared a love of animals and the desire to protect them. Rolpe Dorje was no exception. The Karmapas are believed to teach the animals just as they do humans—or other natural or supernatural beings they may encounter.

Karmapa Rolpe Dorje's life revolved around meditation, and he kept a strict timetable in his camp. According to Karma Thinley, he meditated and did other spiritual practices from the time he awoke in the early morning until nine, after which he taught his students. In the afternoons he did more meditation, in the evenings he studied. He was a vegetarian, too, something uncommon among meat-eating Tibetans. Karma Thinley cites an instance when the garchen arrived in Kongjo where a smallpox epidemic had broken out. "On the night following Karmapa's arrival, people said that they could hear noises on the roof of his house. In the morning Rolpe Dorje said that he had brought the epidemic to an end by manifesting as a *garuda* [a mythic bird] to destroy the imbalances producing the smallpox. Karmapa expressed his surprise at people's claims to have heard the noises of the *garuda,* because he said in actuality it was simply the activity of formless mind."[55]

Since Rolpe Dorje's patrons were often quarrelsome chieftains whose disputes he was called to mediate, he was surrounded by intrigues, and there were plots against him from time to time by those who resented his influence. The period was politically turbulent. The Karmapa was often engaged in calming tensions and preventing wars between local clans. The popularity of the Sakya vice-regents reached a low ebb. They were blamed for introducing the undue interference of the Mongols in Tibetan affairs. During Rolpe Dorje's lifetime, mid-fourteenth century, a staunch Kagyu follower, Jangchub Gyaltsen of the Pagmodru family, orchestrated the Sakya tisris' downfall. He consolidated an opposition power base that finally eroded Sakya authority. After years fraught with intrigue he set up the Pagmodru rulership in about 1350. Jangchub Gyaltsen sought to correct

Mongol-inspired injustices, including brutal punishments and executions without a hearing. The Pagmodru family ruled for about 130 years in relative peace and security.

Politics did not significantly affect the Fourth Karmapa's following in Tibet, and he continued his ministry until his death in 1383. Rolpe Dorje chose the time and place of his death, on a mountaintop where he said his cremation would help repel invaders. Biographers note that rainbows and earth tremors accompanied his passing. He told his disciples he would be reborn in Nyangdam, and they should keep his books and ritual implements for him until then.

THE EMPEROR AND THE YOGI:
DEZHIN SHEKPA, THE FIFTH KARMAPA

The next year a lama and his wife in Nyangdam, Southern Tibet, celebrated the birth of a son. The birth was replete with marvelous omens. Dezhin Shekpa was said to have recited mantras in his mother's womb, and not long after birth declared he was the Fifth Karmapa. Still a child, he healed an injured lama's bruises and broken bones through gently touching the injuries. He promoted nonviolence, and kindness to people and animals.

Most important to posterity was his association with Yung Lo, the emperor of China, who invited him to the court in Nanking, China, in 1406. An idea of what were considered appropriate gifts for respected lamas may be gleaned from the list of what the emperor sent along with his invitation: an ingot of silver, 150 silver coins, twenty rolls of silk, a block of sandalwood, 150 bricks of tea, and ten pounds of incense, the prized commodities of the Silk Route. When he arrived in Nanking the Karmapa was received by the emperor and thousands of monks. The emperor became a proficient meditator under the Karmapa's guidance. Marvelous manifestations were attributed to the Karmapa during his stay: apparitions of buddhas and monks in the sky, a rain of flowers from iridescent, five-color clouds, and other auspicious omens. Tibet expert Hugh Richardson, who saw the "imperial decree" describing the phenomena at Tsurphu Monastery in 1949, wrote: "It is contained in a silk-backed scroll some 50 feet long by

2.5 feet high composed of sections of text beautifully written in five scripts—Chinese, Tibetan, Arabic, Mongol and Uighur—alternating with panels painted in the meticulously elegant Ming style. The inscriptions record the miracles performed by the lama on twenty-two different days, and the paintings illustrate those occurrences, day by day."[56]

It was also Yung Lo who literally gave substance to the legend of the Black Crown of the Karmapas. Tradition has it that all Karmapas wear a spiritual Black Crown, an inner insignia of their yogic accomplishment. It is said that when the First Karmapa Dusum Khyenpa was sixteen years old, celestial beings bestowed upon him the knowledge of past, present, and future and a black crown woven from the hair of a million dakinis, a tribute to his spiritual rank. Though the crown is said to appear above the heads of all Karmapas, it is only visible to those whose consciousness is sufficiently pure. Once, during a ceremony, Yung Lo is said to have perceived the Karmapa's true nature: he saw a Black Crown hovering over the head of his revered guru. So that others might have similar benefit of recognizing the Karmapa's advanced spirituality, he commissioned a physical replica, made from special black material and jewels. This he presented to the Karmapa. From that time on, the Black Crown Ceremony, in which the Karmapa generates the compassion of Chenrezig, has been a part of his activity.

Needless to say, Dezhin Shekpa was acknowledged by his contemporaries not only as a dazzling yogi and brilliant teacher, but as a trustworthy advisor. Yung Lo had enough confidence in him to allow the Karmapa to dissuade him twice from invading Tibet. Je Tsongkhapa sent the Karmapa a statue with a letter that said, "You are like a second buddha. I would like to see you but I am in a three-year retreat. So I am sending you a statue of Maitreya that belonged to Atisha."[57] When Dezhin Shekpa knew he was near death, he told some Khampas who had pressed him to visit Kham that he couldn't come but assured them he would be seeing them soon. He indicated he would be born in Kham near Karma Gon. His life was short but distinguished, and he died at the young age of thirty-one in 1415.

The next few Karmapas were healers and peacemakers, teachers and poets. They were known to master the weather, bringing rains or quelling storms. Each Karmapa gave letters or other indications of where he would be reborn. The Seventh Karmapa, Chodrak Gyatso (1454–1506), lived austerely and wrote important treatises on dialectics and vinaya. Before dying he wrote down the location and names of the parents in his next birth.

Like so many Karmapas, Mikyo Dorje, the eighth of the line, was born in Dhamchu, Kham, amid extraordinary omens, in 1507. The Third Tai Situ, Tashi Paljor, came shortly after his birth and saw that his family and surroundings corresponded with the details that the previous Karmapa had described. Mikyo Dorje was notable for his poetry and philosophical treatises, which are still consulted. He was one of Tibet's greatest scholars. He was also an artist, painter, and sculptor, his works shot through with mysticism. A famous story about him states that he sculpted a statue of himself in stone and asked the statue, "Do you look like me?" and the statue replied, "Yes, I do." The Karmapa then squeezed a leftover chunk of stone, leaving the impression of his hand. Both statue and hand impression are in the Rumtek Monastery treasure room in Sikkim. The Karmapa foresaw his death, but was entreated by disciples to remain longer. He did and took his peripatetic Karmay Garchen throughout Tibet. Leprosy broke out in southern Tibet, and he went there to offer prayers to stop it. Not long after, he contracted leprosy himself and died in 1554. A letter written when Mikyo Dorje was twenty-eight was left with the Shamarpa. It predicted his next rebirth.

The Ninth Karmapa Wangchuk Dorje was born the following year, 1555, again in Kham. Tai Situ Chokyi Gocha, who heard of the birth of a special child, sent investigators, and seeing that the circumstances conformed to the prediction, he notified Tsurphu. A search party was dispatched to Kham. At Karma Gon Monastery, the boy declared himself the Karmapa, and he identified his own ritual implements from his previous life. He was enthroned by Shamar Konchok Yenlak. Karmapa Wangchuk Dorje wrote extensively. Three important works of his, *The Ocean of Certainty,* and *Eliminating the Darkness of Ignorance,* and *Pointing Out the Dharmakaya,* are in English translations. He, like his two predecessors, was a great mahamudra scholar and practitioner. The Karmapa accomplished all this while moving from place to place in his encampment, the garchen, like some roving religious ambassador.

By this time the Karmapa had a consistent group of reincarnate lamas who were among his core disciples: the Shamarpa, the Tai Situpa, and Goshir Gyaltsapa were three of the most important. In each life the Karmapa located their new incarnations. After the Karmapa's death, one or more of these tulkus performed the same service for him. The Karmapa transmitted all of the teachings to at least one of them before he died, and they would in turn instruct his new incarnation. The Karmapa had cordial relations with Sonam Gyatso, the Gelug teacher who was to be named Dalai Lama by Altan Khan. One thing in particular that Wangchuk Dorje did has bearing on the present. He was invited by the king of Sikkim to visit that country. He didn't go himself, but he sent several lamas in his stead who established three Karma Kagyu monasteries in Sikkim: Ralang, Podrang, and Rumtek, which still function today. Rumtek became the Karmapa's safe haven when the sixteenth incarnation fled Tibet 350 years later, and Ralang is now the Gyaltsapa's monastery in exile. After an active life, Wangchuk Dorje died in 1603. He wrote letters the night before he died that predicted he would be reborn in Kham.

TURBULENT TIMES

Golok, in eastern Tibet, was the birthplace of the Tenth Karmapa Choying Dorje in 1604. Like other Karmapas, it is said he recited mantras, stood up and took one step in each of the four directions, and sat in meditation posture while still an infant. He was acknowledged as a holy child and lived under the protection of a local chieftain in his early years, until he was recognized and enthroned as the Karmapa at the age of eight by the Sixth Shamarpa. Perhaps foreshadowing the tumultuous life to come, a controversy arose over who should be enthroned.

Another candidate, Karma Chagme, was seen by some as the rightful Karmapa, but it was determined through divination and other evidence that Choying Dorje should take the throne. Karma Chagme was thereafter respected as an *outrul,* or "candidate," and became a distinguished writer and meditator. Karmapa Choying Dorje followed the active pattern of previous Karmapas, combining study and good works with almost continual travel in the Karmay Garchen.

Like his predecessors, Choying Dorje was invited to Mongolia by the Mongol Khans who still ruled on the steppes, although it was the time of the ascent of the Gelugpas as spiritual advisers to the Khans. As Richardson observes, it appears "that the Karma-pa lamas did not neglect nor were neglected by the Mongols, but they lacked the missionary fervour of their rivals; moreover their influence and energy were impaired at this time by various internal dissensions."[58]

Some of these dissensions could be traced to the Shamarpa. The Shamarpa incarnations—the name means "red hat"— appeared during the time of the Third Karmapa, Rangjung Dorje, who was the first Shamarpa's teacher. Successive Shamar tulkus settled near the Karmapa's monastery in Central Tibet. By Choying Dorje's time the Shamarpa was a very important Karma Kagyu lama. But unlike the Karmapas, the Shamarpas gravitated toward politics. The political maneuverings of the Sixth Shamarpa Chokyi Wangchuk and his patron, the king of Tsang, provoked hostility among Kagyu lamas who opposed sectarian rivalry and created tension between the Karmapa and Shamarpa. As noted previously, the Karmapas, though never temporal rulers, exercised considerable influence well before there were Dalai Lamas. When the Gelug school founder Tsongkhapa and his disciple Gendun Drub successfully proselytized at the court of the Mongol Khans, the Gelugpas gained not only religious but temporal ascendancy in Central Tibet. The subsequent incarnations of Gendun Drub were revered, and it is this line of incarnations that was dubbed "Dalai" by Altan Khan. Rising Gelug power was resented by the Shamarpa and the Tsang king. It became worse when Gelug sovereignty was institutionalized by the Fifth Dalai Lama's appointment as political ruler by Gushri Khan.

Historically, problems that occur in the *labrang,* or monastery administration of incarnate lamas, have had very negative results. The climate of rivalry among monasteries of different sects during these years encouraged political meddling by those who had other goals besides study and meditation. An illustrative incident occurred during the Fourth Dalai Lama's time, and kept relations between the labrangs of the Karmapa and Dalai Lama frayed into the time of the Fifth Dalai Lama. According to the historian Shakabpa, it began with a poem sent to the Dalai Lama by "the Red Hat subsect of the Karmapa." The "Red Hat subsect" refers to the labrang of the Sixth Shamarpa. The Fourth Dalai Lama, Yonten Gyatso, was the grandson of Altan Khan and was kept in Mongolia until he was about twelve years old, when he was brought to Lhasa for enthronement. The poem was sent on that occasion. The poetic imagery was obscure and the Dalai Lama's attendants couldn't understand it. Instead of sending a similar poem in reply, they fired off a stiff rejoinder to the Shamarpa labrang. This angered the Shamarpa's attendants, who circulated the story that the Dalai Lama's attendants could not understand poetry, an embarrassing lapse for monks who were supposed to be well educated. Some time later, when a Karma Kagyu lama offered a scarf with a poetic prayer written on it at Lhasa's Jokhang temple, the Dalai Lama's thin-skinned attendants again misinterpreted it, thinking it was an insult to the Dalai Lama. Shakabpa says that there are evidentiary letters that show the Karmapa and Dalai Lama corresponded about meeting to sort things out. Such a meeting might have ended the rivalry, but their attendants scuttled the plan. "Poems written at the time blame the attendants on both sides for preventing a meeting which might have led to a reconciliation."[59] It was unfortunate, because the grudges, which festered for decades, ultimately escalated into warfare.

The times were increasingly turbulent politically, and as the Tenth Karmapa Choying Dorje matured, he spent a great deal of energy trying to stop wars. The king of Tsang, Karma Puntsok

Namgyal, was a devotee of the Karma Kagyu school, as was the king's son. When the son came to power, his attempt to take over Tibet and a dispute with the large Gelug monasteries Drepung and Sera triggered a Mongol invasion. It also caused the Karmapa plenty of trouble. The monks of Drepung and Sera, in collusion with the Fifth Dalai Lama's chief attendant Sonam Chopal, invited the Mongols, then under the leadership of Gushri Khan, to help them. The Mongols were asked not only to fight the king of Tsang, but to wage war against the other Buddhist schools. This invitation was made behind the back of the Dalai Lama. It was a classic example of the sort of intrigue cooked up by ministers who overrode the wishes of the Dalai Lama. Such political manipulations punctuate the history of the Dalai Lamas. For almost the entire nineteenth century in fact, no Dalai Lama achieved his majority. His regents clung to their power, sometimes by whatever expedient. According to historical accounts the Karmapas and Dalai Lamas constructively communicated with each other and met occasionally, even if the relations between their followers were less cordial.

Bad feeling persisted between the Kagyu and Gelug monks in Tenth Karmapa's time thanks to the sectarianism of the princes of Tsang, staunch Kagyu supporters who openly discriminated against Gelugpas. Karmapa Choying Dorje disapproved of this and, unlike the Shamarpa, dissuaded the princes from starting a war. When he heard that Lhasa had sent ministers to ask Gushri Khan for military aid, he wrote to the Dalai Lama disassociating himself from the Tsangpa king's activities. He explained he was not in favor of a religious war and did not approve of the king of Tsang's behavior. The Dalai Lama reassured him that he knew this, and war was not his intention, but his ministers thought otherwise. The Karmapa tried to discourage the Tsangpa king from hostilities. The Karmapa warned him that his persistence in war would be personally fatal.

Gushri Khan led his army first into Kham, where he subdued a Bon ruler, then pushed toward Tsang in central Tibet. He attacked the king of Tsang's army in Shigatse and killed the king, just as the Karmapa had foretold. It was then that Gushri Khan installed the Fifth Dalai Lama as supreme ruler of Tibet, giving him both spiritual and temporal authority. Political affairs were placed in the hands of his chief minister Sonam Chopal. The ascent of the Fifth Dalai Lama, Ngawang Losang Gyatso, marked the end of the Rimpung dynasty of rulers. The Gelugpas, led politically by the Dalai Lama, attained a position similar to that of the Sakya lamas who earlier enjoyed Mongol support. The Gelug power base was strong, and they were able to endure in the areas they dominated.

The Tenth Karmapa Choying Dorje, meanwhile, saw more trouble ahead, so he put the able Gyaltsap Drakpa Choying temporarily in charge of Tsurphu and moved off with his garchen to Yam Dar. The Gyaltsapa, or regent, is a significant Karma Kagyu tulku. Once again correspondence between the Karmapa and the Dalai Lama was misinterpreted by the Dalai Lama's ministers, and they used it as an excuse to send the Mongols to the Karmapa's encampment. Many of his monks were killed and the encampment devastated, but Choying Dorje emerged unscathed. Some accounts say he flew away from the camp in the shape of a bird or scampered away as a deer, but by whatever means, he and his personal attendant escaped to a far corner of Tibet. He was sheltered by a loyal follower, the king of Jang Satam, an eastern Tibetan province near the border of Yunnan, China. He continued teaching there. Growing tired of staying in the town, he traveled alone—sometimes in disguise—to find the important Kagyu tulkus that made up his foremost group of disciples. The previous Shamarpa and Tai Situpa had died, so he located Shamar Yeshe Nyingpo and Tai Situpa among others. He was robbed by highwaymen and went about like a beggar until he was finally rescued by his anxious followers.

Choying Dorje remained in Jang Satam for thirty years, and he married, one of only two Karmapas recorded to have taken wives. A son of this marriage was the Sixth Gyaltsapa, Norbu Zangpo (1659–98). The king of Jang Satam offered to invade Tibet and set the Karmapa up as ruler, but the Karmapa discouraged his plan. When he finally returned to Tsang, the Karmapa visited Lhasa, where he met the Fifth Dalai Lama.

There they discussed religious and political matters. The Gelugpas had seized some of his Karma Kagyu monasteries and made them Gelug, but thanks to the diplomacy of the Gyaltsapa, who had been left in charge of the Karmapa's Tsurphu Monastery, most of the Karmapa's monasteries were retained and Tsurphu left untouched. The Dalai Lama promised that in the future Tsurphu would be protected in times of trouble, but this also meant more Gelug political involvement. Karmapa Choying Dorje died at in 1674. He left instructions about his next rebirth with Shamarpa Yeshe Nyingpo, Gyaltsapa, and his own personal attendant.

The Eleventh Karmapa (1686–1702) had the shortest life of all the Karmapa Incarnations. He was recognized and named Yeshe Dorje by the terton Mingyur Dorje, who was a master of both Nyingma and Kagyu traditions. Karmapa Yeshe Dorje was noted for his advanced spirituality.

Jangchub Dorje, the Twelfth Karmapa, was born the son of a pottery merchant in Derge, Kham, in 1703. Like Karma Pakshi, his family descended from King Trisong Detsen. Before his birth his father was told by a holy man from a nearby monastery that a fortunate event in his family would mean he wouldn't have to sell pots anymore. As with other incarnations, the Karmapa identified himself. A search party was sent by the Shamarpa and confirmed his identity. The young Karmapa then embarked on the usual course of studies. During this period the Mongols invaded Lhasa, killed the local prince, and plundered temples, the same events that were recorded by the wandering Jesuit Ippolito Desideri. The Seventh Dalai Lama fled temporarily. On his return, Karmapa Jangchub Dorje met him in Lhasa. The Karmapa then departed on an extensive pilgrimage with his chief tulkus, the Shamarpa, Tai Situpa, and Gyaltsapa. They visited sacred places in Nepal and went as far as Kushinagar, the place of the Buddha's death in northern India. On the way back they visited Mount Kailash, the imposing, striated mountain sacred to Buddhists and Hindus alike, high on the plateau of western Tibet. The Karmapa received an invitation to go to China. After doing a retreat at Tsurphu and discharging some teaching obligations, he entrusted the Karma Kamtsang to the Eighth Tai Situ, Chokyi Jungne. The Karmapa and the Shamarpa left for China in 1725. There, in 1732, Karmapa Jangchub Dorje died of smallpox. The Shamarpa succumbed to the same disease within a month. Before dying, the Karmapa sent a letter with details of his next rebirth to Situ Rinpoche.

The Thirteenth Karmapa, Dudul Dorje, was born in a village near Lhasa, and was discovered after a renowned lama had a vision of his exact location. He mastered his studies and the yogas. His pursuits were those of previous Karmapas. It is said he fulfilled a prophecy of Padmasambhava that if Lhasa was ever threatened by flood, the Karmapa could help avert disaster. When he was called on by the government to help, he prayed, and the river waters that threatened the city subsided. When he visited an elderly Situ Rinpoche in Derge, he stopped at Karma Gon to perform a ceremony sponsored by a noble family. He told the family they would soon meet him again, and they should remember he said this. He recognized the new Tai Situ, Pema Nyingje Wangpo in 1774 after having a vision. The Karmapa subsequently enthroned the Tai Situpa. Before Dudul Dorje died in 1797, he left a prediction letter about his next rebirth with the Tai Situpa.

The following year, biographers record, the Karmapa revisited the noble family in Kham as promised, in the form of their new-born son. Strange phenomena were reported at his birth: unusual rainbows appeared in the sky and flowers bloomed in winter. The Fourteenth Karmapa Tekchok Dorje was recognized and enthroned by Situ Pema Nyingje Wangpo, who subsequently ordained him as a monk and was his principal teacher. At this time Situ Rinpoche's monastery Palpung was the center of a new intellectual development called *rimé,* or "no bias," which strove to bridge sectarian lines and share the wealth of knowledge among all four schools of Tibetan Buddhism. It was a renaissance during which treasuries of sacred art, literature, and science were compiled and new trends were stimulated under the brilliant leadership of lamas such as Jamgon Kongtrul Lodro Taye, Jamyang Khyentse Wangpo, and the terton, or "treasure finder," Chogyur Lingpa. Karmapa Tekchok Dorje lived simply, even austerely, and insisted on strict observance of monastic rules in his monasteries. Jamgon Kongtrul was one of the Karmapa's chief students. Before the Karmapa died in 1868, he transmitted the entire Kagyu teachings to Jamgon Kongtrul.

The Fifteenth Karmapa Khakyab Dorje was born in 1871 in Tsang. Like previous Karmapas, he exhibited extraordinary traits. He was able to read at an early age and composed prayers by the time he was four years old. He was recognized by Jamgon Kongtrul and several other eminent tulkus. Not only did the details of his birth correspond with clues left by the previous Karmapa, but the boy accurately identified pieces of clothing and other belongings of his predecessor. He was taken to Tsurphu and enthroned. He received the lineage transmission from Jamgon Kongtrul and he proved an enthusiastic scholar. Khakyab Dorje took several consorts, and by one of them had a son who was the reincarnation of his guru Jamgon Kongtrul. Another son was the Shamarpa tulku, who was not recognized because recognition of his reincarnation was banned by the government after the Gurkha War in 1792. The story of this ban will be told in a later chapter.

This is perhaps apocryphal, but Khakyab Dorje, after taking two wives, apparently said later in life that he was not so keen on the institution of marriage, and that monkhood is much easier. Sex is famously part of Tibetan tantric lore, but in actual practice—as taught by bona fide lamas in the tantric Buddhist tradition—the lore refers to mastering inner polarities and using that balance to stimulate greater realization, and ultimately freedom from bondage of illusion. There are, of course, accounts of great yogis who, in union with their consorts, light up the sky and dazzle eavesdroppers, but such stories are from a different epoch. The Fifteenth Karmapa lived until 1922, having spent the last ten years of his life in strict retreat. He gave the letter predicting his rebirth to his personal attendant ten years prior to his death.

The Sixteenth Karmapa performs the Black Crown ceremony.

5. The Sixteenth
Karmapa

A NEW ERA BEGAN DURING THE LIfe of the Fifteenth Karmapa Khakyab Dorje that would ultimately draw Tibet into a strange new world. Even before the Fifteenth Karmapa died in 1922, the West had broached the forbidden mountain kingdom in a whole new way: politically. Khakyab Dorje was born at the height of the Great Game, the power struggle between Britain and Russia for influence, if not dominance, over Central Asia. Britain, wary of countries adjacent to India, the jewel in the crown of their empire, maneuvered to create a buffer zone against Russia for most of the nineteenth century. So in addition to the Gelug politics in Lhasa, intersectarian rivalries, and the odd chieftain trying to carve some land out of a neighbor's patch, there was a new ingredient in the mix. The pundit-spies, native operatives employed by the British, and suspicious Russians came and went. While Tibet wrestled with whether or not to relate to the rest of the world, the West coped with rapid change wrought first by the Industrial Revolution and then by the First World

War. New technologies were emerging. The cinema was a wonder that anyone with a few cents could attend. Radios appeared in many middle class homes. Time may have stood still in Tibet, but when the Sixteenth Karmapa was born in Kham in 1924, extraordinary things were taking place in other parts of the world. Modern inventions may well have seemed as unlikely to a Tibetan who heard about them as stories of Tibetan saints' footprints in stone might seem to a Westerner.

The Sixteenth Karmapa, Rangjung Rigpe Dorje, was born near the most important river in eastern Tibet, in the kingdom of Derge, at Denkok, in Kham. It is one of the more beautiful areas of Tibet, with abundant forests and streams. A high lama of a nearby monastery had predicted that a bodhisattva would be born in the noble Atub family. The lama advised the Karmapa's mother to deliver the baby in a cave sacred to Tibet's great saint Padmasambhava, and she complied. Denkok has special significance to Tibetans: in the much-loved folk epic *Gesar of Ling*, the heroic archer Denma was said to have been born there. Auspicious omens were reported by the community at the time of the Karmapa's birth in the holy cave: spontaneous light and rainbows appeared; water turned to milk. Lama Karma Thinley relates: "Before the child's birth he disappeared from the womb for one whole day and then returned the next. On the actual night of his birth, the atmosphere was charged with portents, which everyone in the locality could sense."[60]

The identity of the Karmapa's actual father was debated at the time of his birth. Some old residents of Derge cite a story, widely believed in the locality, that his father was actually a general from Lhasa, Da Na Tapa, who stayed with the Atub family off and on while he was in Derge on business. Old-timers further maintain that the Thirteenth Dalai Lama delayed permission to enthrone the Karmapa for four years, until Da Na Tapa's name appeared on the application as the Karmapa's father rather than Tsewang Atubsang—presumably for the advantage of having a Lhasa official in such a position of influence with one of Tibet's most important lamas. Documents that might prove this tale, however, are filed away at the Potala, if not destroyed. And

A young Sixteenth
Karmapa with the
Eleventh Tai Situpa
Pema Wangchuk
Gyalpo, about 1935

true or not, Tsewang Atubsang treated the Karmapa as his own
son, and the boy was accepted as such.

The identity of the Karmapa's natural father was less important than the identity of the Karmapa himself. This was ultimately determined by an amulet left by the previous Karmapa.
While in retreat he had given it to an attendant by the name of
Golok Gelong Jampal Tsultrim, with instructions to open it
when an urgent message came from Tai Situpa at Palpung
Monastery. Around the time the Atub boy entered the world, Tai
Situpa had specific visions about where to find the young incarnation. He and Jamgon Kongtrul Khyentse Ozer (1904–53) set
out to meet him. After they found him, and were satisfied that
he was the Sixteenth Karmapa, they made the customary offerings of clothing and other things. They also gave him lay ordination[61] and sent a message to Tsurphu that they believed they had
found the Karmapa. Tai Situpa and Kongtrul asked that the
amulet left by the previous Karmapa be sent to Palpung. But the
amulet could not be found. Jampal Tsultrim had gone off to
Mount Kailash on pilgrimage and taken it with him. When he at
last returned, he gave it to Tsurphu Monastery so it could be
decoded. It was a numeric cryptogram, difficult to interpret. The
story goes that a monastery cook accidentally found a page of a
poetry that provided the key to crack the code. When it finally
was interpreted, it revealed birth details that coincided exactly
with those of the boy discovered clairvoyantly by Tai Situpa.
The letter read:

From here to the East, near the river Serden,
In the district held by the Brave Archer,
On top of a naturally formed lion,
The mountain adorned by "Aa" and "tub,"
In the royal house, the case of Chokar Dzeu,
He can be seen dwelling in the womb of a worldly Dakini,
In either an Ox or a Mouse year.
From the emptiness of all-pervading Ati,
There will arise a great lamp of transcendental wisdom, the
unification of appearance and knowledge.
He will be called Rangjung Rigpe Dorje.[62]

The letter said his birthplace would be on a mountaintop locally
called Lion Sky Castle, near the Golden River, or Drichu, far to
the east of Tsurphu. The "Brave Archer" is Denma, the war-
rior of Ling Gesar, and Denkok was his district. "Aa" and
"tub" refer specifically to the Karmapa's family name. He was
born in 1924 to Atub Repo Tsewang Puntsok and his wife
Gyalkhar Kalsang Drolma. Chokar Dzeu refers to the clan of
the royal house of Derge to which they belonged. And so the
Sixteenth Karmapa was found, two years after the death of his
predecessor.

When he was quite young the Sixteenth Karmapa's psychic
gifts enabled him to help his neighbors in practical ways, for
instance, to locate stray animals, a valuable asset for nomads
whose goats might wander. Early in 1931, when he was seven
years old, Tai Situpa and Jamgon Kongtrul gave him novice ordination and escorted him to Palpung Monastery. Karma Thinley
relates that Tai Situpa enthroned him in the main shrine of
Palpung. A few months later he was taken to Tsurphu for his
enthronement, four years after his recognition. It took that long
for permission to be granted by the Lhasa government. Official
permission was necessary since Tsurphu was located in central
Tibet and fell under the jurisdiction of the Lhasa government.
Some of these requirements dated from the turbulent times and
subsequent peacemaking between the Tenth Karmapa and Fifth
Dalai Lama centuries earlier.

The Karmapa, escorted by Jamgon Kongtrul, Gyaltsap Rinpoche, and Pawo Rinpoche, another important Karma Kagyu tulku, traveled with about one thousand monks in the Karmay Garchen, stopping at monasteries all along the way. At a monastery about halfway to Tsurphu, in Nangchen, the Sixteenth Karmapa performed his first Black Crown Ceremony. Not long after reaching Tsurphu the Karmapa visited the Thirteenth Dalai Lama in Lhasa. The Dalai Lama performed the customary hair-cutting ceremony for the young lama. At this ceremony, the Dalai Lama reportedly perceived the inner black hat of the Karmapas, just as the Ming dynasty emperor Yung Lo had done before him. The Karmapa removed his small black hat for the ceremony, as etiquette demands, but the Dalai Lama was heard to ask why the Karmapa had not taken off his hat. Everyone else present saw him bare-headed. There are differing versions of what the Dalai Lama actually said, but accounts agree, and believers concluded, that he must have seen the non-material black crown that may be discerned only by those of advanced spiritual development.

After the Karmapa came to Lhasa, he and the Thirteenth Dalai Lama formed a warm friendship, in spite of the great difference in their ages—the Thirteenth Dalai Lama was then

The Sixteenth Karmapa as young boy at Tsurphu

The Sixteenth
Karmapa with
his principal
teacher Bo
Gongkar
Rinpoche, in
the 1940s

nearly fifty. The Fourteenth Dalai Lama told me this story, which was told to him by the Sixteenth Karmapa: "During the Thirteenth Dalai Lama's time, in the late Karmapa Rinpoche's own words, when he reached Lhasa from Kham, the Dalai Lama kept him there at Norbulingka for some time. Then some of the Karmapa's followers got worried about whether or not they would be able to take the Karmapa to Tsurphu. Finally he did go there. But the Karmapa himself had pleasant memories. From time to time the Dalai Lama sent some treats, Tibetan biscuits and fruit, and these were brought to him by a person on horseback. The horse had a special bell, and he used to recognize the ring of the bell. When he heard this bell he would rush out and wait for this man to reach the monastery."[63]

The Karmapa pursued his studies at Tsurphu under the tutorship of Bo Gongkar Rinpoche. Bo Gongkar Rinpoche's fame as a repository of Karma Kagyu teachings was great, and among his students were the Sakya scholar Dezhung Rinpoche, who later settled in Seattle, and C. C. Garma Chang, who translated the *Hundred Thousand Songs of Milarepa* into English. When the Karmapa was twelve years old he went back to Kham. On the way many strange things happened, among them an oft-told incident where Karmapa seemingly taught snakes that came out of the rocks at a hot springs. The snakes surrounded the Karmapa who, disregarding the panic of his attendants, talked to them. The reptiles appeared to listen for a while, and when the Karmapa was finished, they quietly slithered away. From an early age he demonstrated a special rapport with animals. In one place his pet deer is said to have left hoofprints in stone. After a series of similar supernatural episodes, the Karmapa arrived at Palpung where he was ordained by Situ Rinpoche in 1938. Later that year the Karmapa and Tai Situpa, when traveling together, reportedly both left footprints in stone at a monastery temple in Litang.[64]

The young Karmapa continued his studies and his travels, visiting monasteries all around Tibet. In 1944, when he was twenty, he made a pilgrimage to Samye and to Southern Tibet, to Drowolung Monastery. The same year he was invited to Bhutan by its second king, Jigme Wangchuk, who had ruled Bhutan since 1928. The Karmapas had long-standing relationships with the neighboring kingdoms of Sikkim and Bhutan, and members of the royal families were his devotees. The monasteries in Bhutan were predominantly Drukpa Kagyu.

The Bhutanese trace Buddhism in their country to the ninth-century Tibetan king Ralpachen. According to Dorji Wangmo, one of the four queens of Bhutan, Ralpachen's brother Prince Tsangma was exiled to "Lho Mon," as Bhutan was known.[65] His descendants preserved their Buddhism and eventually became the ruling elite. The Shapdrung, the highest of the Drukpa Kagyu tulkus, virtually ruled Bhutan. The first Shapdrung, Ngawang Namgyal (1594–1651), declared Bhutan a unified state under a Buddhist theocracy, ruled by him and his successors. His death was kept a secret for more than fifty years in the interest of preserving the new country's stability while an acceptable Shapdrung was found. The power vacuum created in the absence of a ruling Shapdrung led to fierce warfare and assassinations among bureaucrats and clans. Later, British annexation of the fertile Duar Plain caused a war. But a skillful governor, Orgyen Wangchuk (1862–1926), finally supplanted

An assembly of top Karma Kagyu lamas at Palpung in the 1940s. Left to right: the Second Jamgon Kongtrul, Ongen Tulku, Beru Khyentse, the Sixteenth Karmapa, Situ Pema Wangchuk Gyalpo, (unknown), and Pawo Tulku.

the Shapdrung as king. Wangchuk curbed civil unrest by stabilizing the country's internal and external affairs. He was elected king in 1907 by monastic, bureaucratic, and popular representatives. The semi-democratic election notwithstanding, Bhutan retained many feudal trappings. And it retained its religion as well: the Bhutanese remain devout Buddhists.

The Karmapa was often inspired by his travels. Like earlier Karmapas, he was a visionary. Visits to valleys sacred to Padmasambhava in Bhutan and Sikkim, or to places frequented by Milarepa or other saints, stimulated his creativity. He wrote poems, often about his own previous lives. There is evidence that his insights went beyond Buddhist philosophy. As scholar Tashi Tsering points out, the young Karmapa's poetry began to show that he foresaw the storm gathering over Tibet. An example is this excerpt from a 1944 poem:[66]

The Sixteenth
Karmapa as a young
man at Tsurphu

I will not stay, but go to uncertain places
to experience the fruit of the karma of my previous lives.
The cuckoo will come to Tibet in the spring.
The day the saddening song is sung,
you will wonder where the man Rigdol is.
Oh! Dependent ones! Don't you realize you will feel
    distressed?

The cuckoo is an unusual bird. It lays its eggs in the nest of other birds. The unwitting mother returns and incubates the alien egg. When it hatches, the hatchling cuckoo often tries to push the unhatched eggs out of the nest, killing the rightful occupants. The cuckoo is an unmistakable metaphor for the Chinese, and the poem foreshadows the Karmapa's own departure from Tibet. He warns of suffering to come. In another poem he wrote, "There is nowhere to turn but India."[67]

After receiving full ordination from Tai Situpa in 1945, the Karmapa received the entire transmission of the Karma Kagyu teachings, also from Tai Situpa. Two years later, when the Sixteenth Karmapa was twenty-five, he made his first visit to Nepal at the invitation of King Tribhuvan Bir Bikram Shah Dev. Buddhist pilgrimage sites in Nepal are everywhere. The Buddha was born there, in Lumbini. The Karmapa went there before continuing to the sacred sites in India: Bodhgaya, where Buddha was enlightened, Saranath, where he first taught, and Kushinagar, where he died. The Karmapa also went to Ajanta and Ellora, where some of the oldest and most exquisite Buddhist murals may still be seen. The king of Sikkim, Chogyal Tashi Namgyal, sent his personal secretary as a guide for the Karmapa during this pilgrimage, and invited the Karmapa to Sikkim.

Sikkim's capital Gangtok is picturesquely perched on a hillside below the great Kanchenjunga massif. Here the Karmapa stayed at the Royal Palace Monastery. He gave sermons and performed the Black Crown Ceremony. From Sikkim he returned to India, journeying across the country to see sacred sites in the north-west, such as Tso Pema, the "lotus lake" associated with

The Sixteenth
Karmapa in
Beijing, 1955

Padmasambhava and consort Mandarava, in what is now the
Indian state of Himachal Pradesh. There are many strange tales
about this place where yogis still meditate in surrounding caves.
That an island in the middle of the lake mysteriously moves
around is but one of these tales. The party returned to Tibet via
Kinnaur, Lake Manasarovar, and Mount Kailash, where the
Karmapa did three circumambulations of the holy mountain,
three days for each round, a fairly arduous task. His travels
entailed thousands of miles, much of it on foot or horse. In

those days—and indeed, even today in some areas—motorable roads were hard to come by in the Himalayas.

In 1933 the Thirteenth Dalai Lama Tupten Gyatso died. His new incarnation, the Fourteenth Dalai Lama, Tenzin Gyatso, was born in Amdo, the northeastern part of Tibet, in 1935. He was located when he was about three years old, thanks to "a number of signs" described by the Dalai Lama himself in his 1990 autobiography.[68] First, the head of the embalmed body of the Thirteenth Dalai Lama provided a clue when it turned from facing south of Lhasa to northeast. Then the Dalai Lama's regent had a prophetic vision while gazing at the sacred Lhamoi Latso lake. He saw a series of Tibetan letters, *Ah, Ka,* and *Ma.* He also envisioned a particular three-story monastery and a house with a distinctive design. The clues led them to Amdo, to Kumbum Monastery, and finally to the small house where a child ran up and recognized one of them as a lama from Sera Monastery. Then items were brought that had belonged to the Thirteenth Dalai Lama mixed up with others that had not. Each time the boy correctly selected the belongings of the previous Dalai Lama, saying, "It's mine." In that way the Fourteenth Dalai Lama was found. He was lodged in Kumbum until 1939, when he was brought to Lhasa and enthroned in 1940.

The Sixteenth Karmapa's relationship with the Fourteenth Dalai Lama, who was eleven years his junior, was strong in times of growing difficulties for Tibet. The two lamas met at intervals, and in 1953 the Karmapa received the Kalachakra initiation from him. This ceremony confers a particular blessing and instruction that is believed to bring peace in dark times. The following year the Karmapa was part of a delegation to Beijing led by the Dalai Lama. During this visit the Karmapa recognized a senior tulku, the Twelfth Tai Situpa, Pema Donyo Nyinje. Namkhai Norbu Rinpoche has a story to tell about this.

Both Namkhai Norbu Rinpoche and Bo Gongkar Rinpoche taught in a Chinese school at Dartsedo at the time. When Namkhai Norbu discovered who his colleague was, he asked him for teachings. Namkhai Norbu had not had Kagyu teachings before, and Bo Gongkar was an illustrious master. "Gongkar

Rinpoche is one of my very important teachers," Namkhai Norbu recalled, "For that reason we had a very good relationship, very, very strong." Bo Gongkar Rinpoche had been very concerned about finding the new Tai Situpa and wanted precise information, since there were rumors in Derge about one or two boys who displayed the special characteristics of a tulku. He went to Beijing to ask the Karmapa. When Bo Gongkar Rinpoche returned to Dartsedo, Namkhai Norbu asked what happened. "He showed me this letter that the Karmapa had given him," Namkhai Norbu recalls, "And on this paper I saw indications of Situ Rinpoche's family, father, mother's name, etcetera. Very, very precise. I was a little surprised, really. I told Gongkar Rinpoche it's too clear. Maybe it's difficult to find everything…He said 'No, don't say this, because Gyalwa Karmapa is very, very skillful at recognizing incarnations. I believe we can find Situ Rinpoche very precisely.'" Bo Gongkar Rinpoche sent his monks with this letter to Palpung Monastery, and Palpung immediately sent a search party using the indications of where to look in the Karmapa's letter. They found Tai Situpa.[69]

On the Karmapa's return he visited monasteries of Kham, and when he reached Palpung he enthroned the infant Tai Situpa. There was little time to waste. The Chinese army was already harassing monasteries in eastern Tibet. The Karmapa knew that worse was yet to come.

The Dalai Lama recalls meeting the Sixteenth Karmapa often in Tibet. After the first formal meeting before a large audience, they met privately for discussions in the Norbulingka. "Then later, on one occasion he invited me, and I went to Tsurphu, and I stayed few days there. I saw all the *nangden,* those sacred things that we usually keep through generations."[70] These are relics of saints, images, and other precious objects. It was an occasion that reminded him of the Karmapa's sense of humor. "My two tutors were also there," he continued. "And of course both tutors were very close friends of the late Karmapa, particularly Trijang Rinpoche. They were always teasing each other." He added, with a twinkle, "Karma Rinpoche himself, you see, had this kind of jovial nature. A very nice person."

It was in 1955, when the Dalai Lama was twenty years old. The visit coincided with Tsechu, the summer ritual dances, in which the Karmapa himself took the lead part. The Karmapa performed the Black Crown Ceremony, and the Dalai Lama, who, like the Karmapa, is considered an emanation of Chenrezig, gave the Chenrezig initiation. "I remember very clearly the few days I spent there, a very happy memory, happy days, like a holiday." The Dalai Lama also said they met frequently later in Lhasa, when the Karmapa came to meetings at the behest of the Chinese.

The Chinese imposed their own bureaucracy in Lhasa, setting up a preparatory committee for the autonomous region of Tibet. But in eastern Tibet they were not so restrained. The People's Liberation Army attacked more monasteries in Kham, showing clearly their intention to employ any means to take over. The Khampas, the people of the eastern Tibetan province of Kham, began organizing a militia to defend themselves. When a charismatic leader who mobilized fighters to defend Litang Monastery was killed, there was a revolt in that province and retaliation upon Chinese camps. Khampa refugees began to stream into Central Tibet as more villages and monasteries were destroyed. In 1956 the Karmapa acted for the Tibetan government when he accompanied a delegation to Chamdo that

Sixteenth Karmapa and attendants crossing the Natu-la pass into Sikkim on his second, and last pilgrimage from Tibet to India.

included Zhabpe Ngaboe Ngawang Jigme, chief government liaison officer with the Chinese. The delegates tried to reason with the Chinese, and finally got them to agree to stop the imposition of "reforms" for five years, but the situation remained grave. Now all the Karmapa's teachings and ritual prayers were offered to preserve the tenuous peace. He returned to Lhasa and conferred with the Dalai Lama.

The Sixteenth Karmapa made another pilgrimage to India, again via Sikkim. He met the Chogyal and the royal family again in Gangtok. From there he revisited holy places in India and Nepal. He came back to Sikkim, and before returning to Tibet he went to a few monasteries, including Podrang. But when requested to visit nearby Rumtek, he declined, saying he would return later for a longer stay. Back in Tibet, he continued his teaching and counseling as strife spread in Kham. A monastery, Dhargye Choling, was being constructed for the Karmapa in Bhutan by a Bhutanese princess. The Karmapa himself was busy restoring Nyide Gon in Lhodrak, in southern Tibet, and

A group portrait taken at Tsurphu from the 1950s. In the first row, second from left, is a teenaged Topga Yugyal. The Sixteenth Karmapa is fourth from left, with a snoozing infant Tai Situpa between him and Sangye Nyenpa Tulku. Next to Sangye Nyenpa is his brother, the eminent Nyingma tulku Dilgo Khyentse Rinpoche.

reassuring the local monks, who were increasingly alarmed by Chinese aggression. His followers had implored him to leave Tibet, but he had told them that the time was not yet right. When it was, he told them, he would be able to leave without difficulty.

During his years in Tibet, the Sixteenth Karmapa preserved the custom of traveling in the Karmay Garchen, his massive, nomadic monastery. Tendzin Namgyal, the current chandzo, or chief administrator, for the Seventeenth Karmapa, participated in the Garchen as a young monk. He said that laypeople who wanted to go along had to qualify as serious Buddhists by completing one hundred thousand Chenrezig mantras.[71] Members of the group would carry volumes of the Kangyur, the Buddhist canon, on their backs and recite the contents as they walked. The Karmapa sometimes was carried in a richly caparisoned palanquin, though he often preferred to ride a horse, which was also adorned with colorful brocades and tinkling bells. When they pitched camp, the Karmapa's personal tent was partitioned into several rooms: one bedroom, one relic room, one small shrine room, and a large shrine room where the people would congregate for the Black Crown Ceremony, observe rituals, and hear sermons. These rooms were hung with precious tangkas and brocades, canopies shining with silk and pure gold. Some of the accouterments were gifts of bygone Chinese emperors. Near the Karmapa's tent were those of the most important monastery officials: the chandzo, the shrine master, and so forth, arranged according their importance in the hierarchy. Chandzo Tendzin Namgyal said the entourage could pitch and strike the tents in very short order. The Karmapa's schedule was worked out ahead of time. People in a region would request certain ceremonies, and he would spend days or weeks in one place, performing whatever rituals were required.

The time came at last when the Karmapa felt that he could no longer stay in Tibet. There were those who tried to dissuade him from leaving, but once he had decided, he was adamant. He could not delay even a few months. Tai Situpa, then six years old, had already been taken to Bhutan by his monks to escape the fighting, which was spreading throughout Tibet. Other tulkus also left. The Third Jamgon Kongtrul, who was the same age as Tai Situpa, was with his family in Kalimpong in India. The Karmapa felt it was necessary to leave in order to preserve Tibetan Buddhism. He told the Dalai Lama of his plans.

In the spring of 1959, on the fourth night of the second month of the Earth Pig year in the Tibetan calendar, in the middle of the night and dressed like a layman, the Sixteenth Karmapa and a party of attendants, monks, and laypeople from the Tsurphu community left for Bhutan. The Karmapa arranged for the most important portable ritual ornaments, statues, relics, tangkas, texts, and brocades to be packed up and taken along. There were two *ushas,* or black crowns—the original one given by Yung Lo in the sixteenth century and a copy, made a few hundred years later, to spare the original some wear and tear. One of these was left at Tsurphu, presumably destroyed when most of Tsurphu was reduced to rubble by the People's Liberation Army. The other was brought with the essential texts and treasures of Tsurphu over the snow mountains to Bhutan and on to Rumtek Monastery in Sikkim. No one is certain today which Black Crown was brought out. Most of the precious relics of Tsurphu had to be abandoned.

Nearly two hundred people were in the Karmapa's party, going on horseback and on foot. The journey took twenty-one days, over rugged Himalayan terrain. Chandzo Tendzin Namgyal, then the Karmapa's personal secretary, was twenty-seven at the time. He recalls a difficult journey by way of the southern route through Lhodrak, where they stopped briefly at Marpa's house. The Karmapa offered prayers at Milarepa's nine-story tower, the same one Marpa made Milarepa build and tear down so many times. Several important incarnate lamas traveled under the Karmapa's protection, among them his own brother, the third Dzogchen Ponlop Rinpoche. Also with him were the young, as yet unrecognized, Shamarpa and the Twelfth Goshir Gyaltsapa. Drupon Rinpoche was with them as was the Fifteenth Karmapa's consort, Khandro Chenmo.

Another incarnate lama who traveled with the group was Lama

Karma Thinley, who later wrote an English-language history of the sixteen Karmapas. He relates how the Karmapa pushed everyone to climb the last pass separating Tibet from Bhutan. His description: "As the group reached the last snow pass, Mon La Gar Chung (elevation 19,855 feet), which marks the Tibet-Bhutan border, Karmapa urged everyone on, saying that they must cross the pass that same day. The party expended their last energy in crossing over into Bhutan, assisted by guides from the local people. During the following night there was a great snow-fall, which blocked all the passes for two or three days. In fact, the military forces had been in close pursuit of the refugees, and had they not done as Karmapa directed they would have been captured."[72] They arrived safely in Bumthang in north Bhutan, and were hospitably received by the Bhutanese royal family and government officials.

While possibilities for accommodating the growing number of refugees were under discussion in Bhutan's capital, Thimphu, Sikkim's ruler, the Chogyal, offered to give the Karmapa and his entourage sanctuary in Sikkim. His prime minister met the Karmapa at Buxa in India in order to extend the royal invitation. The Chogyal valued the relationship that his family maintained with the Karmapas over several hundred years, and he did not hesitate to give him hospitality in his small jewel of a kingdom. The Karmapa felt Sikkim would be an ideal place for his people. It was predominantly Buddhist, with numerous Nyingma and several important Karma Kagyu monasteries. It was a place where he could continue his life's work. Three months after his departure from Tsurphu, the Sixteenth Karmapa arrived in Sikkim to yet another warm royal welcome.

The Sikkimese king gave the Karmapa seventy-four acres of land to be held in perpetuity, in acknowledgment of the old and strong links between the Karmapas and the Chogyals. The Karmapa chose the land because of its excellent location. Tibetans, like the Chinese and Indians, have their own system of geomancy, or auspicious placement according to the lay of the land. This land was located above the old Rumtek Monastery built during the time of the Ninth Karmapa Wangchuk Dorje.

Not surprisingly, after about four hundred years in a wet climate, the old monastery was barely habitable. A mountain protected the site; it had a view of the towering snow mountains; there were abundant streams—seven of them; and it faced a fortunate, southerly direction with a river below. And so the Karmapa made good his earlier commitment to an extended Rumtek stay.

Many of the Rumtek settlers started out living in tents but were unaccustomed to the environment. Weather conditions were moist in semitropical Sikkim, where it rained or was foggy for much of the year and had four solid months of heavy monsoon downpours. It was not the dry, crisp desert of the Tibetan Plateau. Tibetan standards of cleanliness were more suited to the high desert, where bacteria do not proliferate. Bathing was not always *de rigueur*. Favorite foods such as meat and butter would not keep as well as they did at home. The drastically different climate, the trauma of war in Tibet, the loss of family and friends, and relocation in a strange place took its toll. There was much illness. Fevers, gastrointestinal problems, and the scourge of Tibetans, tuberculosis, were common afflictions. Facilities

Sixteenth Karmapa,
circa 1970

were nonexistent. The crumbling old Rumtek Monastery was only partially habitable. Construction—and fundraising to build adequate housing—had to begin immediately. People worked with their hands, using shovels or whatever primitive tools they could find.

Jawaharlal Nehru, prime minister of the now independent India, was sympathetic toward the Tibetans fleeing the Chinese communists. The Karmapa went to Delhi and met Nehru, who promised aid to the Tibetans at Rumtek in the form of food and clothing. The Indian government also granted money for construction and provided materials, including a sum for a dispensary. The Karmapa used his own funds to make up the difference. The new monastery construction began in 1962 after the Chogyal's land grant was legalized. It took until 1966 to complete the project, which became the Karmapa's official residence in exile, the Sri Karmae Dharmachakra Centre, Rumtek. When it was finished, the precious treasures brought from Tsurphu were enshrined in a room next to the Karmapa's personal quarters.

While construction was underway, the Karmapa kept up his

A picnic in Sikkim not long after escaping from Tibet. Left to right: Chandzo Damchoe Yongdu, Chogyam Trungpa Tulku, the Sixteenth Karmapa.

usual pace of travel, teaching, counseling, and generally doing what he could to help the large numbers of refugees who poured into India. The Dalai Lama escaped from Tibet in March 1959, after the PLA shelled Lhasa and then brutally suppressed the subsequent uprising. Under his leadership a fledgling Tibetan government-in-exile was formed, but it was overwhelmed with people in need. The communist crackdown had spread throughout greater Tibet, forcing tens of thousands to flee. Land was given to the Dalai Lama for settlement in mountainous Himachal Pradesh, in an old hill station, Dharamsala. The Indian government had set aside parcels of land in various parts of India to accommodate Tibetan refugees. In Dharamsala the Dalai Lama's government-in-exile gathered the highest lamas of all four lineages of Tibetan Buddhism who had survived the depredations of the Chinese and who had escaped to India. The Dalai Lama asked for their help. At a meeting in Dharamsala, heads of lineages, including the Karmapa, discussed ways to preserve their traditions in exile.

"Whenever there was some big religious meeting, he always came. He was always invited. Then when he visited Ladakh or some nearby area he came to Dharamsala," the Dalai Lama recalled in an interview, "So we were like spiritual brothers,

Laying the foundation stone of Rumtek in 1962. The Sixteenth Karmapa is in the foreground, left. Standing next to him is the Chogyal of Sikkim. The Chogyal's American wife, Hope Cooke, has her arms around a child.

which we remained until his death." The Karmapa resumed his routine of ministering to Buddhists. He visited monasteries and villages in Ladakh in 1967, where he taught monks and laypeople and performed the Black Crown Ceremony. On the way back he returned to Dharamsala to take teachings from the Dalai Lama. Afterward he went to Tibetan settlements in Himachal Pradesh near Dharamsala: Tashi Jong, Bir, Nangchen, and Dalhousie, where many Khampas had settled and were living in very difficult conditions. The Indian government had donated land, but scraping together a living in the new country wasn't easy. Naturally concerned about the people remaining in Tibet, he performed special medicine pujas and sent "blessing pills," made of herbs and auspicious ingredients, meant to carry healing power. These brought at least some comfort to the devout in Tibet in the absence of their revered lamas.

Circumstances had drastically changed for the Tibetans, and perhaps for this reason the Karmapa decided to broach a subject that had been taboo since 1792, when the Gurkha War ended and a law was enacted that forbade the recognition of the Shamarpa tulku. In 1963 the Karmapa asked the Dalai Lama to allow him to recognize the Shamarpa, who, he knew, was his late brother's

The Dalai Lama and the Sixteenth Karmapa.

116

son. He wrote a letter in the accepted style, leaving a space for the Dalai Lama to reply. After the customary honorific salutation, the Karmapa wrote, "Since the tenth reincarnation, the Shamar Tulku has been given only the name but has not become well known. Now, Atub Pon has a son who is twelve years old. When this boy was in Tsurphu Monastery, he displayed, as known to all, portentous signs, such as being able to recognize the monks of Shamar Monastery in Yangpachen. I also sought the Three Jewel's help, and my ignorant mind told me that this must be true. I request you to examine with your wisdom whether or not this boy is the authentic reincarnation and make a pronouncement." The Dalai Lama responded: "The examination conducted with the help of the Three Jewels revealed that Buddhism will benefit if the following son of Atub Pon is recognized as the reincarnation of Shamar Rinpoche."[73] The Thirteenth Shamarpa was subsequently enthroned at Rumtek.

ENCOUNTERS WITH THE RED-FACED ONES

The late sixties and early seventies brought a new breed of disciple to the Himalayan foothills, of the sort most Tibetans had never seen. Fair-haired, fair-skinned hippies began to turn up on their odyssey to find spiritual truth. Most of them at first gravitated to the Hindu ashrams in Rishikesh, Almora, and other places in India. But a few who went to Nepal and the areas where Tibetan refugees were lodged met Buddhist teachers. The Karmapa, Sakya Trizin, the Dalai Lama, Dudjom Rinpoche, Lama Yeshe, and Kalu Rinpoche and other charismatic teachers began to attract a small Western following. To Tibetans these people seemed a bit strange. One lama, who met hippies as a boy while living in fairly straitened circumstances, told me how funny it seemed to him that young people from a rich country would want to go around barefoot wearing ragged, dirty clothing when they didn't have to. A few Tibetans had settled abroad, and more followed them. Some, like the Sakya scholar Dezhung Rinpoche or Chogyam Trungpa Rinpoche, were eminent lamas. Contact with such lamas inspired some Westerners to come to India, hoping to meet other high lamas who had escaped from Tibet.

Eventually, in 1974, the Sixteenth Karmapa carried his vigorous Buddhist ministry far beyond its former scope, to the United States, at the invitation of Chogyam Trungpa. It was a successful tour in which he performed the Black Crown Ceremony in North America for the first time, and brought many people in contact with a venerable tradition of Tibetan Buddhism. He is also said to have performed a miracle, ending a drought on an Indian reservation. When he visited the dispirited Hopi village in the Southwest he was told there had been no rain for two years. Writer Robin Kornman records what happened:

> When visiting the kiva at Polacca, His Holiness stopped to chant beside the entrance. Later that day, seemingly miraculously, it rained. In the evening His Holiness decided suddenly to perform an empowerment rite (that of Avalokiteshvara) for the Hopi. The Hopi came in their pickup trucks through the fresh mud bringing offerings of fried bread...The next day's edition of *Eagle's Cry* ran the headline: "Tibetan Chief Brings Rain."[74]

The tribal elders also recalled a Hopi prophecy that seemed to be fulfilled by his visit. It forged a new sense of connection between the Tibetans and Native Americans, whose customs have striking similarities and whose mutual ancestors may have crossed the neck of land that once spanned the Bering Strait thousands of years ago. After touring various Buddhist centers from coast to coast, the Karmapa returned to Rumtek via Canada and Europe. He made another extensive tour of North America and Europe in 1976. That year a Black Crown Ceremony organized by EST founder Werner Erhard was held in New York.

Meanwhile, at Rumtek, a meditation retreat center was completed. The Karmapa was, like the Dalai Lama, passionate about educating his lamas and monks to preserve, as far as possible, the tradition that was being systematically destroyed in Tibet. He attracted the sorts of people who could help him get things done. Freda Bedi was an Englishwoman who had attended

Oxford and subsequently married a fellow student, an Indian, and settled down in India. She started helping Tibetan refugees, which led her to work with the Central Welfare Board of the Indian government to organize the Young Lama's Home School. She later became a disciple of the Karmapa and took nun's vows, assuming the name Sister Khechog Palmo. She accompanied the Karmapa on his first visits to the West. The Karmapa was always adamant that his monks keep the vinaya, or monk's rule, meticulously, and he didn't like it when any of them strayed from the monastery. A good-natured man, he did have a temper, which was given full rein where erring monks were concerned.

Preservation of Buddhist texts was a project close to the Karmapa's heart. He commissioned many texts to be carved on woodblocks, according to the traditional Tibetan printing methods. Others were published using more modern technology. Monks labored over these texts for years at a small letterpress in the narrow lanes of the Ballimaran district in Old Delhi. E. Gene Smith, then field director of the U.S. Library of Congress in Delhi, made it possible for the Derge edition of the Buddhist canon—the Kangyur and Tengyur—and many other important Tibetan texts brought into exile, to be published, and he had copies purchased for U.S. libraries. Smith, a formidable Tibetan

Rumtek
Monastery

scholar, helped proofread the galleys of the Tibetan texts before they were printed, which earned him the enduring regard of Tibetans.[75] The Karmapa, in this way, published five hundred copies of the Derge Kangyur and distributed them to monasteries of every lineage.

In 1979 the Indian government granted the Karmapa land to build a monastery in New Delhi. He laid the foundation stone with Indian President Neelam Sanjiva Reddy in November of that year. Shortly thereafter the Karmapa became gravely ill, vomiting blood. They rushed him to the hospital where he almost died. It was then it was discovered he had cancer. He was due to visit the United States again, but for a while it looked like the trip would be canceled. His devotees feared for his life. The Karmapa underwent surgery. Much of his stomach was removed. After that he rallied and sent word that he still intended to come to the United States as promised and would arrive in May 1980. Buddhist centers across the country cooperated to organize the visit. Students of Chogyam Trungpa were by now seasoned veterans of the tours of Tibetan religious dignitaries, and the network of centers radiating from the Karmapa's own center, Karma Triyana Dharmachakra, in Woodstock, New York, also geared up. It was the Karmapa's first visit since the Woodstock property had been acquired. The preparations were made, down to the hire of a maroon Cadillac in which a long-time American disciple would chauffeur him. A red and gold brocade silk coverlet was always thrown over the Karmapa's seat.

When he arrived everyone was shocked by his frailty. The robust man in photos of earlier days had grown painfully thin, but there was a quality that made his physical body seem a transparent vessel for a bright and exuberant spirit. The Karmapa's trip in 1980 was memorable and poignant. He was gravely ill but he ignored it. Or, as some said, he overcame the pain through his profound discipline of mind. In the middle of his stay he was stricken with Bell's Palsy, which paralyzed the right side of his face for awhile. But the Karmapa didn't miss a beat, he just carried on with the tour, giving the Black Crown Ceremony, empowerments, and teachings across the country, letting his disciples treat him to dinners, dim sum breakfasts, and a visit to the Bronx Zoo. He was also getting medical tests and treatment. He appeared to be so "up" that everyone hoped that the cancer had been defeated.

He went back to Rumtek to continue working on his pet projects—education and publication. Late in 1981 he fell ill again. Those close to him begged him to go to Hong Kong or the United States for treatment. He went reluctantly. He told intimates that knew he was going to die soon and preferred to stay in Rumtek. But urged by the general secretary and others, he went abroad for treatment. His first stop was Hong Kong, where he was admitted to Queen Mary Hospital on September 17th and was treated there for several weeks with little effect. A consulting American doctor was called in who thought a treatment available in the United States might save him. So the Karmapa was moved to the American International Clinic in Zion, Illinois, near Chicago.

The Sixteenth Karmapa
blesses a Western disciple
after a ceremony at Karma
Triyana Dharmachakra,
Woodstock, NY, 1980.
(Photo by Lea Terhune)

The invasive medical treatment was deeply disturbing to those close to him. The person of the Karmapa is considered so sacred that no one else is allowed to use his belongings, or even touch some of them. When his hair was cut a sheet was put below so the clippings can be saved as sacred relics. Here he was subjected to the same indignities that a hospital stay inflicts on anyone. His blood was transfused. Yet he bore it all, including the pain, with equanimity. He was attentive and friendly toward his doctors, nurses, and those who were with him. He kept up his daily prayer routine until the last day.

Near midnight on Thursday, November 5, 1981, the Sixteenth Karmapa ended his incarnation. Only two of the heart sons were with him: Tai Situpa and Jamgon Kongtrul. Gyaltsap Rinpoche had stayed in Rumtek, in his time-honored role as caretaker in the Karmapa's absence. Shamarpa, who had been in Zion earlier, was sent by the Karmapa to continue Tai Situpa's European teaching program. Tai Situpa had withdrawn from it to be with the Karmapa. It was a painful experience for them to see their spiritual father and guru at the mercy of the Western medical establishment, which had little reverence for Tibetan Buddhist customs. The Karmapa impressed the doctors with his serenity, however. They couldn't understand why he wasn't in agony, because the cancer was so advanced. So when his vital signs stopped, the hospital staff respected the wishes of the lamas and allowed the Karmapa's body to remain undisturbed.

Great lamas who are accomplished yogis are said to sustain meditation for several days after death, sitting upright, with good color and perceptible heat around the heart, the state of *tukdam*—a kind of quietist suspended animation. Though he was unable to sit in the formal yogic posture, he nevertheless remained in meditation for three days, according to Tai Situpa, Jamgon Kongtrul, and others who were there. This was signified by the unique phenomenon of warmth around the heart. One of the Karmapa's doctors was baffled by the serenity of the Karmapa's final days, as the disease ravaged his body: "Every day I'd go in and ask him, 'Are you having pain?' He'd smile and say, 'No pain, no pain.' It was very confusing." The Karmapa, he said, was more concerned about how the others around him felt than about himself. When Jamgon Kongtrul and Tai Situpa invited him to feel the area around the Karmapa's heart after his vital signs stopped, the doctor recalls, "Each day I was amazed how it stayed warm. I wasn't as amazed after 24 hours, but after 48 and after 72 hours I began to be quite shocked." Pointing out that the body normally cools quickly after circulation stops, he said, "As a physician, I have no explanation."[76]

At about 4 A.M. on the third day the heat around the heart dissipated, which signaled the end of the meditation. For the heart sons it was the bleakest moment imaginable. "We felt really bad," Tai Situpa recalls. "We didn't know what to do without him. We just made preparations to take his body back to Rumtek and start the ceremonies. It was hard to think beyond that."

6. Transitions

HIS RESONANT VOICE AND HEARTY LAUGHTER were silenced. For those lamas closest to the Sixteenth Karmapa, he had been the most important person in their lives, a strong father figure, but more significantly, the lineage head and their principal guru, the centerpiece of their personal and Buddhist world. At the time he passed away, of the four heart sons,[77] all but Tai Situpa still lived with him at Rumtek. Gyaltsap Rinpoche had his room beside the main shrine room downstairs; Shamarpa and Jamgon Kongtrul were on the floor above, steps away from the Karmapa's chambers. Most of them had just begun their teaching ministries and had started teaching abroad. Now they had to pick up the reins of the Karma Kagyu, but not before funerary prayers for the Karmapa had been said.

The mourning had already begun in Sikkim, and a melancholy reception in Gangtok awaited the helicopter bearing his *kudung,* a respectful term for the mortal remains of a high lama. The kudung was placed on a temporary shrine constructed beside the helicopter pad, which commanded a spectacular view of the surrounding mountains and valley. For several hours people prostrated before the impromptu shrine, offered scarves, and sat in the presence of the physical remains that had been sanctified by the Karmapa's spirit. Later, as his kudung was brought to Rumtek, villagers along the road ran out to throw scarves and flowers at the funeral procession. Once at Rumtek, the Karmapa's kudung was taken to the Crown Ceremony shrine room upstairs. Ritual gave the bereaved a familiar course to follow.

Custom demanded that, in the last rites for high lamas, the body be packed in salt, which desiccates and mummifies it. This is done as the forty-nine-day prayer cycle begins. The salt is changed several times during the weeks of the ceremony, because the body shrinks as the salt absorbs the bodily fluids. After the packing salt is removed, it is distributed as a sacred relic to disciples. During the forty-nine days, pujas are offered to all the major bodhisattvas and protectors that figure prominently in Karma Kamtsang tradition. Disciples from the affluent and aristocratic families of Sikkim, Bhutan, and elsewhere, tulkus and Buddhist organizations from Sikkim and other parts of India, Nepal, and abroad, all sponsored parts of the service. When

Offering prayers at funerary ceremonies for the Sixteenth Karmapa. From left to right: Beru Khyentse Rinpoche, Gyaltsap Rinpoche, Jamgon Kongtrul, Tai Situpa, and Shamarpa.

spread over seven weeks, the expenses were significant. Daily tea and food for hundreds of monks and visitors was only the beginning. Supplies for the rituals were also required: butter for thousands of butter lamps; the lamps themselves, sometimes made of precious metals; saffron for the holy water that is sprinkled and dispensed; food offerings that are later distributed. The final resting place of a lama as eminent as the Karmapa had to reflect his infinite, precious value: a large stupa fashioned of high-quality metal, gold-plated, and studded with gems.

Ordinarily, the sacred music, incense, chanting of mantras, and prayers are meant to give the departed the most fortunate possible send-off, helping the individual consciousness into the next and better rebirth. But in the case of a very high lama, there is a larger spiritual dimension to the ritual. In the eyes of his followers, the Karmapa doesn't need prayers to guide him. He is already a bodhisattva. In the minds of believers he can choose when he dies and when, where, and how he reincarnates. The pujas offered for a high lama are offered for the benefit of ordinary beings, particularly his disciples. Prayers are said to remove obstacles to the incarnate lama's swift rebirth and recognition—obstacles not generated by the Karmapa but by those unrealized individuals whom he incarnates to help.

From the Tibetan Buddhist perspective, death is perhaps the most important thing that happens in a lifetime. It presents the greatest challenges. In some ways it might be said that in the Buddhist view, life is one long preparation for death. This is not a morbid preoccupation; it is both realistic and opportunistic, like an athlete who trains for competition. Preparation is necessary, and one must know what to expect. Buddhist teachings about nonattachment and impermanence are all linked to the truth of change: meetings bring partings, birth brings death.

The actions taken in life determine the nature of the next rebirth. Humans have a developed intellect and relative freedom compared to beings of less fortunate realms, such as those of animals or hungry ghosts, which is why the "precious" human birth is deemed best.[78] If a person accumulates "good karma" and transforms negative effects of past actions by doing good deeds, the next rebirth will likely provide even more opportunities to achieve awakening. If a person falls into negative habits and performs evil deeds, the subsequent rebirth will reflect that, also. Until the last instant of life it is possible to choose which direction one travels. Vajrayana methods acquaint the practitioner with what to expect, form good habits, and engender astute discrimination. The moment of death is climactic, a time when the departing consciousness is tested. It is often the only point in the course of life when an ordinary individual has a flash of clarity that can give complete understanding. During the transitional phase, the consciousness must distinguish and choose between higher and lower vibrations as it gravitates to the level at which it will be reborn. "Death and the stages after death are profound upheavals in our experience. It is one reason why we do not remember what happened in our past lives. It is like a great explosion that causes amnesia."[79]

While alive, a person will ideally cultivate his or her spiritual side to meet this challenge. Daily life is the perfect training ground. Discipline is imparted by frequent, focused meditation. If done well, this honest introspection will result in rock-like composure, even at that tumultuous moment of final separation from the physical body. At that moment, Tibetan Buddhists believe it is possible to transfer the consciousness into a higher level of being. The highest-possible achievement is complete enlightenment. Next best is bodhisattva realization and birth in a "buddha field." Failing that, the consciousness strives for a human rebirth. The stories of Tibetan saints are full of accounts of transference of consciousness so successful that the adept disappears in a shimmering rainbow at death. But most people are not adepts, and if that moment of "clear light" at death is missed, one is precipitated into the first phase of the *bardo*, the intermediate state between life and death.

The first transitional stage after death may last from a single moment to several days. The entity falls into unconsciousness after the first clear light. So as not to disturb this delicate process in any individual, Tibetans do not cremate or otherwise dispose of a dead body until at least three days have passed. A second chance to be born a bodhisattva comes when the consciousness awakens from the death "faint." If the individual fails to make the leap this time, the consciousness leaves the body and enters the bardo. This intermediate period between actual separation of the consciousness from the old body and reentry into a new one has two stages, and may last up to forty-nine days. During this time, the individual is faced with a variety of tests of judgment. Past actions determine what happens in the bardo. Negative deeds are heavy dross that pull the consciousness down into lower, extremely difficult levels on the wheel of rebirth, levels that naturally attract those who have cultivated hate, anger, jealousy, and so forth in life. True wickedness can land a birth in one of the hot or cold hells. Lesser evils may lead to birth as tortured spirits who are always hungry or thirsty but are unable to eat or drink, warlike demons always murdering and plotting against each other, or gods who live pleasant, long lives but at the end experience the most terrible of deaths. Those who have managed, by their deeds, to merit a human life must still find a birth situation that will offer the best conditions for spiritual progress, the *precious* human rebirth. The human life, although more balanced than the others, still is afflicted by ignorance, pride, anger, hatred, and greed.

Descriptions of the bardo in some ways resemble fairy tales in which the protagonist is confronted with myriad doors and told that one door leads to a treasure room, one to a beautiful paradise, one to the goal being sought, and one to the pit of hell where an unspeakable monster waits. The being chooses according to the amount of discriminating wisdom acquired in previous lives. Prayers and good works done for the benefit of the departed can give a push in the right direction and help the individual stand steady in the onslaught of overwhelming perceptual input in the bardo, which is why the forty-nine-day ritual is considered important. But the being in the bardo can only be benefited when the capacity to respond to such positive influences has been built through past choices. Most beings are just tossed about, with no control over where they are going. Influenced by the consequences of their unenlightened actions, they stay frightened and confused, until they find themselves in a womb and are born into circumstances they have set up for themselves in ignorance.

There is a rich liturgy for death and dying in the Tibetan tradition, and *The Tibetan Book of the Dead,* a Nyingma text that has been translated several times into English, is just one part of the ritual designed to speed a person to the best rebirth. All of this is to some degree in the minds of Tibetan Buddhists during funerary prayers, which are essentially a guided meditation on this mortal transition. In the case of an incarnate bodhisattva like the Karmapa, who is able to choose his next birth even before dying, the rites invoke his presence in the form of various deities, through which he blesses the faithful.

High lamas, politicians, and ordinary villagers came to pray and pay respects beside the Karmapa's enshrined body. The Dalai Lama sent representatives, as his commitments prevented him from attending himself. Hundreds filed past each day, as the pujas continued from early morning into the evening. A small group of Western followers were also present, many of them members of a group led by Ole and Hannah Nydahl, a Danish couple who were longtime disciples of the Sixteenth Karmapa. The Karmapa had given them permission to give provisional refuge and elementary Buddhist teachings in the West at a time when there were few qualified lamas to teach and little awareness about Tibetan Buddhism. The Nydahls opened Buddhist centers in Europe and the Americas in the Karmapa's name, and they visited Rumtek frequently, usually bringing groups of their students whom they led on pilgrimage tours to India and Nepal. According to Ole's account, the last time he and Hannah met the Sixteenth Karmapa, he told the couple to come to Rumtek on a particular date. That is why they were just in time for his funeral.[80]

Devastated that the Karmapa died at the relatively young age of fifty-seven, his followers hoped for his early reincarnation. On December 20 1981, the day of the Sixteenth Karmapa's cremation, nearly a thousand monks and important high lamas were there, and hundreds more laypeople besides. The mummified bodies of high lamas are sometimes covered with gold tissue and preserved in a reliquary stupa, as was the late Panchen Lama. This was discussed among the Karmapa's labrang, his monk and lay administrators, but the decision was made to cremate the body. One lama who was there at the time told me that had the body been preserved, much trouble might have been averted. It is believed that a great deal of positive power is concentrated in the *kudung* of a great lama, and it would have been a potent shield against discord at Rumtek. Someone with no lineage or other religious connection with the Karmapa lit the pyre, according to tradition.[81]

As the cremation progressed, signs appeared indicating the Karmapa would be born in Tibet. The first portent came when Tai Situpa circumambulated the stupa-shaped kiln in which the Karmapa's now desiccated corpse was burning. A large, black, burning mass rolled out of the opening in front of him, an event Tai Situpa describes: "Someone nearby, I don't remember who, pointed to the opening in the cremation stupa and said something was falling out. I saw a black, burning mass drop down into the opening. I sent a monk to tell Kalu Rinpoche, who was the eldest there, to find out what we should do. Then I waited. He sent word back that it was the heart, eyes, and tongue. I used one of the offering bowls to take it up." Though Tai Situpa said it seemed strange that the eyes, heart, and tongue should be fused together, whatever it was, it was regarded as an important relic. Tai Situpa asked that it be preserved at Rumtek in a golden stupa. It was subsequently enshrined in a two-foot high stupa made of pure gold, and rests in the treasure room at Rumtek.

After the ceremonies were over, life resolved into a new normality. The emphasis was on completing the Karmapa's projects. Early in 1981, nine months before he died, the Sixteenth Karmapa had opened an international office at Rumtek, calling it the Kagyu International Headquarters. He did this, it seems, with some reluctance. "I never desired to have an established office, consequently until now I have managed without one, working for the noble cause of Dharma," he said at the time. "On account of great persistence from the various centers all over the world, I am compelled to open an office of this nature," adding, "now it is relevant."[82] The Rumtek chandzo, Damchoe Yongdu, applied himself to completing the small golden stupa and a larger memorial stupa to house the Sixteenth Karmapa's relics. He also oversaw the construction of the *shedra,* or monk's college, named by the Karmapa the Sri Karmae Nalanda Institute of Higher Studies.

Chandzo Damchoe Yongdu was the most important person at Rumtek after the Karmapa. He was completely responsible for monastery administration, had the implicit trust of the Karmapa, and managed all the monastery money and assets. It would not be exaggerating to say that he had more worldly clout on a day-to-day basis than the Karmapa, since he looked after temporal affairs. He was a tough Khampa who wore heavy turquoise and gold earrings and kept his hair tied in the typical tasseled long braid wrapped round his head. He usually dressed in a Tibetan *chuba,* a sashed, tunic-like garment worn over trousers. He took snuff constantly. People addressed him by the honorific "Kungo-la." His word was law and he believed in the old feudal ways. A story was often told of him that in a past life-time he was a demon whom the Karmapa of the day subdued by grabbing him by the wrist, and since that time he stayed by the Karmapa's side. Some Tibetans claimed to have seen the dark line around his wrist believed to be a remnant of that struggle.

Dzogchen Ponlop Rinpoche, Damchoe Yongdu's youngest son, said that his paternal grandfather had been part of the Fifteenth Karmapa's labrang. Damchoe Yongdu became a monk at Tsurphu when he was eleven years old. When he was nineteen he became the Sixteenth Karmapa's attendant and was appointed *chopon,* or shrine master, the monk who looks after the altars and ritual implements. At the age of twenty-five he became the monastery treasurer, an assistant to the Tsurphu chandzo. At twenty-seven he assumed the duties of chandzo, although not the official appointment. He was finally confirmed in the office at the age of twenty-nine by what might be called democratic divination. The labrang voted for four candidates. The names of each were written on separate pieces of paper, which were wadded into balls. The Karmapa then chose the

paper ball with Damchoe Yongdu's name on it. Damchoe
Yongdu later gave back his monastic vows to marry. His first
wife was the Karmapa's sister, who died at Tsurphu. She had two
sons, Drupon Rinpoche and another who died. His second wife
had a daughter, but he was again left a widower. His third wife
had a daughter and Ponlop Rinpoche.[83]

I first met Damchoe Yongdu in 1980, when he came to
America with the Karmapa, and we met subsequently in India.
The chandzo, usually traveled with the Karmapa on any official
tours. Though he was brusque and seldom smiled, Damchoe
Yongdu had a good-natured side and liked a joke. Whatever
faults he may have had, he was completely devoted to the
Karmapa—and the Karmapa's interests. He considered the
completion of the shrine room for the Sixteenth Karmapa's reliquary stupa as an important obligation fulfilled. When the
chandzo invited me for dinner at his house at Rumtek one
evening during my visit there shortly before he died, he told me
how much it meant to him to have discharged this duty. His next
goal was to complete the study center in New Delhi in accordance with the Karmapa's last wishes.

Initially, it was decided that the four tulkus, Shamarpa, Tai
Situpa, Jamgon Kongtrul, and Goshir Gyaltsapa, would act as
regents at Rumtek and supervise the Karmapa's other projects
by rotation, in cooperation with the chandzo. This was decided
at a formal meeting of lamas and the labrang after the
Karmapa's funeral. Each tulku would serve as regent for three
years unless the four tulkus and the Rumtek labrang decided
upon another arrangement. Shamarpa assumed the first period
of regency beginning January 1, 1982. The four wrote a letter to
the chandzo, expressing their solidarity and commitment to
achieving the Karmapa's aims. "When the next Karmapa incarnation appears, we will turn over everything to him intact and
will carry out our responsibility to return the crown jewel of the
Kagyupas to his throne." But the chandzo died suddenly while
on a visit to Bhutan to inspect some of the Karmapa's properties, which included a palace-monastery and a cinema hall. He
had had a meal with Topga Yugyal, a nephew of the Karmapa,

and during a walk afterward, he collapsed and died. The cause of his death was never ascertained, but at the time, in December 1982, people were more concerned with how Rumtek would go forward. The chandzo had completed the memorials to the Sixteenth Karmapa, but the *shedra,* the monastic college, was yet to be fully realized.

It fell to Jamgon Kongtrul to look after the shedra in its first years. He already had started fundraising for Karmae Jamyang Khang primary school, which offered a five-year course where the youngest monks could learn reading, writing, arithmetic, history, and science. Once he found sufficient sponsorship, he went on to raise funds to complete the shedra. The shedra offers a serious, eleven-year course of religious philosophy, ritual, and practice. Students at elementary school and college levels are expected to keep strict monk's discipline, complete the required coursework, and pass examinations.

The death of the chandzo heralded dramatic changes in the Karmapa's domain. Shamarpa and his cousin, Topga Yugyal, took charge. Topga had come out of Tibet with the Karmapa in 1959 as a young man. Topga was the son of the Karmapa's sister, who had died shortly after escaping from Tibet. At the time of the Karmapa's escape, Topga was a learned monk who had a facility for languages, a great asset in the early days in India. He picked up Hindi and English quickly. He became master of studies at Rumtek. But monastery life did not particularly suit Topga. He gave it up to marry a Bhutanese princess, Ashi Chokyi Wangchuk, and settled in Bhutan's capital Thimphu.[84] The late Karmapa had appointed Topga "deputy general secretary" a few years before his death, but few expected him to assume a significant role. It was more of an honorary appointment, through which Topga was entitled to be called by the honorific *dasho* and wear the scarf denoting Bhutanese nobility. No duties were defined.[85]

Shamarpa, the son of the Karmapa's brother, was close to his older cousin Topga and had been since childhood. Their cooperation was long-standing. Shamarpa and Topga established a new management at Rumtek. The two cousins began by trying to sort out Rumtek finances, about which the late general secretary left no clue. The chandzo kept books in the old Tibetan style—in his head and close to his chest. He kept all the money under his personal control and doled it out as needed to run the monastery and its projects. He was signatory to bank accounts. That there was a big mystery about how much money there actually was and where to find it soon became evident. Shamarpa and Topga Yugyal traveled to Delhi to inspect the late chandzo's flat. His elder daughter Dechen lived there with a friend while they both attended college. Pasang and Karma Damdul, Rumtek people who worked on the Delhi monastery project, also stayed there, and there was a spare room for transiting guests, such as myself.[86]

Shamarpa and Topga were worried. Rumtek was in trouble, they said. Hundreds of thousands of dollars could not be accounted for, and the Delhi project would have to be stopped if they couldn't find the money. So far they had only been able to locate a few hundred thousand rupees. A safe that was supposed to be stuffed with cash came up short when it was opened. There were loans for the Delhi monastery from the Sikkim government, and that money, too, was all gone it seemed. Shamarpa and Topga said they needed to look at the paperwork and bank accounts in Delhi. Their search yielded unexpected results fairly quickly. Under the bed in the general secretary's room was a locked tin chest. They broke it open and found stacks of neatly bundled $100 bills, the total amount of which is now a matter of some dispute, though some witnesses claim there was as much as $90,000.

In a matter of weeks a great deal of bitterness had built up and precipitated a split in the Rumtek community. Shamarpa and Topga maintained that more money must be hidden somewhere, and they accused the late chandzo's family of hiding the money. The family denied it. People with lingering resentment toward the old master were all too willing to believe the stories; he had been a strong personality who was affable if you were on his good side but was ruthless to those who crossed him. No further evidence came to light about where the missing money was or if it even indeed existed. The costly building project in Delhi likely absorbed much of the money. A leading architect and a construction company had been engaged, and building had already begun. Money had to be given on an almost daily basis to keep the workers in materials and on the job. A labrang official, Gonpo Tsering, said that the main reason for the general secretary's trip to Bhutan was to secure loans for the Delhi monastery project, observing that if money were indeed salted away, loans would not be necessary.

Rumtek, already depressed in the absence of the Karmapa, became yet more gloomy. Within the next year the general secretary's widow migrated to the United States, soon followed by her daughters. His sons Ponlop Rinpoche and Drupon Rinpoche remained, continuing their work as teachers in the shedra. Ponlop Rinpoche said later, "My father usually didn't tell the family about money or labrang business. If we asked, his answer was 'mind your own business.'" Ponlop Rinpoche invited Shamarpa and Topga to search the house "from top to bottom" if they liked.

An effort was made to regularize bank accounts, putting them in the name of the Karmapa's monastery project with Shamarpa and Topga as signatories. But one entity could not be altered: the Karmapa's Charitable Trust. According to Indian law, trusts can be made in the name of a holy person or guru that legally devolve upon the valid successor to the post. The Karmapa Charitable Trust was one of these singular arrangements according to which the Seventeenth Karmapa can legally assume the property and assets of the Sixteenth Karmapa when he reaches the age of twenty-one. A board of trustees administers the trust while the Karmapa is a minor. This is outlined in the legal documents, signed before the Political Officer of Sikkim, that established the Karmapa's Charitable Trust in Sikkim in 1961. The trust was formed with an initial sum of 251,473.64 rupees contributed by the Sixteenth Karmapa himself and a number of his supporters, the purpose being to conserve and invest money for the upkeep of Rumtek Monastery and its monks. The construction of buildings, food, shelter, medical care, and education for the monks, and performance of religious and cultural activities at all the Karmapa's monasteries are all valid uses of the trust. "His Holiness Gyalwa Karmapa Rangyung Rigpai Dorji as head of Karma Kargyupa Sect as its Sixteenth Incarnation of the Holy Institution of Zvanagpa (Black Hat Lama) representing various monasteries all over the world including in Tibet, Bhutan, Sikkim and India," is his description in the trust document.

The trustees are responsible for managing and investing the money and approving its utilization. As long as the Karmapa was alive, he was sole trustee and had the last word. But after his death? These are the provisions for the succession of the new incarnation and protection of his interests until he reaches his majority: "In the case of the Mahanirvan (death) if the Trustee, i.e., His Holiness the Sixteenth Karmapa as stated hereinabove his successor in office, i.e., His Holiness the next Karmapa, i.e., His Holiness the Seventeenth Karmapa shall become the Trustee. During the intervening period of the Mahanirvan of His Holiness the Sixteenth Karmapa and the incarnation of the next Karmapa, i.e., His Holiness the Seventeenth Karmapa when incarnated and if he is below the age of 21 years then till the time when His Holiness the Seventeenth Karmapa attains the age of 21 years the seven persons named…shall become the trustees for the management of the 'Karmapa Charitable Trust.'"[87] In years following the Sixteenth Karmapa's death, this trust was to become a major bone of contention as various parties sought to control the Karmapa's property and assets,[88] and it remains a source of rancor, even as the maturing Seventeenth Karmapa pursues his studies in India.

Shamarpa and Topga began to travel again, often to Southeast Asia, where there were many Chinese disciples, supporters of the Sixteenth Karmapa's projects when he was alive. There they hoped to raise funds for the Delhi project, the international institute of Buddhist studies, which was a special focus of their attention. Once Jamgon Kongtrul had raised sufficient funds for the Rumtek schools, he turned his attention to his own projects: the monastery at Lava, near Kalimpong, and Pullahari retreat center overlooking Boudha in Kathmandu, Nepal. Gyaltsap Rinpoche, whose traditional role was regent of Tsurphu in the absence of the Karmapa, did what he could for Rumtek, and also started construction on his own new monastery at Ralang, near the old, sixteenth-century monastery. Tai Situpa occupied himself with his Sherab Ling Monastery in Himachal Pradesh, on the other side of India. All the tulkus began to travel more, the pace increasing as each of the four tulkus attracted greater followings abroad. Meanwhile, disciples fervently prayed for the Karmapa's quick rebirth. But as time went on, the wait was shaping up to be a long one.

7. The Four Heart Sons

IN *The Lama Knows,* a novel written by the twentieth-century American missionary to Tibet Robert Ekvall, a young and intelligent tulku escapes from his monastery and its hostile administrators when he realizes that he is up against an invincible force. They fake his death in order to replace him with a more biddable substitute. The real lama returns many years later, a potent magician, and is once again abused by the new set of administrators of his rightful monastery. Remarkable characters populate the narrative: heroic local chieftains, who are often relatives of high lamas and who become even more powerful thanks to their high-ranking religious kin. Like many Tibetan stories, it is peppered with miracles and ends on a mysterious note, with the hero disappearing into the Himalayan mists. Based on a true story, it is an accurate portrayal of the life of eastern Tibetans in Amdo, among whom Ekvall lived like a native for decades. Fluent in Tibetan, he was a careful observer. As he points out in his prologue, it is a story that could only happen in Tibet. "Only against the background of Tibetan culture—the way the Tibetans see the world and pattern their behavior—does it have meaning."[89]

Aspects of the recognition of the Seventeenth Karmapa, especially the ensuing dispute, may seem inexplicable to some, but not to Tibetans. As time went on, disagreements began to surface between the Karmapa's four heart sons, first over the management of the Karmapa's projects and later over the Karmapa's recognition. The disagreements escalated to a dramatic level that shocked those unfamiliar with Tibetan intrigue—which included most of the Western disciples. Around the time that the intrigue began, a Tibetan friend advised me to read *The Lama Knows,* saying simply, "It's all there." A biographical sketch of Ekvall written many years later includes this telling anecdote, which demonstrates Tibetans' pragmatic attitude about incarnate lamas: Ekvall on his travels fell in with some Tibetans…

> who rode to welcome a new lama, a boy of seven who had just been purchased from his family and was being taken to his new home in the monastery. As the child-lama and his entourage approached, Ekvall's friends dismounted, dropped to the ground in worship, and let loose a torrent of prayers. Later when they were asked about the amount of money paid to the parents of the boy, the answer was somewhat profane: "This is just like buying a *mdzo-mo* (milk cow). First you pay for her and then you milk her for butter which is wealth. Now that we have paid for the lama he will be used to produce wealth."[90]

History teaches that this is plainly one of the mundane functions of a monastery and one of the uses of a monastery's tulkus. The earthly entities of family, power, and wealth were served as well in the monastery as in the commercial districts of the town.

Seventy years after Robert Ekvall enjoyed the confidence and camaraderie of his Tibetan neighbors, an expatriate drama that mimics the ethos, if not the story line, of Ekvall's book was being played out in jewel-like Sikkim. To better know the cast of this drama and understand the Tibetan history that feeds into the play of events, a closer look at the background of the four chief Karma Kagyu tulkus is in order. Tulkus headed great monastic estates that often included numerous monasteries and villages that were satellites of the larger monastic seat. Gyaltsap Rinpoche and Jamgon Kongtrul were associated with the Karmapa's Tsurphu and Tai Situpa's Palpung monasteries, respectively, and they were very influential lamas. Participating in the management of one of these organizations—being part of a high lama's labrang, his management organization—involved money, power, prestige, and politics.

Historically, the labrang was sometimes a source of misunderstandings and disagreements in which the high lama himself may have no actual part or even knowledge. The record of the Dalai Lamas reveals one ambitious power struggle after another, frequently orchestrated by ministers or regents keen to hang onto their authority. Influential laypeople were inevitably from the aristocracy. Influential monks were often similarly well connected. Certain aristocratic or otherwise important families generated a suspicious abundance of consequential lamas. Tulkus meant power in a theocracy. While most incarnate lamas are revered as sincere, spiritual figures, these holy individuals can also be exploited by ambitious persons in their entourage. Even strong lamas are not immune to manipulation by people in their families or monasteries. Lamas who cite flaws in the tulku system—including the current Dalai Lama—point out that if a halfway intelligent child is plucked from poverty and oblivion and given every advantage and education, he is likely to make something of himself. And if a child is truly extraordinary, he will naturally distinguish himself.[91]

It is unrealistic to think that migration from Tibet to India caused Tibetans to leave all of the old ways behind them. In exile there have been plots and even occasional murders. The most notorious case was the 1977 assassination of Gungtang Tsultrim in the Tibetan settlement Clementown, in India. He was a leader of a group who opposed the Dalai Lama's brother, Gyalo Thondup. Gungtang Tsultrim particularly opposed a plan

Gyalo Thondup allegedly had to bring all orders of Tibetan Buddhism under the Gelug lineage through the government-in-exile, which had been established chiefly by Lhasa-based Gelugpas and their followers, including aristocrats who fled to India. This perception of Gyalo Thondup's activities created intense resentment, chiefly among independent eastern Tibetans. Opposition in Tibetan settlements, for which Gungtang Tsultrim was a voice, grew stronger. His assassin, when apprehended, claimed he had been paid Rs. 300,000 for the hit, quite a large sum in those days. The assassin also claimed he was told the Sixteenth Karmapa would fetch an even higher price.

A more recent example of old Tibetan disagreements surfacing in exile came to a head in 1997, when three Gelug monks were murdered in Dharamsala. They were stabbed to death, allegedly in connection with a dispute between those Gelugpas who worship a particular protector spirit and those who disapprove of it. Protector spirits are common in the Tibetan Buddhist tradition. They are like guardian angels whose intercession will ward off harm, and they come in benign and wrathful forms. The most powerful of them are believed to be enlightened bodhisattvas, but there are many minor protectors, or *dharmapalas,* who are "good spirits" helping from the other side.[92] The current and previous Dalai Lamas discouraged worship of

The Sixteenth Karmapa, seated, enjoys a picnic with young tulkus and Sikkimese officials. At Karmapa's feet is Chandzo Damchoe Yongdu. Tai Situpa, Gyaltsapa, and Jamgon Kongtrul stand behind.

this particular protector, Dorje Shugden, in the conviction that it is detrimental to the Dalai Lamas and divisive of the Tibetan community in general.

The latter has certainly proved true in recent decades. But the dispute is an old one, dating back to the seventeenth century and a monk who was a rival to the Fifth Dalai Lama. The story goes that this monk (who as a child was a candidate in the selection process for the Dalai Lama, but not chosen) defeated the Dalai Lama in a debate and was mysteriously found dead shortly after, his throat stuffed with a white scarf. The monk's restless spirit became troublesome, so to appease him the government decreed him a minor protector spirit of the Gelugpas. One of his roles was to counter the influence of the Nyingmapas. A number of Dalai Lamas, including the current one, studied and practiced Nyingma meditation methods. This sympathy toward the Nyingma tradition was often the source of sectarian episodes among the Gelugpas. Anti-Nyingma sectarianism was one reason the Thirteenth Dalai Lama forbade the Shugden practice.

The reemergence of this dispute in the 1990s is an example of Tibetan theocratic politics carried along by the diaspora, translated into a new situation. A new ingredient is non-Tibetan involvement, where non-Tibetans take up cudgels on behalf of opponents of the Dalai Lama. Westerners drew international media attention to the dispute over the forbidden practice, and even demonstrated against the Dalai Lama, Nobel Peace Laureate that he is, during his 1996 visit to London. The situation caused Buddhist commentator Stephen Batchelor to ponder, "In the West we are fond of portraying Buddhism as a tolerant, rational, non-dogmatic and open-minded tradition. But how much is this the result of liberal Western(ized) intellectuals seeking to construct an image of Buddhism that simply confirms their own prejudices and desires?"[93]

The Fourteenth Dalai Lama has tried to modernize his government and his monasteries while preserving Tibetan culture and religious traditions. Such hangovers from the past have not made this easy for him. Although he has made a concerted effort to democratize his own government and made a certain amount of progress, it has not been a total success. And the attention that exotic Tibet attracts from outsiders, however well-meaning they might be, can both help and hinder efforts to move ahead. It certainly can complicate further already complicated Tibetan scenarios.

When the old guard of Tibetan lamas escaped from Tibet—the Dalai Lama, the Karmapa, and others—they had the benefit of rigorous traditional training to help them in preserving their religion and culture in the new environment. At Rumtek, after the death of the Sixteenth Karmapa, it was up to this new generation, Shamarpa, Tai Situpa, Jamgon Kongtrul, and Goshir Gyaltsapa, to minister to this new sangha of non-Tibetan disciples as well as the Tibetans. Pressure grew upon them as the older generation of lamas who had come out of Tibet, one by one, passed away. The four tulkus were young, still in their twenties when the Karmapa died, and none of them had the same disciplined training and opportunities for meditation retreat that their predecessors had had. It was a very different world on the other side of the Himalayas, and while the Karmapa ensured they had the best education available and received all the necessary transmissions to continue the Karma Kagyu lineage, their circumstances were not ideal for in-depth study and application. With the possible exception of Jamgon Kongtrul, whose family was well established in Kalimpong, the tulkus were refugees. They had to adapt to hardships. Monasteries established for centuries in Tibet had to be rebuilt from scratch in exile. Not only were monasteries and texts destroyed, many precious teachers were killed in Tibet during 1959 and the ensuing Cultural Revolution in the 1960s. And India did not offer the same peaceful isolation so conducive to meditation retreat as rugged, thinly populated Tibet. India is a bustling place, teeming with people.

Of the four chief tulkus charged with looking after Rumtek, Shamarpa was the oldest at twenty-nine, born in the Dragon year of the Tibetan calendar (1952), while the other three were twenty-seven, all born in the year of the Horse (1954). Each had already begun to attract a following by the time the Sixteenth Karmapa died. Each is historically important in his own right.

A gathering in the 1970s at Kalu Rinpoche's monastery at Sonada, near
Darjeeling. The Sixteenth Karmapa is surrounded by his tulkus. Back row, left
to right: Gyaltsapa, Shamarpa, Tai Situpa, Jamgon Kongtrul, Beru Khyentse.
Kalu Rinpoche is seated, Bokar Rinpoche (wearing glasses) on his right. (Photo
by Bryan G. Miller)

THE SHAMARPAS

The Shamar tulku, or Shamarpa, at one time was considered the
most important lama of the Karma Kagyu after the Karmapa
himself. The Shamarpa is named after the special insignia he
wears, a red ceremonial crown.[94] Some Shamarpa incarnations
were celebrated scholars and meditators. But an interest in power
struggles would ultimately be the Shamarpa's undoing. Successive
Shamarpa tulkus involved themselves in the Kagyu rivalry with
the Gelug and other sects, allying themselves with warlike
princes. This propensity became a point of tension between the
Shamarpas and several Karmapas, who were antisectarian.[95]

The First Shamarpa appeared in 1283 in eastern Tibet. He was
drawn to spiritual pursuits and became a monk and, at the age
of seventeen, a student of the Third Karmapa Rangjung
Dorje. He received the complete transmission of the Kagyu
teachings from the Karmapa and spent much of his life in
meditation. It was the Second Shamarpa who actually received
the red hat from his teacher, the Fourth Karmapa Rolpe Dorje,

in acknowledgment of his spiritual attainment. It certified his ability to transmit the lineage teachings, so essential in the Kagyu sect. The next Shamarpa incarnations followed a similar pattern. He would be recognized by the Karmapa, who became his teacher. The Shamarpa, in turn, often located the next Karmapa incarnation after the Karmapa passed away. The Fourth Shamarpa, Choyang Yeshe, founded Yangpachen Monastery in 1488, near Tsurphu, in Central Tibet. This became his seat.

The Fourth Shamarpa was active politically. He briefly ruled Tibet, and was mentor to the Rimpung princes. The Fifth Shamarpa, Konchok Yenlak, and the Sixth, Chokyi Wangchuk, also demonstrated a predilection for politics, taking an activist role against Gelug incursions upon Kagyu monasteries. The biographies, as interpreted in English by Karma Thinley and others, record that the Karmapa discouraged the Shamarpa from retaliating against Gelug attacks on Kagyu monasteries. The Eighth Shamarpa, Palchen Chokyi Dondrup, was born in Nepal but went to Tsurphu for studies, and eventually settled permanently at Yangpachen.

Political intrigue naturally captures interest more readily than priestly altruism or contemplative seclusion, as the story of the Tenth Shamarpa demonstrates. The Tenth Shamarpa Mipam Chokyi Gyatso was born in 1742 in central Tibet, brother to the Third Panchen Lama, Palden Yeshe. He was recognized by the Thirteenth Karmapa and underwent the usual monastic educational discipline. Like Shamarpas before him, he traveled to Nepal, where he became friendly with the king.

At that time the rulership of Nepal had passed from the hands of the Malla dynasty to the more belligerent Gurkha dynasty, who conquered all of Nepal in 1769. Friction developed between neighbors Nepal, Bhutan, Sikkim, and Tibet. Tibet bought pure silver coins from Nepal for use as currency. Tibet and Nepal also engaged in substantial trade, but relations were upset after the Gurkha conquest. The Nepalese began to adulterate the silver in the coins with copper. The Dalai Lama objected and asked the Nepalese king to stop the practice of

146

debasing the coins. While that issue was left hanging, the Bhutanese incited Nepal to attack Sikkim. Sikkim was in turn aided by Tibet, and Tibetan officials were present when a treaty was finally signed between Sikkim and Nepal, something the Gurkhas resented. China watched and waited, studying the reports from the amban, the Chinese envoy in Lhasa.

The Third Panchen Lama, who had become a formidable figure in diplomacy with China and other neighbors, was strong at a time when the Dalai Lama was weak, and a regent ruled in Lhasa. The Panchen Lama succeeded in establishing a rapport even with the British, when George Bogle[96] was sent on his mission to Shigatse. The Panchen Lama was in Lhasa, giving ordination and teachings to the Dalai Lama, when he was invited to China by the Manchu emperor. There was some discussion and reluctance in Lhasa to release him because of the dangers of the journey, but he did go. He would not return. Shortly after his arrival he reportedly died of smallpox. The current Shamarpa has said he suspects the Panchen Lama may have been poisoned by the Chinese, the rationale being that the Chinese felt their position could be threatened by the Panchen Lama's manifest competence and his flirtation with the British, who were keen to establish a trade center in Shigatse. However death took him, his untimely exit had some significant ramifications.

The Gurkhas had been spoiling for a fight with Tibet. In this they were helped by the Shamarpa, who is credited by historians with instigating the Gurkha War with alluring descriptions of the riches at the Panchen Lama's monastery, Tashilhunpo, and egging on the Gurkha king. For himself, the Shamarpa wanted to claim the properties of his brother the late Panchen (or Tashi) Lama—said to be the richest in Tibet—but was foiled when his other brother, the Panchen's chief administrator, refused to give any of it up. So he went to the Nepalese king with his complaint, carrying a certain amount of portable treasures from Tashilhunpo with him. Bogle, in the narratives edited by Markham, mentions that the Nepalese were "tempted by stories of the great riches in the Teshu Lama's palace, brought by a refugee Tibetan monk named Sumhur Lama."

To stir things up the king of Nepal made some provocative demands on the Tibetan government and threatened to invade Tibetan districts bordering Nepal if the demands were not met. He also said he would hold the Shamarpa hostage pending the Tibetan government's reply. The Kashag—the Tibetan cabinet—replied in a measured way, making some concessions, but also making it clear they did not take responsibility for the Shamarpa. He, they said, chose to go to Nepal of his own accord and his fate was no concern of theirs. They wrote the Shamarpa in a similar vein, adding he was welcome to return to Tibet, but ended the note with an apt proverb, "Knowing how to shoot, you bought the bow."[97]

The Gurkhas promptly attacked remote southern districts of Tibet, close to Nepal's northern border, using a servant of the Shamarpa as a guide. They moved into the border districts of Nyanang, Rongshar, and Kyirong, getting as far as Dzongka and Sheggar on the Nepal-Tibet route to Shigatse. Tibetan troops were dispatched. The Manchu amban in Lhasa informed the emperor, who also sent reinforcements. Two thousand Chinese troops went as far as Shigatse, where the Chinese general dithered and hoped for a truce. Shakabpa quotes a young kalon, or cabinet minister, Tendzin Paljor Doring, who recorded the incident with some degree of contempt, saying he finally exhorted the Chinese general in exasperation, "We had been sent to Shigatse to fight, and fight we must!" They did push on to Sheggar, where they sat out the winter as half-hearted negotiations went on. Meanwhile, the Gurkhas attacked the Sikkim king's winter palace. The royal family fled. The Gurkhas were repulsed with the help of Tibetan troops.

The Shamarpa appears to have been directing negotiations for Nepal, and asked that the Tibetans send representatives for talks with him and a Gurkha official. The Chinese liked the idea, but the Tibetans did not trust the Shamarpa. A delegation was sent to Kyirong, where "the Shamar tulku appeared very proud and pleased with himself," according to Shakabpa. The treaty that was signed by Tibetan and Gurkha officials and witnessed by the Chinese was heavily weighted in favor of the aggressors. The

Chinese, as Shakabpa observes, were more hindrance than help in the situation. He quotes a letter from Kalon Doring that says, "There was little difference between the Gurkhas and the Chinese. The former looted and killed because they came as enemies; but the Chinese did the same thing and they came as friends."[98]

The Dalai Lama's regent, Ngawang Tsultrim, had been in Peking through all this. When he returned he berated the Kashag, the Tibetan cabinet, for caving in to Chinese pressure by accepting the humiliating terms of the Nepalese treaty. A hot-tempered man, he threw a bowl of barley flour at the assembled kalons, "coating them in flour in the best slapstick fashion," Shakabpa notes. The regent took action. He demoted those who were failures and exiled the corrupt; he rewarded the conscientious. Again negotiations were undertaken with Nepal to reduce the tribute payment extracted by the terms of the treaty, but Nepal refused to deal with the Tibetan envoys, saying they were not of sufficiently high rank. This infuriated the regent, who refused to send any more envoys, telling them if they wanted their tribute they could come and get it, and the Tibetan armies would be waiting when they came.

Unfortunately, this spirited regent suddenly dropped dead of a heart attack in the spring of 1791. His deputy, the vice-regent, was on his way to China and had to be recalled. Once again the Kashag bowed to Nepalese demands, and sent the requested ministers Doring and Yutok to negotiate with the Shamarpa and the Gurkhas. After reaching Shigatse they were warned that the Shamarpa and Nepalese were up to no good and were preparing for war. The kalons relayed this information to the Kashag in Lhasa before they proceeded to the rendezvous in Nyanang. There they fell into a trap. Local Nepalese requested the use of the Nyanang fort courtyard to celebrate a Hindu holiday. In the course of celebrations, Gurkha soldiers came in disguised as coolies. As the party wound down and revelers fell asleep, they attacked the Tibetans, killing dozens of them and taking the two envoys prisoner.

When the news came to Lhasa, officials began packing their bags and prepared to flee. The infant Panchen Lama was sent from Shigatse to Lhasa for his safety as the Gurkha army advanced. The Gurkhas sacked Tashilhunpo and the wealthy houses of Shigatse, but the combination of attacks by the Tibetan army and an epidemic that broke out among the Nepalese drove them back to Sheggar. Again the Chinese troops mobilized, joining the Tibetan troops to take back Tibetan territory and enter Nepal. Tables were turned. The Nepalese ruler, Rana Bahadur Shah, requested British aid and then left Kathmandu in a hurry. Around this time the Shamarpa is said to have poisoned himself. The Nepalese placed all the blame on the Shamarpa and tried to broker a truce. The Tibetans demanded that all the plundered wealth from Tashilhunpo be returned and the Shamarpa's followers, including his wife, be surrendered.

A deal was struck in which, this time, the Chinese became the tribute takers. A stone pillar erected by the Manchus still stands in Lhasa, commemorating the defeat of the Gurkhas in Tibetan, Chinese, and Manchu. The treaty gave the Tibetans very little and increased their problems by furnishing the Manchus with more power to interfere in Tibetan affairs. To exert more control they instituted a "golden urn" lottery, the purpose of which was to settle disputes about the recognition of the Panchen or Dalai Lamas with a lucky draw. It was largely ignored by Tibetans, but from time to time it has been re-invoked by the Chinese, most notably in their recent attempts to appoint their own choice of the Panchen Lama over the boy recognized by the Dalai Lama in 1995.

After the Gurkha War, the Tibetan government seized the estates of the Shamarpa and turned his seat, Yangpachen, into a Gelug monastery. It was decreed a crime to recognize his incarnation, or, indeed, for the Shamarpa to reincarnate at all. There was one last indignity: his red crown was buried under the cobblestones of Lhasa, near one of his confiscated properties that was converted into a courthouse. This was done so that people would walk over it, perpetually delivering what is considered in Tibet an extreme insult.

Until recently, the standard Kagyu account of the Tenth Shamarpa's life was considerably sanitized. What had occurred was a combination of a great embarrassment and an affront to the lineage. The story was put out that the Shamarpa was actually trying to make peace with the Nepalese king and went to Nepal on pilgrimage. The current Shamarpa has claimed that the Tenth Shamarpa fled Tibet for Nepal because the Gelug government was out to get him; he went to Nepal on pilgrimage and he tried to talk the king out of making war on Tibet. But Tibetan and Chinese historical documents support the political involvement of the Tenth Shamarpa in the Gurkha War.[99] After that, the Shamar tulkus were acknowledged only clandestinely by the Karmapas. According to an unofficial record, a Shamarpa was a son of the Fifteenth Karmapa Khakyab Dorje. Another died in infancy. The current Shamarpa[100] was born in Kham into the Atub family, a nephew of the Sixteenth Karmapa.

According to the Shamarpa,[101] both his uncles, the Karmapa and Dzogchen Ponlop Rinpoche, recognized that he was an incarnate lama. When the Karmapa heard his sister was pregnant, he told her to care for herself and the baby well because the child was a tulku. Ponlop Rinpoche also dreamt about it. The Shamarpa was born in Derge in 1952. When he was a year and a half old, his father died, helped along by alcohol, which he used to numb his increasing frustration and despair. He saw that the Chinese takeover of Tibet was imminent, yet he also saw people ill-prepared and worse, doing nothing to avoid the inevitable communist onslaught. He was among a group of local leaders who sent letters to the Tibetan government through then governor, Lhalu, expressing the willingness of Derge to mobilize forces against the Chinese. Their offer was rebuffed by Lhalu,[102] who told them it was none of their business.

Several months after his father's death, Shamarpa's mother married again, a man named Yeshe Raru, who joined the CIA-supported guerilla group "Four Rivers Six Ranges." Characterized as "a pan-Khampa resistance movement," it took its name from an ancient name for Kham.[103] Raru was trained by the Americans, parachuted into Tibet, and wasn't heard from again. It later came out that he was shot during some nighttime warfare; he drew on a cigarette and was sighted by a sniper and killed. The Shamarpa was sent to Tsurphu and, at the age of seven, traveled to Bhutan and Sikkim with the Sixteenth Karmapa.

The Shamarpa has described the early years at Rumtek as harsh. No road had been made, not even the potholed, poorly maintained road that is there now. Supplies were sent by pack mule from Gangtok, a six-hour trip. The Karmapa asked the Tibetan government in Dharamsala for permission to recognize and enthrone the Shamarpa, and in 1964 the permission was granted. He was enthroned shortly thereafter at Rumtek at the age of thirteen, the first Shamarpa enthroned in 250 years. He was educated with other tulkus in the monastery school.

He began traveling abroad in his twenties. I first encountered him in New York in late 1979 when he made his first visit to the U.S. He appeared casual and urbane, and very interested in political methodology. He used to tell us that he was more interested in politics than in teaching, and enjoyed recounting stories of the political power of previous Shamarpas and the history of his own family and the kings of Derge. One book he asked to read was Machiavelli's *The Prince*. It was amusing at the time to see him walking around the Woodstock center, a copy of Machiavelli in hand.

THE TAI SITUPAS

The Tai Situ line dates back to the days of the Indian *mahasiddhas,* or great adepts. He is believed to be an emanation of Maitreya, the coming Buddha. One noteworthy lifetime was spent as the mahasiddha Dombipa. Dombipa was king of Magadha and a disciple of Virupa who eventually abdicated his throne to lead a contemplative life in the wilderness. He took a low-caste woman as a consort and was more or less forced to abdicate. He became a great yogi.

Another important incarnation of the Tai Situpa was Denma Tsemang, one of the twenty-five main disciples of Padmasambhava. The special connection of the Tai Situpas with Padmasambhava is reflected in the names of the incarnations since the ninth, all of which begin with Pema.[104] Marpa the translator, who is discussed in chapter 3, is also considered an incarnation in the Tai Situ line of tulkus.

Jamgon Kongtrul and Tai Situpa at Lava Monastery, near Kalimpong, in 1992. (Photo by Michele Martin)

The incarnation that directly links the series of incarnations with the Karmapas is Drogon Rechen (1088–1158), one of the main disciples of the First Karmapa Dusum Khyenpa, and it is from this incarnation that the standard list begins. Next came two more incarnations, Yeshe Nyingpo followed by Ringowa Ratnabhadra, both accomplished yogis. The first incarnation to bear the Situ title was Situ Chokyi Gyaltsen (1377–1448), who became a disciple of the Fifth Karmapa Dezhin Shekpa. He traveled with the Karmapa to China, where the Ming emperor Yung Lo conferred the long honorific title upon him that the Situ lineage of incarnations bears today. It is often shortened to Kuang Ting Tai Situ, which may be translated "far-reaching, unshakable, great master, holder of the command." The numbering of the Situpas was not applied retroactively, as has been done with other lamas of his rank. The First Tai Situpa was appointed by the Karmapa as Master of Studies at Karma Gon and spent much of his life in solitary meditation.

The Second Tai Situ, Tashi Namgyal (1450–97), was recognized and enthroned by the Sixth Karmapa and later given Karma Gon by the Karmapa. The Third Situ Tashi Paljor (1498–1541) and the Fourth Situ Chokyi Gocha (1542–85) continued to develop

Karma Gon, which became famous for its library and the fine paintings and carvings that embellished its walls. Most of this art did not survive the destruction of the monastery by the communists, although some of the old buildings still stand. Situ Tashi Paljor recognized the Eighth Karmapa, Mikyo Dorje, and was one of his main teachers. Mikyo Dorje, in turn, recognized the Fourth Tai Situpa and became his teacher. The Ninth Karmapa Wangchuk Dorje bestowed the Red Crown upon the Fifth Tai Situpa Chokyi Gyaltsen Palzang as a sign of advanced spiritual attainment.

The Tai Situpas were based in Kham, in eastern Tibet, and most of the Karmapas were born there, so the Tai Situpa was frequently among first to investigate and discover a Karmapa incarnation. The Sixth Tai Situpa, Mipam Chogyal Rabten (1658–82), was noted for miracles and is remembered in the biographies for leaving footprints in stone and hanging prayer beads on a sunbeam. The Seventh Tai Situpa, Mawe Nyima, was a son of the king of Ling but died young.

By far the most remarkable of the Situ line was the Eighth Tai Situpa, Chokyi Jungne (1700–74). He is one of the most eminent figures in Tibetan religious history. A phenomenal scholar and linguist who was literate in Sanskrit, Nepali, and Chinese, his text on Tibetan grammar is still used in schools today. He was a doctor and wrote prolifically on astrology and medicine. He was an innovative painter who initiated a new school of tangka painting. He was known for his great spiritual insight and could predict future events. A story is told that he once complied with a minister's request for a prediction by telling him that there would be a coup and the minister himself would be assassinated. It happened as foretold.

Situ Chokyi Jungne founded Palpung Monastery in Derge in 1727, which became the seat of the Tai Situpas. Though he was invited along with the Shamarpa to accompany the Twelfth Karmapa on his trip to China, Situ Chokyi Jungne stayed behind. When the Karmapa and Shamarpa both died during that trip, tremendous responsibility fell upon Situ Chokyi Jungne, who had to look after the Karmapa's monasteries in addition to his own. He recognized and became the teacher of the Thirteenth Karmapa.

Another of his famous works was the printing press at Derge, which he set up with the help of the king. The king of Derge, Tenpa Tsering, sponsored the revision of the Kangyur and Tengyur, the entire Buddhist canon. The texts printed there were of such high quality that modern facsimile reprints have been made and reside in libraries around the world. At the Derge printing press texts were meticulously carved on rectangular wooden blocks, one for each page. Each block was painted with ink and the impression transferred onto handmade paper. Tens of thousands of such blocks were required to produce the more than three hundred volumes of the canon. At least half of the task of editing was undertaken by Tai Situpa himself. He drew up the index and edited the Kangyur pages for the carvers to copy, a huge task. Original texts of this kind that survive, on still-supple paper often embellished with paintings and gold ink, are priceless works of art and printcraft. The Derge printing press was renowned throughout greater Tibet for the quality of its texts.

The Tai Situpa did not stop with this but sought out other sources to translate and interpret. Situ Chokyi Jungne kept diaries that give a fascinating view of the intellectual climate of the time. E. Gene Smith, in his tantalizing introduction to the Tibetan reprint of these diaries, notes that "his diaries are filled with his quest for Sanskrit manuscripts," and details some of the color that abounds in his informal writings.[105] The Eighth Situ commented on daily events, his travels, and people he encountered. He moved throughout Tibet, teaching and accumulating more knowledge. He also visited Nepal and China. He was an original thinker who followed his own path. Situ Chokyi Jungne had tremendous influence during his own time and after through his many disciples. The Dalai Lama's labrang requested him to come to Lhasa to teach the young Dalai Lama, but the Derge king refused to let him go. His activities presaged the flowering of Tibetan religious culture that bloomed in his own monastery, Palpung, in the nineteenth century and spread throughout Tibet.

It was under the Ninth Tai Situpa, Pema Nyingje Wangpo (1774–1863), that this nonsectarian, or *rimé,* renaissance of thought reached its zenith. Rimé was essentially the effort by several great scholars to collate and conserve the rich teaching traditions available in Tibet. It was accomplished partly through one of Situ Pema Nyingje's chief disciples, the First Jamgon Kongtrul, Lodro Taye. Famous as a meditator, the last thirty years of the Ninth Situ's long life were spent in retreat, and his clairvoyance sometimes discomfited his monks. One was supremely surprised when the high lama, immured in retreat, admonished him to stop drinking.[106]

Tai Situ Pema Wangchuk Gyalpo (1886–1952) continued the vigorous activity that previous incarnations began. He was recognized by the Fifteenth Karmapa. The Karmapa and Jamgon Kongtrul Lodro Taye were his main teachers. He expanded Palpung, which by his time incorporated thirteen monastic estates in central and eastern Tibet. There were 180 monasteries under his care, and he traveled much of the time, ministering to their spiritual needs. There are still people alive who knew this colorful figure, noted for his tough discipline and the wrath he would let loose on those who trespassed monastic rules. His beatings were legendary, and the glowering figure in photographs lends credibility to the legend. As mentioned earlier, Situ Pema Wangchuk Gyalpo recognized the Sixteenth Karmapa without benefit of seeing the predictive letter left by the previous Karmapa. Later in life he spent his time alternating teaching with meditation.

After Tai Situ Wangchuk Gyalpo died in 1952, his monks were anxious to find his reincarnation. He was located by the Karmapa in the following way. In 1955 the Sixteenth Karmapa was out shopping with his attendants in Beijing. He was in China with a delegation accompanying the Dalai Lama for the purpose of discussing problems in Tibet. According to one of his monks who was with him, he suddenly wanted to go back to the guesthouse, but he didn't say why. He went into his room and asked not to be disturbed. The reason for the abrupt end of their shopping expedition, they later discovered, was that he had become aware of where the Twelfth Tai Situpa had been born. He wrote a letter to Palpung Monastery describing where the Palpung monks would find him, giving it to Bo Gongkar Rinpoche to deliver.

The Twelfth Tai Situpa, Pema Donyo Nyingje, was born in 1954 in Palyul, Derge. His parents were farmers by the name of Liu. His father died shortly after his birth, and his mother later married his father's brother, a common Tibetan practice. He was an infant when the search party came from Palpung, guided by the Karmapa's letter. Auspicious signs occurred at his birth: there was an earth tremor and a rainbow that appeared inside the house. The Karmapa's letter was very specific, and at the age of eighteen months he was escorted to Palpung to await the Karmapa's return from Beijing. He was enthroned at Palpung by the Karmapa shortly thereafter, with local dignitaries and two representatives of the Dalai Lama present. Hostilities between the Khampas and the Chinese escalated, and he was taken to Tsurphu. There he performed his first Red Crown Ceremony of this lifetime. This ritual is similar to the Black Crown Ceremony of the Karmapas except that the Tai Situpa recites the mantra of Maitreya instead of Chenrezig. He remained at Tsurphu with the Karmapa for a year.

When he was five years old, in 1959, his attendants took him to Bhutan for safety. The Bhutanese king, Jigme Wangchuk, and the queen mother had been devotees of the previous Tai Situpa. Ongen Rinpoche, Mingyur Rinpoche—both Palpung tulkus—and about forty of his monks accompanied him out of Tibet. From Bhutan they went to Sikkim, to be near the Karmapa. Since the Sikkimese ruler, Chogyal Tashi Namgyal, was also a Palpung tulku, he offered Tai Situpa and his monks hospitality. Tai Situpa lived in the royal palace and occasionally visited Rumtek for instruction. But he fell ill with tuberculosis and moved to Darjeeling, where he could receive medical treatment at a sanatorium. He stayed there for several years, living under straitened circumstances with a handful of his monks. A Tibetan aid organization, the Tibetan Refugee Assistance Committee (TRAC), put him in contact with American Nola McGarry, who became his foster mother from afar and who helped support him and sent him books, encouraging him to learn English. She did not meet him until he was an adult, during his first teaching tour in the United States in 1982. When he recovered from the tuberculosis, he returned to Rumtek and took instruction with the other tulkus.

He remained with the Karmapa until he went to teach in Ladakh at the age of twenty-two. While traveling in Ladakh, disciples from Derge and Nangchen offered him some land in Himachal Pradesh, land that was part of the Bir Tibetan settlement. It is located in forested foothills near the town of Baijnath, and not far from Palampur in the Kangra Valley. The monastery overlooks the village of Bir, just a few kilometers away. The monastery began in tents. Then a small building was completed. Eventually a small monastery rose on the hillside, floor by floor, as money became available. A new, much larger monastery was built during the 1990s that houses about four hundred monks of all ages.

THE GYALTSAPAS

In some ways the Gyaltsap tulkus have meditated in the shade of the Karmapas, their constant root lama. *Gyaltsap* means regent in Tibetan, and the Karmapa, who frequently traveled, entrusted Tsurphu to his care as hereditary regent. The Gyaltsapa's influence was considerable, for when the Karmapa was between births or roaming with the Karmay Garchen, he was the highest ranking lama at Tsurphu. The monastic seat of the Gyaltsapas adjoined the Karmapa's at Tsurphu.

There have been twelve Gyaltsapa incarnations, beginning with Goshir Paljor Dondrup (c. 1427–89), who was a disciple of the Sixth Karmapa and a noted meditator. He recognized and enthroned the Seventh Karmapa and transmitted lineage teachings to him. Before he died at the age of sixty-three he predicted that he would return in many successive incarnations. The Second Gyaltsapa, Tashi Namgyal (1490–1518), was recognized by the Seventh Karmapa, and his spiritual accomplishments were acknowledged when the Karmapa bestowed an Orange Crown upon him. Gyaltsapa Tashi Namgyal later recognized the

Gyaltsap
Rinpoche,
formal
portrait

Eighth Karmapa, Mikyo Dorje, and became his teacher. The Third Gyaltsapa, Drakpa Paljor (1519–49), was recognized by the Eighth Karmapa and spent his short life as a distinguished meditator. The Fourth Gyaltsapa, Drakpa Dondrup (1550–1617), was also recognized by the Eighth Karmapa, who again transmitted the lineage teachings to him.

Drakpa Choyang, the Fifth Gyaltsapa (c. 1618–58), was recognized, enthroned, and taught by the Sixth Shamarpa and was a contemplative most of his life. At a time when the Gelug government was confiscating properties and closing non-Gelug monasteries down, the Gyaltsapa managed to maintain good relations and control of the Karmapa's monasteries. He was evidently quite a diplomat. The Tenth Karmapa Choying Dorje had a love affair that produced a son, Gyaltsapa Norbu Zangpo (1660–98), the sixth in the line. Recognized by the Karmapa at the age of three, Gyaltsapa Norbu Zangpo was a precocious child who could recall former lives, and he became a yogi of great merit. Together with the Seventh Shamarpa, he recognized the Eleventh Karmapa, Yeshe Dorje. The Seventh Gyaltsapa, Konchok Ozer (1699–1765) was recognized and enthroned by Karmapa Jangchub Dorje, who was his teacher. He was ordained by the Eighth Tai Situpa at Tsurphu. He was also taught by the Eighth Shamarpa. The Eighth through the Eleventh Gyaltsapas all led lives of study and contemplation that exemplified the best of the Kagyu tradition.

The Twelfth Gyaltsapa, Drakpa Tenpai Yaphel, was born in Nyemo, near Tsurphu, in 1954. When he was four years old he was recognized by the Sixteenth Karmapa. His father was a well-known *ngakpa*, or yogi. The Karmapa brought Gyaltsap Rinpoche with him out of Tibet when he escaped, and for a while the young tulku lived at the royal palace monastery in Gangtok, looked after by Sikkim's queen mother. Her relationship with the Karmapa was a bit sour. According to Martam Amala, who knew her, the queen mother had sent a text to Tsurphu for copying, and she claimed the original was never returned. Whatever her reasons, she did not want Gyaltsap Rinpoche to join the Karmapa at Rumtek. But Gyaltsap Rinpoche was determined to go. He wanted to learn the rituals and receive the teachings from the Karmapa and other teachers who were there. So one day, when he was thirteen years old, he escaped from the palace monastery and walked all by himself to Rumtek. The ties with the queen mother were severed, but he was able to apply himself to what really interested him, study and meditation practice.

He tells the story of his escape to Rumtek in a simple, matter-of-fact way. The important thing to him, he told me, was to be with his guru the Karmapa. Of the four heart sons of His Holiness the Karmapa, he is the one considered the most studious, spending much of his time poring over Buddhist texts. He has acted in his traditional role as regent of Rumtek much of the time since the Karmapa's death and the recognition of the Seventeenth Karmapa, who remained in Tsurphu. Since the Seventeenth Karmapa's escape to India in 2000, the Gyaltsapa has continued his stewardship of Rumtek even as the young Karmapa is prevented from going there. Gyaltsap Rinpoche divides his time between Rumtek and his own monastery, Ralang, in western Sikkim. He now is one of the principal teachers of the Seventeenth Karmapa and regularly visits him to give teachings and initiations.

THE JAMGON KONGTRULS

The line of Jamgon Kongtrul tulkus is relatively short but quite illustrious. The First Jamgon Kongtrul, Lodro Taye (1813–99), was born in Derge to a family of serious Bon practitioners.[107] His father was a Bon lama, so at an early age he mastered Bon teachings. It appears Kongtrul believed his natural father to be a Buddhist lama, Yungdrung Tendzin. In any event, he went on to master whatever traditions there were, Bon and Buddhist alike.

His first Buddhist training was in the Nyingma tradition, and he was ordained in that tradition at Shechen Monastery when he was nineteen years old. Shortly thereafter he was named as a tulku by Situ Pema Nyingje Wangpo at Palpung Monastery and was compelled to be reordained in the Kagyu tradition, a requirement that disturbed him for its pettiness and sectarianism, but to which he consented. He was ordained by Situ Rinpoche, who became his root lama. But Kongtrul received teachings from eminent lamas of all lineages. The Nyingma master Chogyur Lingpa acknowledged him as a terton, a "treasure finder." Kongtrul, Chogyur Lingpa, and Jamyang Khyentse Wangpo, a scholar of great repute in eastern Tibet, launched the *rimé* renaissance. Kongtrul was a physician and scholar, and in his long and energetic career he helped to settle disputes between monasteries and authored close to a hundred volumes on the philosophy and practices of Nyingma, Kagyu, Kadam, Sakya, Zhiche, and Bon sects, among others. He recognized the

Fifteenth Karmapa, the most eminent of his numerous disciples. His imprint upon Tibetan religious history is indelible.

The Second Jamgon Kongtrul, Khyentse Ozer (1904–53), was recognized by the Fifteenth Karmapa, who was his father. He received the lineage transmission from the Karmapa and from the Tenth Trungpa tulku. He led a largely contemplative life at Palpung and took responsibility for transmission of teachings to the Sixteenth Karmapa. Before dying he predicted where he would reincarnate.

The Third Jamgon Kongtrul, Lodro Chokyi Senge, was born in Lhasa to the Sadutsang clan, a trading family whose importance and riches were legendary in Tibet. The Sixteenth

The Second
Jamgon
Kongtrul,
Khyentse Ozer

The Third Jamgon
Kongtrul Lodro Chokyi
Senge Tenpai Gocha,
late 1980s

Karmapa recognized him in 1955, but he was the firstborn son, and his grandfather refused to relinquish him to Palpung Monastery. The family needed a son to carry on the business. The Karmapa met with the family and asked the grandfather if another son was born, would he let Jamgon Kongtrul go to the monastery? His grandfather agreed, and eighteen months after Jamgon Kongtrul was born the family was blessed with another son. In 1956 the family assented to Jamgon Kongtrul being educated as a tulku and brought up in the monastery, although he remained at home for the time being, since he was still an infant. Conditions were worsening in Tibet, so the Karmapa advised the family to take Jamgon Rinpoche away to India. They moved to their home in Kalimpong, near Darjeeling, where they had a house and a trading office.

When he was six years old, Kongtrul went to Rumtek to receive teachings and was enthroned at Rumtek that same year by the Karmapa. In 1973 he received full ordination, and he accompanied the Karmapa on his tours to Europe, North America, and Southeast Asia in 1976 and 1980. The Karmapa sent him on his first solo teaching tour to Southeast Asia in 1981. His relationship with the Karmapa was like son to father, and

163

after the Karmapa died in 1981, Jamgon Rinpoche devoted himself to fulfilling the Karmapa's projects. Jamgon Kongtrul became a well-loved teacher, and he was deeply committed to the Buddhist way of life. He death in a road accident in 1992 will be a topic of a later chapter. His reincarnation was discovered by the Seventeenth Karmapa in Tibet in 1996.

SEEDS OF DISCORD

With each successive year more questions arose about why it was taking so long to find the Karmapa's new incarnation. When Topga Yugyal became Rumtek chandzo in 1982 he appeared, at first, to be a person who could bring some modern innovation and even transparency into the old-fashioned system entrenched at Rumtek. He was modern, a learned monk before marrying a Bhutanese princess, and a nephew of the Sixteenth Karmapa. One observer suggested the secret of his success was that he could carry off diplomacy in the old world and the new—sometimes playing one against the other. He could be very charming.

But there were other sides to his character. He was known to exploit his connection to the Bhutanese royal family for personal gain. An example was documented in May 1982, when he was detained and his luggage impounded at the Calcutta airport. The customs officials had been tipped off that he and his wife were smuggling gold from Hong Kong on their diplomatic passports. The luggage was found to contain 150 kilos of gold and twenty expensive watches—contraband in the eyes of the Indian Government. His royal connections, and, perhaps, the unwillingness of the Indian government to upset the delicate relations with Bhutan, spared him from prosecution.[108]

According to sources within Rumtek, Topga Yugyal seemed to relish power. He systematically sidelined any who dared to differ with him. One of those was the Sixteenth Karmapa's personal secretary, Dronyig Tendzin Namgyal. Topga Yugyal behaved as if the Karmapa's assets were his own. He took the Karmapa's Mercedes Benz to Bhutan for repairs and never returned it. Rumtek residents worried that less replaceable treasures could have been spirited away. Gradually, disapproval grew in the

Rumtek community about the way Shamarpa and Topga Yugyal managed the monastery's affairs.

One thing that shook Rumtek Tibetans was when Topga and Shamarpa "sold" the Karmapa's monastery in Bhutan, Tashi Choling, for the reported sum of forty lakh rupees, about 120,000 U.S. dollars at that time. Price aside, that a monastery could or should be sold at all flabbergasted many at Rumtek. According to Bhutanese sources, however, it was a misapprehension that an outright sale took place. For one thing, Topga and his wife owed quite a lot of money to the Bhutanese government, and when they couldn't come up with it, and the palace monastery was relinquished to the government to obtain forgiveness of part of this debt.[109] Another factor was the xenophobic tendencies of the Bhutanese government, which took advantage of Topga Yugyal's indebtedness to diminish the Karmapa's strong influence in central Bhutan. The government did not want foreign labrangs entrenched in Bhutan. Tashi Choling and its extensive adjoining land was offered for the Karmapa's use by aristocratic devotees after he was forced to flee Tibet, but it was evidently not deeded to him. There were several Bhutanese properties besides Tashi Choling that had been given to the Karmapa by aristocrat devotees. But in any case, in a feudal society such as Bhutan, aristocrats can do what they please—give or take away. Whatever the justification, in this murky mixture of politics and finance the Rumtek labrang lost out.

The Sixteenth Karmapa, like other lamas, attracted sponsors for his projects among non-Tibetans. Some of these donors were very generous. One of them, C. T. Shen, raised money to buy the land in Woodstock, New York, where the Karmapa's North American seat was established. Estimates of the Karmapa's assets, however, have been greatly exaggerated in press accounts that imply his "estate" includes all of the Kagyu centers around the world. A figure of 1.2 billion dollars, arbitrarily floated by a journalist, caught on and was repeated endlessly in media accounts. In reality, most Buddhist centers in the West barely scrape together the rent unless they are lucky enough to have a benefactor or are an old, established trust. Tibetan

Buddhist centers are typically supported by the subscriptions of center members, and even when a high lama does visit, he by no means takes home all the revenue from the seminars, but instead is given an honorarium. The rest of the income goes to defray center expenses. The network of centers that have been erroneously described as the Karmapa's property would doubtless be an unwelcome financial burden.

The Karmapa's real assets besides the partly reconstructed Tsurphu Monastery in Tibet and Karma Triyana Dharmachakra in New York are in India—Rumtek in Sikkim and the Karmapa International Buddhist Institute (KIBI) in New Delhi, which was appropriated in fact, if not legally, by Shamarpa during the interregnum. KIBI now hosts the Shamarpa's followers.

The murmurs of dissatisfaction grew louder over time. Relatives of Shamarpa and Topga began to prosper in a manner inconsistent with their business activities. Hotels came up run by members of the family of the Shamarpa, such as one that sits today on the main road into Gangtok. Topga Yugyal's attitude and behavior were viewed by many Rumtek residents as increasingly detrimental to the monastery and the assets of the Karmapa. It didn't help when in 1983 Jamgon Kongtrul, Tai Situpa, and Gyaltsap Rinpoche fell out with the Shamarpa over his attempt to substitute his own name in place of the Karmapa's in some documents related to the Karmapa's properties. Shamarpa maintained it was a misunderstanding, but a climate of mistrust was seeded by the incident.[110]

In 1985 the four tulkus announced that "a letter" had been opened, leading people to believe the next Karmapa would soon be found. But all that happened was a request for a great many prayers to be said and offerings to be made for the removal of obstacles blocking the discovery of the next Karmapa. It turned out later that the announcement was a bit of a white lie to buy time, because no actual instructions from the Sixteenth Karmapa had yet been found. The letter had been a group effort of sorts in which all four participated. Gyaltsap Rinpoche, with his scholar's memory, recalled an appropriate prayer that had been composed by the Sixteenth Karmapa, and Jamgon

Rinpoche wrote it down in red ink on a legal pad and put the prayer in a reliquary. They were desperate to have some words of the Karmapa to guide them. Initially positive about finding the Karmapa quickly, by the late 1980s the four tulkus became discouraged. Meetings held over the next few years generated no substantive action; less and less was said by the principals. It became an awkward subject.

8. Search and Recognition

IN LATE 1990, TAI SITUPA went into a meditation retreat. He was thirty-seven years old. In the Tibetan system of astrology certain days, months, or years in a person's life are said to bring good or bad influences. The thirty-seventh is considered an obstacle year, and such periods are believed to feature exceptional difficulties and occur in everyone's life. An individual's birth chart reveals what to expect and when. Forewarned is forearmed, and Tibetans will often have special prayers said in a "black year" to ward off negative influences. If Saturday is someone's unlucky day of the week, another day will be chosen for an important interview, meeting, or marriage. High lamas customarily devote more time to prayer and meditation during their obstacle years. Their monks pray to prevent harm befalling their guru. So Tai Situpa went into retreat at his monastery, Sherab Ling.

The biggest obstacle for all the Kagyu tulkus at this time was their inability to locate the Seventeenth Karmapa. It was much on their minds. Daily prayers were said for his discovery. Tai

Situpa recalls, "During that retreat, I remembered the talisman the Karmapa had given me in Calcutta in 1981. I thought maybe I should look there." This small packet sewn up in brocade was not an unusual gift. Tai Situpa had never opened it because it was not the custom to do so. It is a common practice for lamas to give their disciples blessing prayers or holy scripture or sacred mandalas sewn into cloth pouches. These are believed to ward off negative influences, and recipients do not usually open up such a talisman. Such things are treasured for the blessings they convey and are worn on the body or kept on a personal shrine. Tai Situpa describes the event: "At that time His Holiness [the Karmapa] was staying in the Oberoi Grand Hotel Calcutta and I went to meet him. According to the wishes of His Holiness I stayed with him for a few days. One evening His Holiness gave me a protection amulet wrapped in brocade. He said that in the future this will be useful to me. At that time I thought that His Holiness must have foreknowledge of a bad phase for me and had, for that reason, given this protection amulet to me. So I kept it on my body all the time."[111]

For ten years the four tulkus had looked in all the logical places where instructions might have been left: among the Karmapa's papers and books; in reliquaries; they interrogated attendants and associates and listened to reports about precocious children carried by hopeful relatives from Tibet and nearby countries. All efforts had yielded nothing. This packet Tai Situpa always carried with him was one unexplored place. After the idea to look there occurred to him, he says he opened the amulet and he found an envelope. On the envelope was written: "To be opened in the Iron Horse year." It was the Iron Horse year. Inside the envelope was a letter. Tai Situpa did not open the letter, but sensing this could be important, he immediately sent letters to the other three tulkus and the Rumtek labrang, asking for a meeting at Rumtek. He told them that he had some news to impart regarding the Karmapa. Shamarpa and Topga Yugyal would not agree to meet at Rumtek. One old member of the administration who had been appointed by the Sixteenth Karmapa, Assistant

Shedra, circa 1989, with (seated left to right): Thrangu Rinpoche, Gyaltsap
Rinpoche, Jamgon Kongtrul, Shamarpa, Khenpo Tsultrim Gyamtso, and
Khenpo Chodrak Tenphel. Sangye Nyenpa Rinpoche stands center.

General Secretary Gelek Tendzin, known as Lama Kyap,
announced Tai Situpa's message to the public and was immediately fired by Topga.

By this time considerable tension was building up in the
Rumtek community and among the four tulkus—Tai Situpa,
Jamgon Kongtrul, and Gyaltsapa on the one hand, with
Shamarpa and Topga as focal points on the other. Jamgon
Kongtrul was very upset about the two cousins' attempt to gain
control over the Karmapa Institute in New Delhi. It did not get
better after Shamarpa took over the shedra. The four had followed the previous Karmapa's wishes and served as co-principals, with each regent taking a three-year term as chairman.
Kongtrul and then Gyaltsapa had taken their turns and worked
diligently to make it a disciplined monk's college. One thing
Kongtrul had set in motion was getting the shedra accreditation
with Sanskrit University in Varanasi through which monks could
earn shastri and acharya degrees.[112] This duty was neglected by
Shamarpa, who spent much of his time away from Rumtek.
Jamgon Kongtrul often had to cover for things Shamarpa had
left undone.

Jamgon Kongtrul's longtime English secretary, Kunga Wangmo, who was then secretary for the shedra, wanted to resign when Shamarpa took over, but Kongtrul urged her to continue. Devoted and conscientious, she had done much of the arduous legwork for the shedra as well as Kongtrul's other projects. When I asked her about it again while researching this book she told me, "Shamar had tried his best to undo the very extensive sponsorship program which was in place when he took over the thing. Needless to say, it was a most stressful period." She added, "Jamgon Rinpoche, always following the middle path, told me not to resign, even though I wanted to do it with a flourish and throw the keys at Shamar and his cronies. So I had to continue for a few years."

When Tai Situpa's turn came to serve as chairman in 1992, Shamarpa would not hand over the office keys and files. Instead he gave the monks of the Karma Shri Nalanda Institute an eight-month holiday and ignored their annual examinations, which were not held. The shedra, to run properly, demanded a good deal of the principal's time, which Shamarpa appeared unwilling to give. It contrasted with Jamgon Kongtrul, who was very attentive to the shedra and was personally concerned with its students. This deficiency prompted the chief abbot, Khenchen Thrangu Rinpoche, to write to Tai Situpa imploring him to do something: "Now the Institute has been left without proper care, as a result of which its administration has totally collapsed. Even the lecturers are on foreign trips without any concern about these developments. To add further injury, there are speculations about the intention of closing down the Institute. The very reputation of the Institute is at stake." He asked Tai Situpa, whose turn as principal it was, to take control "to save it from future damage and to revive the system which is already collapsed" and "to resolve the present crisis."[113] In this he was seconded by Khenpo Tsultrim Gyamtso and the students of the shedra, who wrote Tai Situpa they had been prevented from sitting for final exams and feared that the same thing could happen again the following year or that the Institute would be closed altogether.

Pressure was mounting from people impatient for the new Karmapa to be identified. It had been ten years since the Sixteenth Karmapa had died. Letters began to arrive at Rumtek from various Tibetan organizations in different parts of India, Nepal, and Bhutan asking pointed questions. Some of these organizations were religious, with members who are devotees of the Karmapa, some were followers of the Karma Kagyu, and some were connected to Tibetan social and cultural causes. The theme of the letters was the demand that the four rinpoches find the Seventeenth Karmapa as soon as possible. A letter from the Derge Tibetan Buddhist Culture Association from Nepal alleged that Topga Yugyal "for the past couple of years has been trying to allocate an incarnation for the Gyalwa Karmapa on his own, a fake incarnation," and accused him of manipulating a Bhutanese princess who was a relation of his by marriage to do so. Saying they had run out of patience, they scolded the four regents: "This is a very dangerous transition, the main pillars of the Kagyu lineage, Rinpoches, you cannot stay quiet, just like this."[114]

So when Tai Situpa tried to bring the four tulkus together to tell them about his discovery of the letter, the divisive currents were strong. The fact that they all had committed to busy travel schedules made it difficult to arrange a meeting as well. The best that Tai Situpa could do was to meet Jamgon Kongtrul and Shamarpa one afternoon in New Delhi. They met in Tai Situpa's hotel room. Gyaltsap Rinpoche was not present, and Tai Situpa did not want to share the news unless all four were there. Tai Situpa then consulted the Dalai Lama on the best means to remove obstacles. The Dalai Lama suggested that a fire ritual be done, 100,000 times. In such a ceremony, purificatory prayers are said and offerings are made, some of which are burned at the end of the ceremony. This was done at Rumtek.

Early in 1992 Tai Situpa again requested a meeting, one week after Tibetan New Year. His first letter of invitation met with no response. Determined, he sent a second letter appointing a meeting for the 15th of March. When he arrived at Rumtek, Jamgon Kongtrul was there. Gyaltsap Rinpoche, who was at his monastery at Ralang, Sikkim, came soon after. Shamarpa was out of the country, in Nepal. Tai Situpa requested him to come. He then called a general meeting of the Rumtek administration, informing them of his purpose for coming there. He said he would do retreat until all the four tulkus were assembled. He went into his retreat in the shrine room where the large reliquary stupa of the Sixteenth Karmapa is kept. Before the retreat, and several times during it, Tai Situpa and Jamgon Kongtrul had lengthy discussions. That was when Tai Situpa showed him the letter, according to Tai Situpa's account. When Tai Situpa emerged from his retreat on the morning of the 19th of March, he recalled, "I saw a good omen as soon as I came out. Three children were carrying full pails of milk up the hill." For Tibetans, such mundane events take on significance when they occur at a sensitive moment: the abundance of milk, the upward as opposed to downward progress of the children, were good signs.

Since all four tulkus were at last assembled at Rumtek, the first of several meetings was held later that day. Outside, government officials and delegations from Buddhist associations waited for news. Inside, Tai Situpa was finally able to do what he had waited a year to do: present the prediction letter that the Sixteenth Karmapa had left with him to the other three lamas. They read the letter and discussed it. Jamgon Rinpoche and Gyaltsap Rinpoche were very happy about it. Shamarpa looked at it and tossed it down. He took Jamgon Rinpoche out on the balcony and talked to him. He then came back and called Tai Situpa into another room and asked him, "Did you write it or did the Karmapa? If you wrote that letter, you tell me and I trust you and I have no problem with accepting that." Tai Situpa said later that he was shocked by this reaction. "I told him that while I did not see the Karmapa write it himself, it was given to me by the Karmapa, and I had no reason to doubt that it was his handwriting. I certainly did not write it myself." Later Jamgon Kongtrul said that when Shamarpa took him aside he also accused Tai Situpa of forging the letter, but Kongtrul responded that he had no need to forge a letter. If Tai Situpa knew where the Karmapa was he had the authority within the lineage to write his own letter. Then Shamarpa accepted the letter and said that he wanted to be the one to show the letter to the delegation waiting outside and explain the circumstances. Gyaltsap Rinpoche, recalling these events, said in his typically laconic way, "Situ Rinpoche called us together several times but we couldn't meet. When we did, there was no result. The first meeting we asked for *shapten* [prayers to remove obstacles]. At the last meeting Situ Rinpoche produced the letter that all of us accepted, including Shamar Rinpoche."[115]

Ringu Tulku, a Kagyu lama who resides in Gangtok and regularly teaches abroad, was among the group of anxious Buddhist leaders and government officials who waited outside. He said they waited all day for the four to come out. When the four tulkus at last emerged, the Shamarpa was the one who showed the letter to the group. Inside the meeting, it had taken all day for the tulkus to decipher the letter, which was written as poetry and included some obscure symbolism. A search party could be commissioned to find the Karmapa only once the letter was interpreted. All the tulkus were, at that time, in agreement that the letter was genuine, and at least three of them saw no cause for delay. Members of the Karma Kagyu, the local Buddhist groups, Sikkimese government officials, and others, were elated, eager for the child to be found. Shamarpa announced that the enthronement date of the Seventeenth Karmapa would be given no later than October 15, 1992. Plans went forward to send a search party.

But on April 26, 1992, a shocking calamity left people stunned: Jamgon Kongtrul was killed in an automobile accident. He was only thirty-eight years old. He had been staying with his family in Kalimpong, near Darjeeling, and was coming down from there with a driver and two monks. They were headed toward Kalu Rinpoche's monastery in Salugara, on the outskirts of Siliguri, taking a brand new car on a test drive. The BMW was a gift from his brother. Whatever happened on the Sevoke Road straightaway, Jamgon Rinpoche and the driver of the car in which they were riding died instantly. One monk attendant, according to accounts in local newspapers, lingered for a few hours before he succumbed to his injuries. Initial accounts said the driver had swerved to avoid some animals that had run into the road. Kongtrul's chief attendant Tendzin Dorje survived, and though dazed, he managed to take Rinpoche the few miles to the monastery in Salugara, but it was too late. At the time of the accident which killed Jamgon Kongtrul, 6:30 A.M. on April 26th, Shamarpa and Gyaltsap Rinpoche were at Rumtek. Gyaltsap Rinpoche recalled, "No one at Rumtek informed me personally about Jamgon Rinpoche's death. I heard it from Lopon Konchok from Dharamsala." Within hours Tai Situ Rinpoche, on tour in Southeast Asia, was notified, and he immediately canceled his program and booked a flight back to India.

Whether the driver veered on the road to avoid something, whether there was a problem with the car, or whether it was simply reckless driving, was never clearly determined. Tendzin Dorje, the only survivor, wrote a letter to the effect that some birds ran out in the road; the BMW had just been serviced. The obituary in the *Sikkim Observer,* however, which called Kongtrul "perhaps the main pillar of Rumtek monastery," also noted, "While no one has so far openly questioned the manner in which the 'accident' took place, many people are now quite doubtful and suspicious about what has been described by many as a 'mysterious' death."[116] There was an investigation, but the investigation was cursory at best, and nothing came of it. An attempt to bring in agents from BMW to investigate was scuttled when the person deputed to call Germany to confirm arrangements tried to bargain down the already agreed-upon price. This angered the investigators, who refused to come.

It turns out that Jamgon Kongtrul was preparing to leave for Tibet within a few days to find the Seventeenth Karmapa. The other tulkus had appointed him leader of the search party; he was ideally suited for the task and was planning a trip to Tibet anyway. His maternal grandfather, Ngaboe Ngawang Jigme, was the highest-ranking Tibetan bureaucrat in China. Ngaboe was formerly the Dalai Lama's cabinet minister and was controversial because he cooperated with the communist Chinese during and after their takeover of Tibet. Ngaboe subsequently became governor of Tibet and managed to float above the muck through all policy shifts since 1959. Many Tibetans viewed him as a traitor. Jamgon Rinpoche used to laugh when asked about it, saying "Some say he is a demon, others do not. I don't know what to say about it. He's my grandfather." Ngaboe was a strong ally if it came to convincing the Chinese to allow the Seventeenth Karmapa to be recognized and enthroned. The loss of Jamgon Kongtrul at this juncture was indeed an obstacle. Kongtrul was one of the most devoted of the close disciples of the previous Karmapa and the one who put the most effort into fulfilling his unfinished works. He had looked forward to finding the Karmapa's new incarnation.

Tai Situpa arrived in Calcutta on April 30th and reached Rumtek the next day, where he met Gyaltsap Rinpoche and Jamgon Rinpoche's family. He was engaged in meetings from the moment he arrived at Rumtek. On the morning of May 2nd he had a formal meeting with the family and labrang of Jamgon Rinpoche to discuss the forty-nine-day ceremonies. At that meeting it was decided that Kongtrul's body should be preserved and a stupa built to house it at Pullahari in Nepal, the place where Jamgon Kongtrul established his seat outside of Tibet.

Shamarpa went into retreat at his house less than a mile down the hill from Rumtek on the evening of May 1st, the day Situ Rinpoche reached Rumtek. Although Shamarpa let it be known it was "a loose retreat," he did not meet Tai Situpa and Gyaltsap Rinpoche to discuss the death of Jamgon Kongtrul or the search for the Karmapa—although he was reportedly sighted in Gangtok, meeting the chief minister and other officials. He left India within days of Situ Rinpoche's arrival without revealing his plans or his destination to Situ Rinpoche or Gyaltsapa. Topga Yugyal also left Rumtek shortly after Tai Situpa's arrival. Tai Situpa had been consoling Jamgon Kongtrul's grieving family when Topga Yugyal came to his sitting room. He requested Topga to wait a few minutes until the family had left, but Topga elected not to wait and, like his cousin, left without meeting Tai Situpa. Shamarpa's other cousin, senior monk and shedra teacher Khenpo Chodrak Tenphel, also avoided Tai Situpa and left Rumtek.

People began to arrive from near and far to pay respects to Jamgon Kongtrul—tulkus, lamas, monks, nuns, lay students, and friends of Jamgon Rinpoche. Tai Situpa and Gyaltsap Rinpoche addressed a gathering in front of Rumtek Monastery on May 17th. They each spoke in Tibetan and Tai Situpa gave a summary in English. First they spoke of Jamgon Rinpoche: "Losing him in such a quick and unexpected manner is very difficult to accept, but we try not to think about it and try to concentrate on doing the right thing, the prayers and the offerings," Situ Rinpoche said. After announcing what had been decided about Jamgon Kongtrul's ceremonies, Tai Situpa went on to say that he and Gyaltsap Rinpoche felt it was urgent to meet with Shamarpa "to discuss the whole situation all over again and make necessary plans on how to proceed." They waited to do this until after his retreat, "But a few days ago we learned that Shamar Rinpoche has left for a tour in the West and, therefore, we have had no chance to meet with him." He explained that they had no choice but to continue with the plans to find the Karmapa made by all four of them in March, and would discuss it with Shamarpa when he returned.

Gyaltsap Rinpoche then cited the prophecy that there will be twenty-one successive Karmapa incarnations, and emphasized the importance of preserving the tradition of all past Karmapas for the Seventeenth and his successors. Both affirmed "the leader, the owner of this monastic community is the Karmapa," with all the relics, holy objects, and texts brought from Tibet and all the properties. "The whole complex will return to the Seventeenth Karmapa, who is the same as the Sixteenth Karmapa," Tai Situpa said, "The only difference is the body: they have a different body, but they are the same person, same mind, same wisdom." He concluded by urging everyone to continue their prayers that Jamgon Kongtrul's "incarnation should come quickly and there be no obstacles...It is very important for all of you to look forward to serving the Seventeenth Karmapa as you have served the Sixteenth Karmapa."[117] Both the tulkus were shattered by the loss of their close friend, and it showed on their faces as they conducted the sad business of his funeral.

Shamarpa's absence grew longer, with no word of when he would return. Later it was discovered that one purpose of his trip was to consolidate assets. Judy Cutler, director of Rigpe Dorje, Jamgon Kongtrul's main fundraising organization in North America, told me that at one time Shamarpa tried to influence her to raise funds for him instead, and said that after Jamgon Kongtrul's death, Shamarpa tried to get her to sign over control of Rigpe Dorje to him. She refused on both occasions. According to sources in Hawaii, Shamarpa tried the same thing there during his travels at the time of Jamgon Kongtrul's funeral ceremonies.

Feeling the urgency of locating the Karmapa, Tai Situpa and Gyaltsap Rinpoche sent a message to Drupon Dechen Rinpoche at Tsurphu Monastery with a copy of the Sixteenth Karmapa's instructions and the interpretation so a search could begin. They did this through Akong Tulku, director of Samye Ling Buddhist Centre in Scotland, and Sherab Tharchin, Gyaltsap Rinpoche's chief administrator. They were going to Tibet to sponsor prayers for Jamgon Kongtrul's swift rebirth at the holy places there. It would be easy for them to courier the instructions. The two set off but were delayed in Nepal waiting for visas. To minimize delay, Akong Tulku sent the message ahead to Drupon Dechen Rinpoche at Tsurphu with instructions to dispatch a search party.

On the 19th of May, Sakya Trizin, head of the Sakya lineage, and his eldest son visited Rumtek. He prayed before the kudung and later met Tai Situpa and Gyaltsap Rinpoche. The next morning the rinpoches asked that the relic room be opened for Sakya Trizin so that he might see the prediction letter written by the Sixteenth Karmapa. This required the consent of the labrang and the Sikkim government, who had placed it under guard. The authorities agreed. When Sakya Trizin read the letter he expressed his approval, respectfully placing the letter on his head in front of lay and religious witnesses. He had often corresponded with the Sixteenth Karmapa and said he recognized the handwriting as his. Afterward, all who wished to visit the relics of the Sixteenth Karmapa were allowed to do so under the watchful eyes of guards and officials before the relic room was later resealed.

During the next days Tai Situpa and Gyaltsap Rinpoche were occupied with ritual and hospitality obligations as a stream of visitors came and went. A letter arrived from the Dalai Lama's Department of Religious Affairs requesting that a comprehensive biography of the Sixteenth Karmapa be written by senior abbots and tulkus of the lineage. The senior tulkus organized a committee to research and write the biography. Chatral Rinpoche, one of the oldest and most venerable surviving lamas in exile, arrived from Nepal on the 29th. He had a long meeting with Tai Situpa and Gyaltsap Rinpoche in which he encouraged them to carry out the instructions of the Sixteenth Karmapa regarding the recognition and enthronement of his successor. Almost every day eminent lamas arrived to offer prayers.

The fifth week of the ceremonies had begun when Sikkim government officials asked the two rinpoches to send copies of the Sixteenth Karmapa's letter of prediction to the Dalai Lama. But Tai Situpa and Gyaltsap Rinpoche wished to deliver the copies in person. Government officials were sent to accompany them. Tai Situpa, Gyaltsap Rinpoche, and the Sikkimese officials left for New Delhi on June 6th. They were in New Delhi when they received news from Tibet that a boy had been identified according to the instructions of the Sixteenth Karmapa's letter. The Tsurphu Monastery search party had set out as soon as permission could be obtained from the Chinese government to go. An official of the Tibetan Autonomous Region went with the search party, which included four Tsurphu monks and a driver. The regional government supplied cars for the trip. They headed for the area where they believed they might find the boy. Their plan was to do it secretly, not betraying their true purpose to the people they met. They decided to pass themselves off as pilgrims. Discretion was advisable, also, because permission notwithstanding, the Chinese government viewed reincarnation as superstition. The letter that guided them, in its entirety, is translated as follows:

Emaho! Self awareness is always bliss;
The dharmadhatu[118] has no center or edge.
For here to the north (in) the east of (the land) of snow[119]

is a country where divine thunder spontaneously blazes.[120]
[In] a beautiful nomad's place with the sign of the cow,[121]
the method is Dondrup and the wisdom is Logala.[122]
[Born in] the year of the one used for the earth[123]
[with] the miraculous, far-reaching sound of the white
     one,[124]
[this] is the one known as Karmapa.
He is sustained by Lord Donyo Drupa;[125]
being nonsectarian, he pervades all directions;
not staying close to some and distant from others, he is the
     protector of all beings:
The sun of Buddha's Dharma that benefits others always
     blazes.[126]

The search party reached a monastery called Karlek Gon in
Lhatok, a province of eastern Tibet. There a quiet investigation
was conducted. They were eventually directed to the village of
Bakor, near Lhatokgar, the main town of Lhatok. During the
search the monks put out the story that they had come from
India with letters for a Mr. Loga. They were told that there was
no man by that name, but there was a woman. This coincided
with one detail of the prediction letter. They inquired about her
husband's name and were told it was Dondrup, the same given
for the father in the Sixteenth Karmapa's letter. Another clue
confirmed. They discovered that the couple had a young son,
born in the Wood Ox year (1985), around whose birth were
many signs the locals deemed miraculous, including "the sound
of the great white one," a sacred conch. All the points in the prediction letter were fulfilled.

By the time Akong Rinpoche and Sherab Tharchin reached
Tibet, the advance search party had successfully located the
family. The monks in the party briefed the new arrivals when
they all met in Chamdo. After hearing the details from the original search party, the two representatives went to Bakor to offer
traditional gifts to the Seventeenth Karmapa on behalf of Tai
Situpa and Gyaltsap Rinpoche. Akong Rinpoche, as he recounted
what he witnessed, said, "It was more and more fascinating as

Amdo
Palden
(photo:
Bryan G.
Miller)

each part of the story unfolded," adding that it was uncanny how the search party was expected by this nomad child—and that the child had been making his own preparations to leave for several months! The boy's parents told the party that when asked why he was packing up his things, he did not explain, he just told them he was going away. He insisted that the family move one month ahead of schedule to the spring pasture, and he became so upset when they dawdled that his parents finally decided to go along with his wishes. By doing so they were able to be at the place predicted in the Sixteenth Karmapa's letter when the monks from Tsurphu arrived.

But even before his discovery, the Seventeenth Karmapa's history has a marvelous quality, like an old-fashioned fairy tale. Dondrup and his wife Logala are nomads. They were not well off, though they had sufficient livestock to provide food and clothing for their large family. They are simple people, respected in their community. Their first child was a son, and he was followed by five girls. They badly wanted another son, and consulted many lamas for help. They said prayers and made offerings to monasteries, but their seventh child was another girl. Now desperate, the father went to a holy man that he knew of, Amdo Palden. Amdo Palden was a respected yogi, a *ngakpa*. This type of lama leads a life of complete renunciation and spends a great deal of time meditating in austere circumstances. Such sages are often credited with supernatural abilities that result from their many years of spiritual focus.

Dondrup approached the ngakpa and explained his predicament. Amdo Palden, not one for idle talk, told him, "I will think about it." A few days later Dondrup returned to see Amdo Palden, who told him that there was a possibility that his wish for a son could be fulfilled. But if a boy is born, Amdo Palden stressed, "He must be given to me." The father promised, and the old yogi agreed to do what he could. The mother was required to undergo special instruction and blessing ceremonies to pave the way for this, which Amdo Palden conferred. These were meant to purify her of negative karma that might interfere and also bring good influences, so that she might conceive the son she desired.

Logala became pregnant again. On the first day of the fifth Tibetan month in the Wood Ox year, June 26, 1985, she gave birth to a son inside their yak-hair tent in the Bakor encampment, near the spring pasture. It is a peripatetic village of seventy-two nomad families, about 430 people in all. At the time of his birth the family and their neighbors reported hearing strange sounds that lasted for about two hours. Some said it was the sound of a conch shell being blown, others heard an odd droning sound, still others heard musical instruments reverberating from the surrounding hills. None of them could pinpoint the source of the sound. The Karmapa's mother said a bird perched on the top of her tent and warbled a beautiful song after he was born.

In a diary he kept of the search, Tsurphu monk Lodro Nyenpa noted that people all over the valley reported the same unusual phenomena, corroborating the story of the boy's family. Flowers sprouted that had not been seen in the area before. Perhaps the

The first photo of the boy, "Apo Gapa," the Seventeenth Karmapa, after the search party found him at the Bakor nomad encampment, Lhatok, Tibet, May 1992.

most dramatic of the many signs that the villagers reported were a trio of suns that shone in the sky, all the same size, lined up in a row. Over the middle sun arched a rainbow, each end dissolving in the flanking suns. According to people in the region, these phenomena were observed throughout eastern Tibet. After the boy's birth, Khatza Tapa, a local wise man proficient in "mirror divination," made a prediction when he saw in a mirror a conch shell spiraling clockwise. The boy, he said, would greatly benefit sentient beings. When he is eight years old (by Tibetan reckoning) everything about who he is and where he belongs will be clear, but until then no one will be able to confirm who he is.

Dondrup took his son to Amdo Palden and asked him what he should be named. Amdo Palden replied, "I am not capable of giving a name to this boy, and you should not ask others, either. Only Tai Situpa can give a name to him." He directed Dondrup to keep the boy in a clean place with a spiritual atmosphere and faithfully perform religious observances. Although he did not say so explicitly, it seems that Amdo Palden had a clear idea of who the boy might be. Because of the signs that accompanied

The Karmapa's
parents, Dondrup
and Logala
(Photo by Ngyen
Thinley)

his birth, it was widely believed that the boy was a special incarnation—a tulku—and monks from a nearby monastery suggested that the boy be brought there. The parents tended toward
this arrangement, since Amdo Palden's monastery was far away
from where they usually camped. When the head of the
Nyingma lineage at that time, Dilgo Khyentse Rinpoche, visited
the region, he was consulted. He agreed that it would be a good
thing to put the boy in the local monastery. But at this point
Amdo Palden reminded the boy's father of his promise to give
the boy to him, and from then on he took responsibility for
looking after the boy.

When he was old enough, about four years old, the boy was
taken to Amdo Palden's monastery Karlek Gon and installed
there as a tulku, though he was not given a name. Later, in
1991, Amdo Palden accompanied the boy and some of his
family to Palpung Monastery in Derge when Tai Situpa was visiting. Amdo Palden was a striking figure, tall and gaunt, with
fine, high cheekbones and large almond-shaped eyes, matted
hair piled high on top of his head in the tradition of Tibetan
ngakpas.

Apo Gaga became the child's nickname in infancy after one of
his sisters, while getting water at the stream, heard a voluble

magpie say the name. She came back and told the family the magpie had given them a name for him. His elder sister, Ngodup Palzom, who is the only member of his immediate family who came out of Tibet and who now stays with the Karmapa in India, recalls one July when he was about three years old, "Our father was away on business and the weather was bad. It was raining. Suddenly my brother said, 'Oh, Apa (Father) met with an accident.' My mother and I told him he shouldn't say such bad things. Then he said, 'Oh, don't worry, he's fine.'" Soon his father returned with an injured finger and a story that tallied with what his son had said. The truck was in an accident, but he was fine except for the finger. Though they didn't know who he was—what incarnate lama, that is—they knew he was special. When he was five or six, Ngodup Palzom says, he twice told his mother, "I am the Karmapa." Every day after churning butter, their mother offered the first bit of it to their home altar, where they kept a photo of the Sixteenth Karmapa and the Eighth Khamtrul Rinpoche, who had headed nearby Khampagar Monastery before he fled to India. Ngodup Palzom relates, "One day as Amala was doing this he said, 'You should give that to me, then.' When our father told him, 'You shouldn't talk like that,' he ran away."[127]

Ngodup Palzom recalls he was always troubled whenever the time for slaughtering animals came, in October and November. They would have to enlist a babysitter to stay with him all day to distract him. He had a pet billygoat who was born the same day as he. The goat had three ears and no horns, a white head, and a black body. He called him Kayi and the goat followed him around everywhere. It lived to an advanced age for a goat, eight or nine years, until it was toothless. Not long before he was to leave, he planted a tree in their pasture beside a spring that had dried up. It was an important water source, and the nomads worried about having to go elsewhere. After planting the tree he said some prayers, and the spring again began to bubble from the ground.

The boy stayed at Karlek Gon on and off for several years. A few months before the Tsurphu party was to appear, he

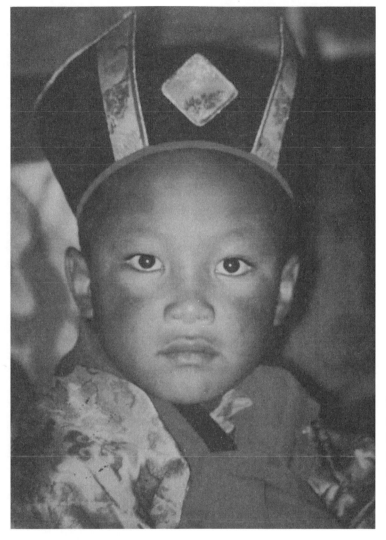

The first
official por-
trait of the
seven-year-
old Karmapa
to be widely
circulated.

announced that he preferred to be with his family, and so he was
returned to them. Lodro Nyenpa recorded in his diary that
"When the first party to receive His Holiness Karmapa arrived
at Karlek Monastery, on that day His Holiness got up very early
and said, 'I'm ready to leave,' and asked his mother, 'Will Karlek
Monastery send a box along with me?' His mother said, 'Where

187

will you be going?' He indicated that he would be going toward central Tibet. His elder brother Yeshe Rabsal had been at Karlek Monastery and arrived at Bakor at midday. He told his family the news that the Dalai Lama says that 'our Apo Gaga is the lama of Tsurphu Monastery.'"[128] Before the search party came for him he told his mother it would be good for Karlek Gon to give him a parting gift, "because I am leaving for my own monastery," he told her. But when the search party came, Ngodup Palzom says, he refused to meet them because it was not an auspicious day. "Only on the second day he came out."

The salient details of how the boy was discovered were received over the telephone by Tai Situpa and Gyaltsap Rinpoche in New Delhi. The rinpoches told the Tsurphu monks to wait until the Dalai Lama was informed before bringing the boy to Tsurphu. After their arrival in Dharamsala Tai Situpa and Gyaltsapa gave the details received from Tibet over the telephone to the Dalai Lama, who was at the Earth Summit in Rio. They also faxed copies of all relevant documents to him. After making extraordinary and traditional examinations, His Holiness later gave a message of confirmation by telephone to Tai Situpa and Gyaltsap Rinpoche through his private office. Tai Situpa and Gyaltsapa requested the Dalai Lama's officials to give his confirmation statement in writing, to serve as the preliminary confirmation letter. A message was then sent back to Tibet, instructing the Tsurphu lamas to go ahead with all necessary procedures and to bring the Seventeenth Karmapa back to Tsurphu.

About his role in the recognition, the Dalai Lama told German filmmaker Clemens Kuby that before he received any information about the Karmapa's discovery he had a dream about the location of his birth that seemed to coincide with the letter and the information from the Tsurphu search party. "Then also I proceeded with my usual method regarding the choosing reincarnation. The indication is positive."[129] The "extraordinary" methods rely on meditation and dreams. The Dalai Lama once explained it at a conference I attended as a technique that is taught to those who have the knack for it. Not all lamas have the gift of finding tulkus, but those who do are trained for it. These methods may include meditation involving objects such as candle flames, mirrors, or burning incense, natural objects that give indications through color or direction of movement. When asked to elaborate on what he saw in his dream, the Dalai Lama said, "Oh, one valley—you see naturally the stones and the lawns, looks like high altitude, facing south, and some small beautiful streams. That is the main sort of picture. Then someone is there and told me—actually without form, someone, some source, telling to me 'Oh this is the place where Karmapa is born.'"

Now that the Karmapa had been found and his recognition confirmed both by the Kagyu lamas and the Dalai Lama, the Tsurphu labrang again approached the Chinese government officials, asking permission to go ahead with the ceremonies to install the Karmapa at Tsurphu. No major religious event may take place without government approval. On the 15th of June official permission was granted. Akong Tulku and Sherab Tharchin remained to assist with arrangements for the enthronement of the Karmapa and as the representatives of Tai Situpa and Gyaltsap Rinpoche until the latter could complete Jamgon Kongtrul's funeral ceremonies and come themselves.

The Chinese response to the recognition of the Seventeenth Karmapa was as surprising as it was swift—but it came well after the Karmapa had been found by his own monks and confirmed by the Dalai Lama. Within days of the announcement in June, *Xinhua* issued a statement of government approval of the reincarnation, the first time since 1959 that they have acknowledged a tulku. "The choice of any important tulku must be approved by the central government," a press release dated the 29th of June stated, after affirming that an eight-year-old boy had official sanction as "the first reincarnated Living Buddha approved by the Chinese government since the Tibetan democratic reform in 1959." A *Reuters* report, dateline Beijing, June 28, 1992, notes, "The New China News Agency has said the boy 'was chosen in accordance with the will of the Sixteenth Living Buddha' and that his predecessors had a long history of paying tribute to China's emperors as a sign of fealty." A typical Chinese touch, although Karmapas did not fall into the category of those who would be paying tribute, if tribute were paid. *Xinhua* continued in the same vein, that the "Living Buddhas of Karma Kagyu...constantly paid tribute" to Yuan, Ming, and Qing emperors and received imperial titles, and that the boy "was chosen in accordance with the will of the Sixteenth Living Buddha of Karma Kagyu."[130] It was clear from the start how the Chinese intended to utilize this fledgling Buddhist master.

While Tai Situpa and Gyaltsap Rinpoche were in Dharamsala and Delhi, Shamarpa returned to Rumtek from his travels abroad. He had been gone for five weeks. The morning after his return, he called a meeting of the Tibetans. He repeated his message in English for the benefit of non-Tibetans the next day. He denounced the actions of Tai Situpa and Gyaltsap Rinpoche in "rushing ahead" with the recognition of the Seventeenth Karmapa. He told the audience, "There is plenty of time." He found it objectionable that the letter was shown to Sakya Trizin, saying, "Up until Sakya Trinzin Rinpoche opened it, it was there, after that I don't know. We are investigating all this. Formerly we wanted to do this secretly...While I was absent I kept receiving information from Tibet that representatives of Gyaltsap Rinpoche, a search party, had found the family. Surprising to me because it was not a decision made by all of us together."[131] He said that Jamgon Kongtrul was supposed to investigate and come back before any decisions were made. "There is no reason for urgency, but people are doing things very quickly." He questioned the authenticity of the Karmapa's letter, asking for "forensic" evaluation of the handwriting. He gave an account of what transpired at the March meeting, something that had been kept confidential until then by mutual agreement among the rinpoches. He claimed Jamgon Kongtrul didn't think it was authentic and Gyaltsap Rinpoche didn't read it properly, going so far as to say, "The other two rinpoches are bad people, really bad people."

He attributed statements to Jamgon Kongtrul that were questioned by a number of people in the audience. Translator Ngodup Tsering was among them. He accused Shamarpa of unnecessarily bringing the late Jamgon Rinpoche into the controversy and misrepresenting the views of someone who was dead and unable to speak for himself. When one woman asked "Why would Situ Rinpoche lie?" Shamarpa replied, "Maybe he had a reason," adding, "Maybe he had a dream...maybe he invented the letter to convince better." He accounted for his absence during most of the forty-nine-day puja by saying that he had a very important meeting, and that only Jamgon Rinpoche knew what it was about. Other members of the audience questioned why he made these allegations in the absence of Tai Situpa and Gyaltsap Rinpoche, whom he had made no attempt to meet since Jamgon Kongtrul died.

Jamgon Rinpoche had been very happy about the recognition letter and expressed no doubts about it. He was captured on film in an interview videotaped by Clemens Kuby before he died in which he states his satisfaction with the recognition letter. "It is very clear and very precise. And that is why we are all confident about the finding of His Holiness," he said.[132] Contrary to Shamarpa's claims of perfect harmony with Kongtrul, their relations were often strained because Kongtrul was worried that Topga's and Shamarpa's activities were detrimental to the Karmapa's legacy. Their disagreements over the running of the shedra and the disposition of the Karmapa's Delhi institute were just part of the problem. To save face for the Karma Kagyupa Kongtrul put up a good front, but according to people closest to him at that time, he was deeply concerned about the state of affairs at Rumtek.

As a result of Shamarpa's speech of June 9th, the split between Shamarpa and the other tulkus was made public. It also became evident that the split was affecting Western followers. Many left the meeting angry, especially those who knew Jamgon Kongtrul personally and knew what his views actually were. Others, most of them students of the Sixteenth Karmapa's disciple Ole Nydahl, appeared to accept what Shamarpa had to say. People were thrown into confusion, Tibetans and non-Tibetans alike.

A few days later, on the 12th of June, immediately upon their return from Delhi, Tai Situpa and Gyaltsap Rinpoche called meetings of the Tibetans and the Westerners to announce the recognition of the Seventeenth Karmapa. Toward the end of the second meeting, which was conducted in English for the Westerners, as Tai Situpa was concluding his speech, Shamarpa entered with a number of Indian army soldiers, disrupting the meeting. The late Trinley Atuk, a retired Indian Army Colonel who ran a travel agency in Gangtok, and a devout Buddhist, had come to hear the rinpoches. Atuk described what happened: "After some time, while His Eminence Tai Situ Rinpoche was speaking about the finding of the sacred letter and its contents, His Eminence Shamar Rinpoche drove into the monastery complex followed by an army jonga [truck]. His Eminence Shamar Rinpoche drove through the bewildered crowd closely followed by one officer of the rank of a captain who was carrying a carbine, escorts carrying automatic rifles, and a radio operator who was unarmed. They were of the Kumaon Regiment of the Indian army."[133] When the armed soldiers threatened to enter the shrine room with their weapons, people objected and stopped them. Col. Atuk identified himself to the officer and the soldiers as a retired Indian army officer: "I explained to them about the sensitive situation created by their entering the monastery with arms and convinced them to return outside the gates of the monastery." But a fight that began between the Shamarpa's supporters and the people defending the shrine room—monastery staff and bystanders—took about an hour to quell, with the help of the Sikkim armed police. Tai Situ Rinpoche and Gyaltsap Rinpoche retreated to their rooms at the insistence of their attendants and the senior lamas.

The unauthorized use of Indian army soldiers created a furor in Sikkim. "While the deployment of the army in Rumtek without the consent of the State Government has been met with justified condemnation and strong disapproval, the entry of the jawans (Indian soldiers) into the main temple of the Rumtek monastery has greatly hurt the sentiment of all Buddhists in the state," led a story in the *Sikkim Observer*.[134] The incident was strongly denounced by then Chief Minister Nur Bahadur Bhandari, who pointed out that it was the state's prerogative to call in the army, and the central government must be involved.

"You will be surprised to know that the deployment of the army was not known even to the Defense Minister and the Union Home Secretary whom I had immediately contacted on this incident," Mr. Bhandari stated in a letter he wrote to Prime Minister P. V. Narasimha Rao demanding an investigation. He alleged there was Bhutanese involvement and further noted that there was no law-and-order problem in the state, and such a move was uncalled for, even if it were not in violation of the established order for deployment of security forces.[135] A statewide strike was called in protest. Rumors circulated about how soldiers came to be involved. However it came about, many in the outraged community blamed Shamarpa and his cousin Topga Yugyal. A year later, Bhandari maintained that some Bhutanese princesses were involved, though not the king: "There is no hand from His Majesty of Bhutan, because there is a very good relationship between Sikkim and Bhutan, but at the lower level, in the name of the prime minister, in the name of the king—people, they always try."

Bhandari was a controversial figure in Sikkim, often criticized for corruption. However, he respected the Sixteenth Karmapa and frequently assisted Rumtek Monastery while he was politically powerful. "He was a big personality," Bhandari said of the Karmapa. Needless to say, the Sixteenth Karmapa's prediction of Bhandari's electoral success at a time when his future looked bleak made a profound impression upon the politician.[136]

Sikkim had been a monarchy for centuries, ruled by the Chogyals and their ministers and aristocrats. In British times things became more complicated. The British gained a degree of political control over Sikkim, and this was passed on to independent India in 1947. Eventually people began to demand more say in government. Opinions differ about whether Prime Minister Indira Gandhi's move to annex Sikkim was really in the interest of greater democracy. When the Indian government took over Sikkim and the Chogyal was rendered powerless, his American wife Hope Cook took their children and fled. A new government of elected officials emerged. Political patronage of the new state government became important for Rumtek. Bhandari and others provided this. Monastery projects sometimes required government approval. Now, with internal problems becoming politicized outside of Rumtek, help of the government was sought for the Karmapa's speedy enthronement.

There was protocol to follow after the Karmapa's recognition. The Kagyu tulkus present at Rumtek wrote to the Dalai Lama, thanking him for his role in acknowledging the Seventeenth Karmapa.[137] Tai Situpa and Gyaltsap Rinpoche called the master of ritual, the chant master, and the master of discipline, asking them to arrange a special ceremony to celebrate the recognition of the Karmapa. But the next morning these three key monastic officers had decamped. They left a letter stating they had to leave because of the conflicting instructions that were being imposed on them. In the letter they said they profusely regretted "due to confusion and bad influence of mental darkness, we ceased to fulfill our obligations temporarily." Shamarpa evidently had told them not to cooperate. Nevertheless, they had made some of the arrangements for the ceremony, and the *gyaling* horns blew from the Rumtek rooftop in acclamation of the new Karmapa.

Around this time the late Tulku Urgyen, an important Baram Kagyu tulku who was close to the Sixteenth Karmapa and one of the revered elders, had gone to reason with Shamarpa. Presently he sent a message up the hill that Shamarpa would accept the incarnation of the Seventeenth Karmapa and end the dispute he had begun. A letter was drafted and signed by Shamarpa, witnessed by Tulku Urgyen, to wit: "A little doubt arose in my mind, but now I have attained complete confidence in Situ Rinpoche and the contents of this letter, according to which the reincarnation has definitely been discovered."[138]

Tai Situpa and Gyaltsap Rinpoche accepted Shamarpa's recantation letter, "not for the sake of the Karmapa, but for the benefit of the Shamarpa," they said in a joint statement. The comment reflected the belief in the grave karmic repercussions that the Shamarpa's actions in opposition to the recognition of his own guru brought upon him. The Shamarpa came up to the monastery from his house below. A long exchange took place between the three tulkus to settle the issue. But trust was not part of the meeting. The Shamarpa and the other rinpoches separately recorded the proceedings on audio cassette. Any *detente* this meeting signified was to be short-lived. The fissure opened up again in Dharamsala.

Tai Situ Rinpoche and Gyaltsap Rinpoche went together to Dharamsala to meet the Dalai Lama, who had returned from Brazil. During a morning audience with the Dalai Lama they detailed the events surrounding the Sixteenth Karmapa's affairs from 1981 until his recent recognition. The Dalai Lama reiterated his confirmation and said that he wanted to meet all three of them together. He hoped that it would be possible for them to work in harmony, he told them, for the sake of Buddhism. The two rinpoches expressed their appreciation of his support and their willingness to do as he wished.

Shamarpa arrived the same day in Dharamsala and had an audience with the Dalai Lama that afternoon where he gave his version of events. During their meeting His Holiness advised Shamarpa as he had the other tulkus, requesting him to attend the meeting with the other two. But the Shamarpa left Dharamsala that evening instead. The next morning Tai Situpa and Gyaltsap Rinpoche were surprised to find that the Shamarpa was not at the audience. He had not contacted them. The Dalai Lama discussed the state of affairs with the two rinpoches and advised them on how to go forward. Of these meetings the Dalai Lama later said, "The relations between them—that is quite, quite unfortunate. I expressed this to both sides—to Shamar Rinpoche as well as to Situ Rinpoche and Gyaltsap Rinpoche...Even besides the spiritual thing, simply, they should follow the convention of ordinary people, when a father treated them as his own children, I think, with every care. The father is passed away. They should cooperate jointly. If that is not possible, I told them—I expressed to both sides—if you cannot work together, don't harm each other." He continued, "Shamar Rinpoche told me he was convinced fully that there would be some other true reincarnation of the late Karmapa. Then I told him, all right, if you bring one or two more, it doesn't matter, like the late Khyentse Wangpo," citing the example of an incarnate lama who is believed to have multiple incarnations. "There are five reincarnations: the manifestation of body, the manifestation of speech, the manifestation of mind, the manifestation of quality, and manifestation of energy. It doesn't matter. One or two or even if you say a hundred Karmapas, it doesn't matter. As far as the throne-holder, there is only one. That is who is now already recognized. He is that one. This I told Shamar Rinpoche."[139] Before Tai Situpa and Gyaltsap Rinpoche left Dharamsala, he gave the *buktam rinpoche,* the final seal of confirmation from the Tibetan government. The Dalai Lama sent a message recorded on audio cassette to all Kagyu monasteries. He sent a scarf woven with the eight auspicious signs and eight auspicious prayers, his own personal mala, a blessing cord, and a blessing ribbon for the Seventeenth Karmapa. Tai Situpa and Gyaltsap Rinpoche then departed for Tibet.

9. The Karmapa Returns

THE SUMMER OF 1992 was an eventful one for the Karma Kagyupa. Tremendous anticipation overtook Tibetan Buddhists as preparations for the Seventeenth Karmapa's enthronement began. Devotees streamed to Tsurphu Monastery from inside and outside Tibet to get a long-awaited blessing from their guru's hands. People made plans to attend the Karmapa's enthronement at Tsurphu in September. The Chinese government gave special permission for visas to be issued to foreigners who wanted to come. Tai Situpa and Gyaltsap Rinpoche arrived in June to help the Tsurphu monks and the young Karmapa prepare for the big day.

Shamarpa did not remain long in Sikkim. He headed in the opposite direction, for Europe. His brother Jigme was in charge of a Kagyu Buddhist center in Dordogne, France, Dhagpo Kagyu Ling. There Shamarpa was joined by Hannah Nydahl and a core group of Nydahl students and Western followers. As noted above, Ole and Hannah Nydahl were among the Sixteenth

Karmapa's earliest Western disciples, and they started Buddhist centers in his name in Europe and elsewhere. They have been staunch supporters of the Shamarpa, first in his dissent and later in his bid to set up his own Karmapa candidate a few years later.

The Nydahls' story is amply described in Ole Nydahl's own published accounts of his life and times on the Dharma trail. He relates how the Karmapa gave his and Hannah's lives a new and powerful direction after they encountered him in Kathmandu in 1969.[140] An intelligent, well-educated, and irrepressible personality inclined to rebel against the establishment, Ole tells of his exposure to drugs at Copenhagen University and his subsequent experimentation with them. Being a natural entrepreneur, his interest and the times led him to smuggling: "We made short trips to North Africa, Lebanon, and Afghanistan to bring back hash for our friends," he writes. This eventually led to arrest and some time in jail for both of them. They gave up smuggling and later the drugs in favor of meditation. Because there were few lamas in the West in the early 1970s, the Karmapa permitted them to start study groups and give talks on elementary Buddhism. They began to do this, starting centers all over northern Europe in the Karmapa's name, and then branched out to other continents.

Ole and Hannah maintained high visibility as purveyors of Buddhist teaching and became well known in the Buddhist circuit. I first met Ole myself in New York in 1979 when he was busy giving lectures on a characteristic whistle-stop tour of the United States. He was one of those individuals whose animal magnetism attracted attention. His presentation was often evangelical and his bearing proud. He was able to convert the masses to Buddhism, as he went from place to place giving talks and tapping people on the head with a large reliquary filled with fragments of Tibetan saints, "giving Karmapa's blessing." His was an overpowering "love bomb" approach, with whiff of the con artist about it, but his warm and friendly energy often neutralized negative perceptions of his character. His wife, Hannah, was quieter, though his match in tenacity. A striking natural beauty with classic high cheekbones and large, almond-shaped eyes, she learned the Tibetan language and became a translator. She was Ole's indispensable helpmate.

The Karmapa obviously saw their ability and appointed Ole as head and Hannah as deputy head of the group of centers they had founded in Europe, "to continue to be instructors to the people who are first entering into the understanding and practice of the Buddha Dharma and also to continue to help to establish new Dharma centres."[141] While Ole and Hannah doubtless had a special connection to the Sixteenth Karmapa and a gift for leadership and teaching, they nevertheless did not have the extensive training of lamas. According to Ole's account, they received the same teachings and did the same practices as many other Westerners who found their way to India and to the monasteries of Tibetan teaching lamas in the early 1970s. The Karmapa permitted Ole and Hannah to give only provisional refuge, meaning that it was temporary, and the recipient would have to take the commitment again the next time a qualified lama visited.[142] They could also give talks or lead discussions in study groups. The term in Tibetan that the Karmapa used was the Tibetan term for discussion leader *(kyorpon)*, a role taken by certain monks in the college.[143] Ole and Hannah's experiences of attending teachings for a few weeks or months in India over a period of years did not qualify them to transmit profound teaching lineages to others. The responsibility to preserve an unbroken teaching lineage is taken very seriously, and teaching lamas must have many years of disciplined study and practice behind them before they are cleared to teach profound aspects of Buddhist philosophy or give initiations into special meditation practices.

A decade later the Karmapa still saw the Nydahls as introductory study group leaders, although Ole did not. He began to give initiations. When the Sixteenth Karmapa heard that Ole was giving advanced initiations to people in places like Latin America and the former Soviet Union, where access to qualified Buddhist teachers of the lineage was very difficult, if not impossible, he told him to stop. This is according to Achi Tsepal, who was the Sixteenth Karmapa's secretary and translator at the time, and others who were there. The Karmapa naturally was concerned that Ole might distort the teachings because of his insufficient training. Despite the Karmapa's order, Ole went ahead an gave the empowerments according to reports from people who were in his Dharma centers at the time.

After the Karmapa died in 1981, Ole and Hannah continued on their international trajectory with new energy. Ole's first auto-biographical work, *Entering the Diamond Way,* was published in 1985. By the time *Riding the Tiger* was published in 1992, now under the name Lama Ole Nydahl, his voice had changed from one with something to learn to one who knows it all. "I had viewed myself as a lama once the main purifications were over," he writes,[144] though neither he nor Hannah completed the three-year retreat required to qualify as a teaching lama.

In increasingly self-adulatory language, he denigrates those who do not follow his lead, "As we grew sometimes stiff-minded people wanted to join our happy yogi groups. Possessing narrow, church-like minds, they frequently had difficulties with my joy. My driving style, fascinating female helpers, and lack of human weaknesses disconcerted them."[145]

New Yorkers, who had contact with eminent Tibetan teaching lamas of several sects, were not sufficiently responsive to Ole's overtures. He is dismissive: "I really gave my best in that city, day and night, but despite all efforts, people grew more zombie-like by the year. It was like an incurable disease. I suspected Trungpa Tulku's Dharmadhatu organization of being its origin."[146] Ole had been banned from teaching in Dharmadhatu centers. A lengthy letter circulated within that organization accused Ole of confusing students by deviating the teachings: "His teaching style, more than the content, runs contrary to everything we have been taught and have come to recognize as genuine. Our students' basic perception of his approach is one of self-aggran-dizement accompanied by a so-called 'spiritual zap' which he seemingly transfers to other people."

Jamgon Kongtrul also became more cautious about Ole and Hannah after they went against the Sixteenth Karmapa's wishes. Ole, in turn, dismissed Kongtrul as a youngster who had a lot to learn. I heard Ole speaking in this vein at Kalu Rinpoche's

The Seventeenth
Karmapa Orgyen Trinley
Dorje is escorted with
ceremonial attendants as
he arrives in Tsurphu,
June 1992. (Photo by
Ward Holmes)

monastery in Sonada in 1983. Ole claimed he knew better than
the lineage holders about how to teach Buddhism, saying they
were young, or in the case of septuagenarian Kalu Rinpoche,
who was bestowing a cycle of advance initiations at the time,
old-fashioned.[147]

When Shamarpa dissented against the recognition of the
Seventeenth Karmapa, Ole and Hannah sided with him. Ole
cited fears of a takeover of the Kagyu lineage by communist
China as his reason. He later echoed Shamarpa's allegations that
Tai Situpa had been co opted by China. His group got to work
on a refutation of the Seventeenth Karmapa's recognition.

ENTHRONEMENT

Meanwhile at Tsurphu Monastery, the child Karmapa appeared
to approach his destiny with equanimity. The trip from his home
in faraway Lhatok was made in modern four-wheel-drive vehicles
that traversed the vast Tibetan Plateau until, at last, they snaked

through the narrow Tolung Valley, a place that seems untouched by time. It probably looked much the same when the First Karmapa rode in on horseback a millennium earlier. Just outside the monastery entrance the string of cars stopped. Videos of the event show a monk attendant help the boy out of the car and lift him onto a waiting horse. The boy rode into Tsurphu like Karmapas of old, dressed in traditional brocades, all yellow, red, and gold, wearing a golden, lacquered traveling hat, and escorted by his own monks. It was June 15, 1992, a few days before his seventh birthday.[148] His demeanor was serious. He had a natural dignity. Once again the *gyaling* horns broke the Tolung's stillness to welcome a Karmapa after a gap of thirty-three years.

Waiting to receive him were the Tsurphu lamas and monks, a depleted group since the previous Karmapa left in 1959. There were nearly one thousand monks at Tsurphu then, but they were eventually dispersed, forced to marry or were otherwise removed by the communist Chinese and their cadres. The monastery itself was destroyed with its holy statues and reliquaries during the Cultural Revolution in 1966. The huge idol of the Buddha cast by Karma Pakshi was dynamited. Tsurphu was largely ruins still, although some reconstruction was done after the Chinese relaxed their attitude toward monasteries in the 1980s. The government gave permission to rebuild in the early 1980s, and even granted 100,000 yuan for the project. More funds were raised, and a comparatively small monastery was completed in 1984.

When Karmapa Orgyen Trinley Dorje arrived 1992, nearly two hundred monks were in residence, partly because senior Kagyu tulkus had visited at different times to ordain monks and nuns, restoring the ordination lineage there.[149] One of these elder lamas, Drupon Dechen Rinpoche, had stayed on. He was among the group welcoming the Seventeenth Karmapa. Drupon Dechen had lived exiled in India for decades, mostly in Ladakh. He returned to Tsurphu in 1984 to assist the monks in reviving their Buddhist traditions and to oversee the rebuilding of the monastery. He turned down an earlier offer by the Sixteenth Karmapa to send him to a center in Canada. He lived at a small monastery in Ladakh until he went to Tsurphu.

The Karma Kagyu
protector, Mahakala,
"Great Black One," is
depicted on a rock face
near the Tsurphu
Monastery entrance.
(Photo by Lea Terhune)

The communist regime had done its best to obliterate
Buddhism: killing or imprisoning qualified proponents,
destroying texts, and forbidding religious practice. Yet
Tibetans, in the privacy of their hearts and minds, tried to preserve their religion as well as they could. In the absence of
guidance, however, teachings and practices became garbled and
fragmented. The chief reason many exiled lamas returned to
their Tibetan seats during the political thaw in the 1980s and
early 90s was to restore the Buddhist teachings where distortions had grown up and try to rebuild their destroyed
monasteries.

The Karmapa had six weeks to adjust to Tsurphu before the formalities began. A few days after his arrival, a public blessing ceremony drew three thousand people, even though the event was not publicized.[150] On June 27 a group of Chinese government officials arrived from Lhasa to present the document giving political sanction for the Karmapa's recognition. This was unprecedented. The only other lamas to receive such sanction in modern times were those chosen by the Chinese themselves, not those selected through traditional means and approved by the Dalai Lama. The first step in his investiture came in the dark, early hours of August 7th, when the Seventeenth Karmapa had his traditional hair-cutting ceremony at the Jokhang in Lhasa. Tai Situpa and Goshir Gyaltsapa had arrived from India to perform this important ritual before witnesses from Tsurphu and the Chinese government. Presentation of gifts from the Dalai Lama was the first order of business. It was then that the child was formally given the name Orgyen Trinley Dorje, the name that the Seventeenth Karmapa bears in prophecies about this line of tulkus.

The day was crystal clear, the sun bright in the wide, blue sky above the Tolung Valley on the morning of the enthronement, September 27, 1992. On the mountains above the monastery snow had fallen, an auspicious sign. The canyon in which the once-large Tsurphu Monastery nestles is as stark and striking as it must have been when the Karmapas' story began centuries earlier. The monastery site, with the winding stream that runs in front of it, holds its charm despite the surrounding ruins. On enthronement day, not even the dust clouds beaten up by the feet of thousands of Tibetans who gathered at Tsurphu to receive the blessing of its long-awaited living buddha could dispel its magic. Trucks, buses, and jeeps rumbled in, adding to the billowing, gritty dust and hubbub. The smell beside the holy stream was ripe where it was used as an impromptu toilet by the campers. Here the facilities are what you bring with you. Accommodation in the reconstructed part of the monastery was quite limited and full to capacity with monks, lamas, and the Karmapa's family. On enthronement day Chinese official estimates of the crowd ranged from twenty to forty thousand.[151]

Many people, myself included, stayed in Lhasa hotels at night and left before dawn in hired vehicles to get to Tsurphu in time for each day of the ceremonies. It is a two-and-a-half-hour journey from Lhasa if conditions are good.

Once the ascent was made from the parking area outside, up the stairs, and into the courtyard, the chaotic din of revving engines and shouts fell away and was replaced by a new atmosphere. Inside, a Tibetan-style carnival was underway. Knots of people formed around gaily costumed performers in several parts of the courtyard. They were watching *lhamo*, the Tibetan opera. Lhamo is distinct from Tibetan religious dance in that it is performed by laypeople and takes the secular themes of folktales, although there is often a Buddhist moral to the story. Players sing, declaim, strum on musical instruments, beat drums, dance, and recite poetry, all arrayed in their brightest clothes, with tassels and turquoises braided into their hair. Some are in masked costumes, some not, according to the demands of the play. Clowns run about and play pranks on unsuspecting members of the audience. These skits about saints and heroes continued from morning until evening for several days. The Sixteenth Karmapa's late chandzo Damchoe Yongdu was a proficient lhamo dancer. He must have danced here many a time. From the windows above, the young Gyalwa Karmapa could, and frequently did, look out on the entertainment below.

The moment arrived. It was about 11 A.M. when the gyaling horns began to blow and the Seventeenth Karmapa descended the stairs from his quarters. He entered the shrine room, accompanied by his attendants, as the people who had managed to get inside craned their necks for a look at him. Attired in monk's robes and his traditional black hat—the small, informal version—he walked unhesitatingly to his place. He looked around with large, solemn eyes at the assembly. Following him were Tai Situpa and Goshir Gyaltsapa, dressed in the heavy brocade robes with swirls of color that are worn, these days, only on the most splendid occasions.

The actual enthronement ceremony was preceded by a secular function: Chinese officials presented a letter from the Beijing government to the Seventeenth Karmapa, putting the

Tsurphu
Monastery
(Photo by
Lea Terhune)

bureaucratic seal of approval on his recognition and enthronement. Officials included Director of the Religious Bureau Ren
Wuzhi, and local Tibetan Autonomous Region functionaries. All
were seated on chairs, all at the same level. With the small tables
in front of the Karmapa and his lamas, it was reminiscent of a
Chinese banquet. Ren Wuzhi, who had come from Beijing, read
a letter formally designating the boy "the seventeenth living
Buddha Garmaba [sic]." White scarves, *khatag,* were exchanged
in greeting, according to Tibetan custom. Speeches of felicitation
were made and gifts given to the Karmapa and the monastery.
After a half an hour, the officials departed.

The principals also left the hall so that it could be rearranged
for the religious rites. Another half an hour went by before the
Karmapa returned. He climbed the ornately carved and painted
stairs to take his seat on the high Tsurphu throne. The others
who accompanied him took their seats and the ceremony began.
It commenced in the Tibetan, rather than the communist egali-
tarian style, with every tulku mounted on the appropriate number of cushions according to his rank, the Karmapa rising above
them all.

Agility and resourcefulness, and a good deal of elbowing, were
required to get into the small shrine room on enthronement day.

Tai Situpa
officiates at the
enthronement.
(Photo by
Bryan G.
Miller)

I was among the lucky ones who managed to get through the
crowd and slip inside. The ancient spectacle enacted there was in
ceremonial contrast to the wild melee in the corridor and the celebrations outside. The young Karmapa, one of the highest lamas
of Tibet, conducted himself with sober dignity and tolerance
during the proceedings, which lasted five hours. He bore the bar-
rages of camera flashes and high-intensity video lights with
impressive aplomb, enduring the often tedious rituals that caused
even adults to fidget. Once or twice he fiddled with his hat. He
hugged his attendant. Important tulkus from all parts of Tibet
and all sects were there. The immediate family of the Karmapa,
including his two brothers and six sisters were on hand, dressed
in colorful Khampa gear. Amdo Palden sat serenely. The shrine
room was jammed. The two hundred passes officially issued were
magically multiplied by black market alchemy so that by the end
of the day more than a thousand people sported red badges.

The event the roiling crowd had come so far to see, the
enthronement of the Seventeenth Karmapa, had begun. The
Twelfth Tai Situpa was the preceptor of the enthronement ceremony. From the steps leading up to the high throne on the
Gyalwa Karmapa's right, Tai Situpa respectfully approached and
offered the Karmapa the *buktam rinpoche,* the confirmation letter

Karmapa during
ceremony
(Photo by Lea
Terhune)

written by the Dalai Lama. It said, "The boy born to Karma
Dondrup and Loga in the Wood Ox year [of the Tibetan calen-
dar] identifies with the prediction letter [left by the late
Karmapa] and is hereby recognized as the reincarnation of the
Sixteenth Karmapa. With prayers for his well being and for the
success of his activities. The Dalai Lama."[152] Tai Situpa then gave
him a copy of the prediction letter of the previous Karmapa,
and the confirmation of the Nechung Oracle, the official seer of
the Dalai Lama's government-in-exile. The Nechung Oracle had
been consulted in June, at the request of officials from the religious department of the Sikkim government, and had said while
in trance, "It is certain that my master, Tongwa Donden, the
bodhisattvas and sentient beings of Tibet, land of snow, will

gather together and the sun of joy and delight will appear. The time is close when you will hear speech like nectar. Be at ease then and remain in a state harmonious with samaya. Palden Lhamo and I, Zugme, never deceive."[153] This was interpreted as additional confirmation of the recognition of the Seventeenth Karmapa.

Offering prayers by the monks followed. At this point Tai Situpa began the ancient enthronement ritual by consecrating Orgyen Trinley Dorje with the eight auspicious ingredients, the eight auspicious signs, and the seven possessions of universal monarchs. After this was completed, speeches were made by eminent lamas on aspects of Buddhist doctrine.[154] Gyaltsap Rinpoche concluded the talks with an exposition of the five auspicious conditions that insure progress toward enlightenment. Such oratory is taken very seriously and is seen as a trial of education, eloquence, and grasp of Buddhist philosophy, poetry, and style. The speakers prepare these recitals carefully.

Gyaltsap Rinpoche was chief celebrant of the mandala offering. He stood before the Karmapa, holding a mandala plate so huge it needed several people to steady it. The mandala offering is a prayer that always accompanies important rituals. The chief celebrant, dressed in the yellow robe of a fully ordained monk, stands before the high lama's throne. He intones the mandala offering prayer, joined by all those present who know it. He grasps the rim of a slightly rounded plate upon which he pours rice in a deliberate pattern while he prays. The essence of the prayer is a symbolic offering of all good things in the universe for the benefit and enlightenment of all beings.

Tai Situpa again moved from his seat on the Karmapa's left to the steps of the throne to offer the boy a Buddha image, a long-life sutra text, and a stupa, objects that represent enlightened body, speech, and mind. This concluded the main part of the ceremony. It was time for the presentation of gifts. These customarily include precious items such as statues, reliquaries, silk brocades, musical instruments, ritual implements, and tea, a convention set centuries before when emperors of China sent bountiful gifts to distinguished lamas. People notice who

A closeup of the lhamo performances celebrating the enthronement. (Photo by Lea Terhune)

gives what, and comments are often made about it later. Gifts flowed from all Buddhist sects: Gelug, Sakya, Nyingma, and Kagyu, from inside and outside Tibet.[155] Close to three hundred tulkus and monastery representatives were there. Buddhist centers in Southeast Asia, the USA, Europe, Africa, Australia, and New Zealand sent delegates. Outside, an irrepressible crowd cheered and flung offering scarves to the newly enthroned Karmapa.

Sitting in the shrine room that afternoon was a real test of nerve. Huge waves of humanity seemed about to inundate the modest hall at any moment. There was no door out of there but one. Finally the hordes who had been pressing against the door, a few of whom were propelled through the entrance each time the door was opened during the ceremony, queued up for blessings. The Karmapa blessed them all, from child to oldster, with grace and patience, using a traditional tasseled wand. When the crowd became unruly, as often happens with Tibetans en masse, the blessings were adjourned until the following day. Lamas have been knocked off their thrones by over-enthusiastic devotees. It had been a long day. About four o'clock the Karmapa and his attendants went upstairs. The dancing resumed outside in the courtyard.

The next morning, September 28th, around thirty thousand people filed by the young Seventeenth Karmapa in an orderly fashion, this time efficiently managed by the monks. It took four hours. They received blessing taps from the Karmapa, Tai Situpa, and Gyaltsap Rinpoche, and a red sacred string to wear. Such "protection cords" are believed to be efficacious for warding off evil. Celebrations continued in the courtyard late into the day, and another queue of people wishing a private audience or advice from the high lamas led upstairs. In between visitors, the young Karmapa went out on the roof to watch the performances going on downstairs. Evenings in the tents outside, where most people stayed, were lively, with merrymaking fueled by a little chang and beer. The people were happy to have their high lama back. Many of them had traveled all the way from Kham to see him, about five days' journey by car.

Another debut performance came on the 29th of September when, after receiving people on the roof of the monastery for several hours, Orgyen Trinley Dorje performed his first formal ritual, an initiation into the practice of the Red Standing Chenrezig. This is an aspect of the bodhisattva of compassion, and meditation on bodhisattva qualities are believed to inculcate the same in the meditator. To perform the rite so that more people could see him, the Karmapa sat in an upstairs window, flanked by Tai Situpa and Gyaltsapa. A huge crowd was again assembled in the courtyard below. Assisted by the two older lamas in much of the ritual, the eight-year-old read the core of the ceremony himself, in a clear and steady voice. This was a powerful moment. It signaled that the Seventeenth Karmapa, like each of his sixteen predecessors who had lived at Tsurphu, had formally assumed his role as head of the Karma Kagyu lineage. This was acknowledged by thousands of ordinary Tibetans, who threw hundreds of white scarves, making the courtyard look like an undulating sea of silk. Coincidentally—or perhaps not, in the Tibetan worldview—a contingent of large, graceful birds hovered in the valley. Their vast wingspans suggested stately lammergeyers, and they circled in an auspiciously clockwise direction above the monastery during the ritual, as if

During a break in the enthronement ceremonies Tai Situpa, the
Karmapa, and Gyaltsap Rinpoche sit on the roof of Tsurphu.
(Photo by Bryan G. Miller)

to mark the event. One couldn't help but recall that the
Sixteenth Karmapa had been particularly fond of birds.

After the enthronement ceremonies were over, people trick-
led homeward, ebullient with blessings after so many decades
of being denied the sight of the Karmapa and, indeed, the
open practice of their religion. They were thrilled to have the
Karmapa restored to Tsurphu. Tai Situpa and Gyaltsap
Rinpoche stayed on two additional weeks before they, too, had
to leave. Though Chinese officials had told them the Karmapa
could eventually study in India and that they had no objections
to his traveling abroad, providing "conditions are suitable,"
their terms remained vague. Until Beijing actually let him go to
India, Tai Situpa and Gyaltsapa intended to come back to give
the Karmapa necessary instruction in Buddhist philosophy,
liturgy, and spiritual practice.

On the way back, in Kathmandu, I spoke with several lamas
who had known the previous Karmapa and were deeply moved
when they met Orgyen Trinley Dorje. One of them, Choling

Rinpoche, spoke to me in his monastery in Boudanath. His eyes filled with tears as he recounted that during his visit to Tsurphu, the boy recalled past incidents that only the Sixteenth Karmapa would have known about since only Choling and the Karmapa were present when they occurred. The mood was celebratory, although people were still anxious about the young Karmapa's fate under Chinese control.

PLOTS AND PROPHECIES

Meanwhile, the Shamarpa and his followers had been busy with their efforts to promote their own position. By the time Tai Situpa and Gyaltsap Rinpoche returned from Tibet, controversy was stirring. It began with a series of letters circulated by fax, some acrimonious, from Ole and Hannah Nydahl and other disgruntled people. Private communications had been faxed around the world, as with the case of a letter that Drupon Dechen Rinpoche sent to the Nydahls admonishing them not break their sacred trust with the Karmapa, their root lama, and their dismissive response.

Then, within weeks of the Karmapa's enthronement, a book entitled *The Karmapa Papers* appeared. It was the result of the summer spent by the Nydahl group in the south of France, compiled by editors who refrained from publishing their names.[156] The collection of annotated documents, the editors claimed, told the real story. It made insinuations against those who recognized Orgyen Trinley Dorje as the Karmapa and presented as fact the claims of the Shamarpa. For instance, it claimed that Jamgon Kongtrul doubted the authenticity of the recognition letter. *The Karmapa Papers* treated the Shamarpa's declarations, uncritically, as credible, distorting facts, and in some places offering pure fiction in an attempt to substantiate the dissenters' objections. The book fanned the controversy and incensed many Tibetan Buddhists in India and Nepal. A large portion of it involved analysis of the Karmapa's handwriting and commentary by the Shamarpa. As a refutation published in America noted, "One of the regents is much more extensively quoted than any of the other three. Further, material from and about him is given a different, and more intimate treatment. For example, we are told at what hour he received a phone call from an Army general, and how he feels about a particular event. And for all information concerning the late Jamgon Kongtrul Rinpoche's wishes and ideas, we are referred only to the same Regent who is always being quoted."[157] Although it appeared in few bookstores, *The Karmapa Papers,* lavishly produced, was widely distributed free of charge in the days following the Karmapa's enthronement.

During the previous emotional six months, a beloved lama had been lost, the Karma Kagyu lineage regained its head lama, and the peace at Rumtek was disrupted. This book compiled by people perceived as naïve outsiders was about the last straw for many Tibetans in Sikkim. After problems arose following the death of Jamgon Kongtrul, two old predictions were recalled. In the wake of the controversy around the recognition, the poems containing these predictions continued to be read and discussed.

The first of these predictions emanated from a vision by the nineteenth-century terton Chogyur Lingpa. In this vision he saw the entire line of Karmapa tulkus from the first to the last in colorful detail. Fourteen Karmapas had already incarnated by his time. He foresaw twenty-one. He also foresaw the circumstances of their lives and gave names for the future Karmapas. Of the seventeenth incarnation he said, "Nearby, at the foot of a lush tree on a rock mountain, is the seventeenth incarnation together with Khentin Tai Situpa. This image symbolizes that, through the unity of their minds, the tree of the Buddha's doctrine will flourish, laden with the ripe fruit which is the essence of the teaching of the lineage of Gampopa."[158] Like most mystical writing, Tibetan poetry is highly symbolic and multilayered. There are many different avenues of interpretation, but the same details emerge clearly in various translations. Chogyur Lingpa also commissioned a scroll painting that depicts his vision. This tangka still exists in a private collection and was photographed for a recent book on the subject, *Karmapa: The Sacred Prophecy,* published by Kagyu Thubten Choling in New York.

The second prophecy was made by the Fifth Karmapa in his biography. He described the difficult conditions that would arise

between the sixteenth and seventeenth incarnations, some of
which are specific to the lineage, some characteristic of the times:

> …In the line of Karmapa incarnations, between the
>   Sixteenth and Seventeenth,
> Buddhist teachings in general and the Karma Kamtsang in
>   particular
> Will hibernate like bees in the winter.
> The family line of the Chinese Emperor will come to an
>   end,
> and his country will be dominated by whomever is
>   strongest.
> From the north and east, Tibet will be invaded
> And encircled like a ring…
> Whatever is done is wrong;
> Whomever you speak to will oppose you.
> Good conduct will degenerate and the bad will flourish…
> In the succession of Karmapas, during the later part of the
>   Sixteenth Karmapa's life
> And the beginning of the Seventeenth, one with broken
>   samaya[159] will surface
> As a lama having the name Nata[160]
> And appear at the main seat.
> By the power of his twisted aspirations,
> The Dharma of the Karmapa will be nearly destroyed.
> At that time, one with previous, positive aspirations,
> A heart emanation of Padmasambhava, will come from the
>   West.
> With a necklace of moles and a mind that is swift and
>   furious,
> He will wrathfully proclaim words of the Dharma.
> This one with a dark complexion and protruding eyes
> Will vanquish the emanation who has broken samaya.
> He will protect Tibet for a while, and at that time
> There will be happiness like that of seeing the sun.
> This is the way I think it will happen within the Tibetan
>   community.

Even if one comes whose previous aspirations arise as
   positive karma,
Because the Dharma is on the wane and evil intentions of
   the maras have come to fruition,
It will be difficult for happiness to arise.[161]

Reading Tibetan prophetic verse can be like trying to make sense of Nostradamus because of symbolic language that is difficult to interpret and words that have multiple meanings, several which may be intended at the same time. For example, *Nata* can mean "nephew" or "relation," and it has been suggested that two nephews, Shamarpa and Topga, wished to retain power at Rumtek, though their proper role was as "protector"—another meaning of the word—of the Karmapa and his properties. But it can mean other things as well, and its usage in the text is ambiguous. Even so, the two-hundred-year-old prediction seems astonishingly prescient.

The first international Karma Kagyu general assembly was convened at Rumtek not long after the enthronement, in November 1992. The purpose of the meeting was to plan the Karmapa's enthronement at Rumtek, which most of the Rumtek community hoped would be soon. Topga Yugyal disagreed. Until now, his opposition to the Seventeenth Karmapa was known mostly among those who worked closely with him or held positions in the Rumtek labrang. He was still the chief administrator and treasurer. Now he publicly distributed a letter he addressed to Tai Situpa containing a strongly worded attack. He stated the Seventeenth Karmapa "should never set foot" at Rumtek. This was too much for the people at Rumtek, already dismayed by many of Topga's activities during his tenure. The assembly voted him out as general secretary and appointed as the new chandzo the Sixteenth Karmapa's personal secretary Dronyig Tendzin Namgyal, who had been made unwelcome at Rumtek by Topga after the Karmapa's death. He had been trusted by the Sixteenth Karmapa and was generally known to be an honest man of integrity.

Shamarpa also began to speak openly on his tours around the world about the rift between himself and the other tulkus. In April

1993 he gave a talk in Malaysia in which he accused Tai Situpa and Gyaltsap Rinpoche of being in league with the Chinese government. He accused them of sullying their faith by practicing politics. "Since the Buddhist Dharma (was) established in Tibet as their culture, then politics and Dharma went together for many, many generations in Tibet. Majority, very few teachers were not involved in politics but politicians involved in Dharma. That's why Dharma became very useful for politicians," he told the Malaysian Buddhists, and added that he knew the Karmapa's prediction letter was forged "because I am his family." Shamarpa wished to cast Tai Situpa, Gyaltsapa, and others who acknowledged the Seventeenth Karmapa as politicians eyeing Rumtek riches. Yet neither Tai Situpa, with his large monastery Sherab Ling in Himachal Pradesh to look after, nor Gyaltsap Rinpoche, who now had his own monastery at Ralang, Sikkim, had expressed any desire to control Rumtek. They simply wanted the Karmapa to be installed in his rightful place and educated to continue the work of the Karmapas. As close disciples of the Sixteenth Karmapa, the lamas saw his safe reinstatement as their biggest responsibility, coming before their own concerns. But it was becoming their biggest headache.

Several violent incidents between the Rumtek monks who supported the Seventeenth Karmapa and the Shamarpa's followers—now supported by Shamarpa and living at his house down the hill from Rumtek—pushed the Sikkim government to act. Sikkim Armed Police were permanently posted at Rumtek. Both Shamarpa and Topga were banned from Sikkim for being troublemakers. "They are not entitled to create problems. If they are going to do these sort of activities here, certainly we will take serious action against them," said then Chief Minister Bhandari, adding "This Bhutanese (Topga Yugyal) and Shamar Rinpoche, they are playing this for commercial (reasons). They want to capture the whole property and centers."[162] The relic room that was sealed in 1992 during Jamgon Kongtrul's funeral remained sealed by the government, with a guard outside the door. Later Central Reserve Police Force bolstered the state police outside.

In 1993 Topga Yugyal and Shamarpa began filing court cases through their agents to gain control of the Karmapa's property.

Early in 1994 articles began to appear in the English daily the *Indian Express*.[163] These articles frequently ran on the front page, often above the fold. Focused on Rumtek Monastery politics, the content was chiefly a twisted version of events which amounted to disinformation. The most cursory fact-checking would have yielded more accurate reportage. And among those familiar with the Karmapa's recognition, this series of stories in the *Indian Express* was seen as another power play by the Shamarpa and Topga Yugyal.[164] This was confirmed when, in March, the announcement came that Shamarpa was going to produce his own Karmapa selection.

10. Strife Within

DURING THE TWO YEARS since the Seventeenth Karmapa's recognition there were occasional reports of Shamarpa's search for a different candidate. He attempted to nominate a son of the king of Bhutan—the boy was coincidentally a nephew of one of his staunch supporters in Nepal, lama-politician Lopon Tsechu, who is uncle to the Bhutanese king's four wives—but the king declined to be drawn into it. The boy who Shamarpa settled on was the son of a somewhat controversial man from Tibet who claimed to be an incarnation of an important Tibetan master, Mipam. According to Tibetan sources, the accomplished Mipam himself wrote, before he died, that there would be no future Mipam incarnations, making the man's claim questionable to Tibetans familiar with Mipam's writings. This Mipam had two sons, both of whom he brought around to monasteries, hoping to get them recognized as tulkus, say Tibetan sources who know about his background. None of the monasteries he approached were interested, so he lodged the boys at a Gelug monastery for their studies. He was said to be connected with Chinese government officials through his friend Katog Shingchong Tulku. Katog Shingchong had come to India after 1959 and was subsequently involved in some political activities in Dehradun. He opposed the Dalai Lama, the Dalai Lama's brother Gyalo Thondup, and the Tibetan government-in-exile. He left India, presumably, when things got too hot for him. He now lives in Chengdu, China.

Somehow the Mipam seeking tulkuhood for his sons and the Shamarpa looking for an alternative Karmapa connected, possibly through Katog Shingchong, who was also thought to be a Shamarpa supporter. The Shamarpa's account has developed over the years since 1994. One version posted on Ole Nydahl's "Diamond Way Buddhism" Web site in 2000 says that Nepal-based lama Lopon Tsechu was a middleman in locating the boy, who was then called Tenzin Chentse. The boy's father had by that time made some claims that his son was the Karmapa. Shamarpa told his followers some years later that a lama had come to him in Delhi in 1986 telling him of the boy.[165] Shamarpa says he investigated the boy with the help of Lopon Tsechu and others, but he did not inform the other three chief Karma Kagyu tulkus concerned. Shamarpa made a trip to Tibet himself during which, he says, he failed to see the boy. He spoke of a mysterious old man who held information but wasn't ready to reveal it. Tenzin Chentse subsequently left China and ended up in Bhutan, though there is no clear, independent description of the circumstances of his departure to be found. A biography about Tenzin Chentse on his official Web site provides little substantial information. Shamarpa's story as conveyed by the Nydahl group is that the father got permission from the Chinese government to go to Nepal with his family, and they went to New Delhi from there in January 1994. Later they went to Bhutan where Topga and Shamarpa used their connections to settle the boy's family.

On the morning of March 17, 1994, at the Karmapa International Buddhist Institute in New Delhi, a thin, pale-looking

Tenzin Chentse
with his father
and younger
brother

boy was brought around to the main shrine room. His age was
given as eleven. Inside the shrine room were a few Tibetans, but
Europeans, of whom there were several hundred, predomi-
nated. Most of them were Westerners from the Nydahl centers,
Hannah Nydahl among them. I attended the ceremony as a
reporter for Voice of America. But before the ceremonies
began, I was recognized by Hannah Nydahl, and soon a Tibetan
man in a suit appeared to ask me and my colleague Tim
McGirk, then correspondent for the *Independent* (UK), to leave.

We protested that we were journalists, but that had no effect
and we left.

Outside, a contingent of monks from Delhi and Himachal
Pradesh were assembled to demonstrate against Shamarpa and
what they saw as a sacrilegious introduction of a fake Karmapa.
It was meant to be a silent protest. It was unclear who cast the
first stone. Brickbats were hurled from above and returned from
below. One journalist who wasn't thrown out reported that pro-
jectiles such as coke bottles and bricks were stockpiled on the
roof of the monastery, apparently for just such an eventuality.
Unfortunately, some people were injured, one man quite seriously when he was hit on the head. Some of the rabble-rousers
were piled into police vans and taken to jail to cool off.

The Shamarpa strove to get the Dalai Lama to recognize his
candidate, whom he had given the name Thaye Dorje. He took
the boy to Dharamsala for the Dalai Lama to perform his hair-
cutting ceremony, but the Dalai Lama refused, returning the gifts
Shamarpa sent as inducements. During these years the Dalai
Lama was forced to reiterate the status of the Seventeenth
Karmapa several times, and press statements were issued from
his cabinet. One of these, issued March 30, 1994, gave a summary of the recognition and added that since the recognition
people "who failed to understand clearly the actual situation
caused false rumors and doubts to circulate. Likewise, there
appeared in Indian newspapers distorted reports alleging that
His Holiness the Dalai Lama had withdrawn his confirmation.
Due to these, people did not comprehend the true significance
of the confirmation, and therefore, needless doubts arose
among them as well as a lack of patience, happiness, and peace.
If these distortions are allowed to lead people astray, the harmonious connections within our community will be destroyed, and
the present campaign of the Chinese government, which
attempts to shatter the sacred connection uniting our people,
will only be strengthened."

But the campaign to promote the rival candidate and disparage
the enthroned Karmapa continued. In August the Tibetan government-in-exile took out quarter-page display ads in major

newspapers to restate that the Karmapa who was enthroned in Tibet is the genuine Karmapa, giving his vital statistics, and asserting "His Holiness the Dalai Lama granted his final seal of approval and recognition to the Seventeenth Gyalwa Karmapa, not randomly or hastily for any reason, but after satisfying himself by means of hearing a series of reports from all those concerned; studying and paying due consideration to the overall matter; and reconfirming the final indications with exclusive traditional examinations. While other candidates may come forward, he is the only one who will be entitled to the position, Rumtek Monastery, the black crown of the Karmapas, and other assets." Shamarpa, for his part, insisted that he had proof that Tenzin Chentse was the real Karmapa, that an old monk had a letter that would be produced "when the time was right." No satisfactory evidence has yet been produced.

Tai Situpa had teaching commitments abroad, so in July 1994 he left India on an international tour. In September he was surprised to find that he had been banned from entering India for "anti-Indian activities." He had recently visited Beijing and met the concerned Chinese authorities in hopes of bringing the Karmapa to India, but with inconclusive results. Tai Situpa had not traveled to Tibet any more often than countless other expatriate lamas, monks, and lay persons who continued to visit their families and monasteries there while maintaining residence in India or elsewhere. Shamarpa, Gyaltsapa, and Jamgon Kongtrul had all been there at least once. When this news broke, Tai Situpa was lecturing on Buddhism in Southeast Asia and had not officially received the order, nor did he know who had signed it. "It must be a misunderstanding," he said. He had lived in India since he was six years old and looked upon it as home. He had built a monastery in Himachal Pradesh. "I have always had and continue to have great respect and deep appreciation for India and the Indian people, and I have great faith and trust in the Indian Government," he told the Tibetan Information Network at that time. He also pointed out that he had consulted with the Indian authorities—then Minister of State for Foreign Affairs, the late Rajesh Pilot among them—and the Dalai Lama prior going to China, and both "seemed perfectly happy about my trip." He emphasized he had no political involvement with any government.

He was backed up in this by officials from the Dalai Lama's government, who confirmed this and expressed their concern to the Indian government. Kalon Tenzin Tethong, speaking for the Tibetan government-in-exile observed, "I am totally unaware that he is involved in anything that could be considered anti-Indian and I think it is very unlikely." He added, "I don't think these allegations have any currency beyond the *Indian Express,* and I really don't know what is behind this except that he traveled to Tibet and China."[166] Not long after the ban order was issued, I asked then Foreign Secretary Kris Srivavasan if the government had anything against Tai Situpa. He was well informed about the whole story, and he told me that they did not. As far as the External Affairs Ministry was concerned, Tai Situpa was not considered a threat.

In India "speed money" is a euphemism for bribes required to get things done quickly, or get things done period. Supporters of the Seventeenth Karmapa, such as members of Sikkim's Joint Action Committee, which was formed to bring the Seventeenth Karmapa back to Rumtek, feel that the ban order against Tai Situpa came from greasing the palms of susceptible bureaucrats and agents in the intelligence bureau. Hard evidence of this kind of activity is difficult to come by, of course, especially if the recipients of largesse are in Indian intelligence, where Shamarpa is said to have his strongest allies. Those who do have specific knowledge are unwilling to name names. The effects of the whisper campaign against Tai Situpa appear to persist in both the Home and External Affairs ministries to this day. I was surprised to find that the MEA spokesman at the time of the Karmapa's escape, Raminder Jessel, repeatedly expressed his skepticism to me in our conversations about the Karmapa's escape. Shamarpa and Topga cultivated people who were "good contacts," that is, the rich and powerful, the effective bureaucrats. They wrote letters, made visits, were very charming to the influential. I saw them do this during the period I had frequent contact with them after the death of the old general secretary. They were good at it.

In 1995 Topga Yugyal published a letter in which he accused Gyaltsap Rinpoche and Tai Situpa of doing the things he himself had been banned from Sikkim for doing. He claimed they had promised to distribute the Karmapa's treasures to supporters, something that was patently untrue. He wrote in the letter addressed to Gyaltsap Rinpoche, "We will hold you and Tai Situ entirely responsible for the loss of any single article, including even a 'needle and thread,' preserved in the monastery and found intact by the concerned authorities until early 1992," ignoring the fact that he had absolute control over what happened to the treasures between 1982 and 1992 and that the treasure room had remained under government seal ever since. There were some other things in the letter, such as a challenge to Gyaltsap Rinpoche to "fast to the death" to see who the true "breaker of the sacred oath to the guru" was, himself or Gyaltsapa. He wrote that the "Dharma Protectors" would ensure that the real oath-breaker would die first. Gyaltsap Rinpoche declined to accept the letter, so Topga had it published and publicly distributed instead. Ironically, Topga Yugyal died first, in 1997, of an aggressive form of liver cancer. The relic room was not opened nor was its contents assessed until 2002, when it was inventoried by court order.[167]

During this time Tai Situpa remained outside of India. For four years he kept himself occupied teaching in North America, Europe, and Southeast Asia. He did several extended retreats in a remote part of Canada. He continued to challenge the ban order, requesting a letter rescinding it. He did not wish to return to India without an official document and risk being turned away. Officers at the Indian High Commission, whenever contacted, would tell him there was really no problem and he could return to India, but they procrastinated about actually giving him a letter to that effect. The ban order was finally revoked in 1998.

Meanwhile, the Seventeenth Karmapa was growing up at Tsurphu. Though the Chinese wrote in a 1993 letter that the Karmapa might travel abroad in 1995, that year came and went without his going anywhere outside the People's Republic of China. By that time the progressive trend that allowed the Chinese to acknowledge an authentically recognized incarnate lama had gone into reverse. The Chinese political line in Tibet hardened, and suppression of religion was renewed. The new attitude became chillingly obvious in Beijing's desperation to control the Panchen Lama. The candidate chosen by the Dalai Lama was repudiated, the boy disappeared, and Beijing installed its own candidate in his stead. This occurred over Tibetan protests and the sure knowledge that Tibetans would never accept the Chinese government's selection.

The Dalai Lama's main concern was for the Karmapa's proper education and training according to his position, which is one of great religious responsibility. Buddhism in Tibet had deteriorated under the communists, who had concentrated considerable resources to effect its destruction. There were few qualified teachers left, and important texts had been destroyed. Because of that and for political reasons, the Dalai Lama did not believe the Karmapa could be adequately trained in Tibet but needed to come to India. "For at least five to seven years he must remain here." He added, "I believe both Gyaltsap Rinpoche and Situ Rinpoche should maintain some kind of good relationship with China. From time to time to time they should go to Tibet." The Dalai Lama had reliable information that three things were "problems" for the Chinese in letting the Karmapa stray beyond China's boundaries: "First, they are worried Karmapa may not return. Second, once Karmapa Rinpoche goes outside, he naturally will have contact with the Dalai Lama and be brainwashed by the Dalai Lama. And third, the Chinese government still doesn't consider Sikkim a part of India, so these three points concern the Chinese government and make them reluctant to let him go outside." Although he felt it was a serious situation, he said, "for the long run, perhaps it is all right. The Chinese themselves may not remain for many years," he quipped, laughing.[168]

The Chinese government officials closely monitored the Seventeenth Karmapa, but they didn't interfere much with his daily routine. He was allowed to study with a tutor. Drupon

Dechen Rinpoche remained at Tsurphu to supervise the boy's schedule. During study breaks he played with toys like any boy and had a particular liking for remote-control cars and helicopters. He went on walks around the Tolung Valley with his monks or on picnics when there were holidays. Soon after the enthronement public access to him was restricted to brief, walk-through audiences. The Chinese sometimes inducted the Karmapa into special programs to celebrate state holidays and the like, but he was a child and his participation was therefore limited. That did not prevent them from squeezing the maximum value out of each occasion.

The first public relations tour organized by the Chinese came in September of 1994, two years after the Karmapa's enthronement, when he was ten years old. This was lavishly publicized by *Xinhua*, beginning with his departure from Lhasa after a visit to the Jokhang. This event gave officials a chance to condemn "a handful of separatists inside and outside China" who were using religion "to engage in separatist activities." "This is absolutely forbidden," said Chen Kuiyuan, secretary of the Communist Party of China, and he admonished the Karmapa to "fight sternly against separatists." The ten year old was reported by *Xinhua* to have said, "I will study hard and always follow the Communist Party of China." He was then taken on a pilgrimage to important Tibetan monasteries, culminating with Tashilhunpo in Shigatse—significantly, perhaps, since it is the monastery of the Panchen Lamas.

The Karmapa was taken back to Lhasa and flown to Beijing. News briefs were issued from Beijing on his progress. "Living Buddha Garmaba [sic] chants for Mao's soul in Beijing" ran one headline. VIPs came to meet him. Ngaboe Ngawang Jigme, vice-chairman of the National Committee of the Chinese People's Consultative Conference and grandfather of the late Jamgon Kongtrul, visited the Karmapa at his hotel. The Karmapa also met other officials, including Li Ruihuan, chairman of the National Committee of the Chinese People's Political Consultative Conference and a member of the Standing Committee of the Political Bureau of the Chinese Communist

Party Central Committee, who used the occasion to reiterate Chinese policy on points such as "the freedom-to-believe policy" and "Tibet is an integral part of China." The Karmapa attended a reception given by premier Li Peng. His fellow guests included Jiang Zemin, Qiao Shi, Li Ruihuan, Zhu Ronghi. Cambodian King Norodom Sihanouk and his queen were there along with 3,500 other dignitaries and officials.

The centerpiece of the visit, from the Chinese point of view, at least, was when President Jiang Zemin met the Karmapa in Tiananmen Square on the Chinese National Day. *Xinhua* quoted the young Karmapa in its October 1st dispatch, and it is worth repeating in detail: "'I thank the central leadership for the attention shown to me,' said the Seventeenth Living Buddha Garmaba with a smile on his face when he shook hands with General Secretary Jiang Zemin on Tiananmen rostrum this evening during the National Day ceremony. At about nine o'clock when the 100,000-people grand evening party was going on, General Secretary Jiang Zemin of the Chinese Communist Party's Central Committee, walked over to Garmaba to shake hands with him. Following the Tibetan tradition, the 10-year-old Living Buddha presented a white hada (a piece of silk) as a gift to Jiang Zemin, and Jiang presented one in return." The article goes on to quote Jiang's words to the Karmapa: "'I hope the Living Buddha will study hard and grow up healthily, so that you can contribute to the economic and social development of Tibet.' Jiang also asked the Garmaba's teacher to train the young Garmaba into a patriotic Living Buddha with deep love for his religion." *Xinhua* quotes the boy's expressions of thanks to the "central leadership," and depicts the end of his interview with Jiang, who "gave his best wishes in the Tibetan language, and the Garmaba put his palms together, saying 'Long live the People's Republic of China.'"

This public relations exercise clearly shows what the Chinese government had in mind for the Karmapa. The Chinese trotted him out again from time to time, tactically when it suited them to highlight integration of Tibet into the People's Republic of China. They had him meet their choice for the Panchen Lama

Seventeenth
Karmapa
with the
Fourth
Jamgon
Kongtrul

and made sure the photo of his offering a white scarf was widely
publicized, although the Karmapa declined to prostrate to him.
Once, during the Karmapa's last official visit to Beijing, officials
asked him to read a speech. Later in India, I asked the Karmapa
to tell me the story of what happened. He said that a Chinese
official gave him the speech. The Karmapa asked the man if he

had written it and if it was an official government speech. The official said yes. "I told them that I would read it," the Karmapa said, "but would preface the reading by saying it was a speech I was asked to read by the government but it was not one that I wrote myself." The official took it back and didn't press the issue.

The Karmapa says the Chinese officials treated him very well at all times, in Tsurphu and out of it. But it was increasingly obvious that the Chinese had no intention of allowing the Karmapa to leave Tibet, at least not until they were convinced he could be sent as a willing instrument of their policies. They wanted to use his influence with the Tibetan people, as they tried to use the previous Panchen Lama, as an antidote to the Dalai Lama. The Karmapa otherwise conformed to the exemplar of his predecessors: he studied, practiced, and recognized tulkus, including the Fourth Jamgon Kongtrul.

As is customary when a high lama dies, in 1994 Jamgon Kongtrul's monks requested the Karmapa to locate their departed lama's reincarnation. The following year the monks visited Tsurphu. They were led by Tendzin Dorje, formerly Kongtrul's chief attendant, and the sole survivor of the crash that killed his teacher. Now chandzo, he oversaw the projects of the Jamgon Kongtrul labrang. The Karmapa, after advising them to do a number of special rituals to remove obstacles, told the monks that the time was not right to find the new Jamgon Kongtrul but that next year there would be "good news." When the monks again visited the Karmapa at Tsurphu in 1996, the Karmapa gave a letter to Tendzin Dorje detailing where they would find the young Jamgon Kongtrul. "At that very moment, a single thunder clap roared in the skies. Sonam Choepel and I were together with His Holiness. When we left the room, heading to see the late Drupon Dechen Rinpoche, I noticed a very light rainfall with sunshine which we Tibetans call *metok char pa* (rain of flowers). In our tradition, it is believed to be an auspicious sign."[169] But the monks were puzzled by the description in the letter, so the Karmapa obliged by making sketches of the area with place names. The Karmapa had seen it in visions. It took two trips, but the search party at last located the infant tulku in a place with features exactly as described by the Karmapa. In September the Karmapa and subsequently the Dalai Lama proclaimed the authenticity of the recognition. The young lama now lives at his monastery, Pullahari, outside Kathmandu.

Tai Situpa, besides trying to sort out the Indian entry ban, tried to get a Chinese visa so he could visit the Karmapa again at Tsurphu. This was repeatedly refused. The Sikkim Joint Action Committee met repeatedly with Indian government officials. They challenged the ban order against Tai Situpa and the accusations of Shamarpa that Tai Situpa was an operative in a communist Chinese plot. When the Indian ban order was finally rescinded, Tai Situpa returned to India in September of 1998, and he became immersed in his duties at his monastery, Sherab Ling. He spent most of the following year in India, but restrictions had been placed on his movements. He could not go to Kashmir or to the northeast where militancy was going on. He could not go to Sikkim without special permission. He did go to Salugara, near Siliguri, for a religious ceremony, but had to get the visit approved first.

The standoff persisted between the supporters of the Shamarpa's candidate and the supporters of the Seventeenth Karmapa. Shamarpa continued to file court cases through his agents in Sikkim and elsewhere.[170] Some of the cases go so far as to accuse the Dalai Lama of colluding with the Chinese. Most of the cases, which amount to harassment, were dismissed. Others carry on, or have been refiled in lower courts in states like Bihar, where laws are loosely enforced if it all, and judges entertain cases that have been thrown out by higher courts. Dugo Bhutia, Shamarpa's chief surrogate in Sikkim who keeps the cases alive, announced in a television interview that Shamarpa is the Sixteenth Karmapa's nephew "and so according to tradition the Karmapa's property belongs to him,"[171] a statement that contradicts history. But it does sum up the Shamarpa's point of view. A supreme court lawyer who accepted a pro bono case filed by another Shamarpa ally, Shri Narayan Singh, that was dismissed by the Delhi High Court in August 2001 said that antagonists can continue filing such cases ad infinitum merely by changing some of the wording. And so they do.[172]

By 1998 the Chinese government's cooperation with regard to the Seventeenth Karmapa had evaporated. So did the initial optimism of Tai Situpa and Gyaltsap Rinpoche. It was manifestly clear that the Chinese government had no intention of letting the Karmapa leave the People's Republic of China. They also prevented Tai Situpa from visiting him. The Karmapa himself was talking to his closest aides about escape, but was counseled to wait by advisors inside and outside Tibet. The Karmapa had a mind of his own, however, and his attendants in Tsurphu worried that his strong will in itself might antagonize the Chinese. Escape, in their minds, was out of the question. The Dalai Lama was apprised of Karmapa's wishes to leave, but he, too, advised caution. As the young lama grew older, the Chinese government called on him more often to participate in official functions. That was predictable, although the Karmapa's independent streak may have surprised them. Around him in Tibet there was growing curtailment of religious freedom, but there were other, sinister events that may have ultimately convinced the Karmapa and his loyal followers that if he wished to freely pursue his vocation as a religious leader, his only avenue was escape.

11. The Politics of Reincarnation

A FEW HOURS AFTER a ragtag, exhausted group of Tibetans turned up in Dharamsala, a Tibetan friend who has worked for Tai Situpa for many years telephoned me. He said, "I have some very good news for the new year. The Karmapa has escaped to India. He is in Dharamsala." My first response was, "What? Are you sure?" My informant said that Tai Situpa was on his way to Dharamsala meet the Karmapa; he left immediately upon hearing the Karmapa was there. Agreeing that this was great news, indeed, I thanked my friend for being thoughtful enough to notify me, hung up, and considered this extraordinary development. It was a typical chilly, yellow-tinted winter day in Delhi that suddenly acquired new energy. Taking an educated guess, I called the Bhagsu Hotel in Dharamsala to inquire if a group of lamas were there. The receptionist told me that some lamas fitting the description I offered had come early that morning, but they had checked out a little while ago. What a story! Tempting as it was to email everyone in my address book, I wanted to

The Karmapa waves from the roof of Gyuto Monastery with Dzogchen Ponlop Rinpoche.

speak to Tai Situpa to get more details. If true, and I still did not completely believe it, it was a terribly sensitive development. Early the next morning I reached him. Tai Situpa said he had seen the Karmapa and told me a few details about the escape. The Karmapa was safe. He was well. He was here. The Seventeenth Karmapa Orgyen Trinley Dorje, in the waning months of the Tibetan Earth Hare year, as if taking a hint from that animal, had nimbly leapt to freedom. Or so he thought.

Tai Situpa also told me during our conversation that the consensus of opinion was that it was best to keep it quiet until the Indian government had time to be notified and respond to the Karmapa's escape. But it was easier to stop a wildfire than to stop this news from spreading. The Indian government had hardly been told about his escape when word got out. Within twenty-four hours of the Karmapa's arrival in India, the news was posted on the Internet by U.S. followers, well before the media picked it up. Then Gyaltsap Rinpoche made an announcement at Rumtek, alerting the Indian press.

As soon as it was confirmed that the lanky teenager who appeared in Dharamsala on the cold morning of January 5, 2000 was indeed the Seventeenth Karmapa, the Tibetan government-in-exile attempted to shield him from notice. The new refugees were whisked from the Bhagsu Hotel to the nearby Chonor Guest House. Reporters scrambled up to Dharamsala to begin a watch outside the guest house, waiting for a photo op or a few words with the Karmapa. If the Karmapa crunched through the snow toward the Dalai Lama's residence nearby, reporters followed. He was then driven in a car, but importunate journalists dogged his steps between the hotel door and the vehicle. Interviews were forbidden. The Karmapa soon was moved from the Chonor Guest House and sequestered in Gyuto Monastery, in Sidhabari, a village seven kilometers from Dharamsala. He was not permitted to meet foreigners. Foreign journalists, especially, were anathema to the Indian government, which obviously wanted to be first to debrief the Karmapa. Damaging fallout that might adversely affect relations with China must be contained. The congregation of reporters outside steadily grew, regardless. The familiar Tibetan politics of reincarnation had now acquired geopolitical significance. Photographers camped on a high dirt mound in front of Gyuto Monastery, waiting for the Karmapa to appear. He often strolled on the roof of the small monastery. The timing of these strolls was unpredictable, so photographers mounted daylong vigils.

Security was inordinately tight. Senior officials from the Indian Foreign Ministry and intelligence agencies arrived to interview the high-profile refugees. Comings and goings were carefully scrutinized. The Karmapa was allowed to meet a few Indians and Tibetans privately. Finally, in February, the day before Tibetan New Year of the Iron Dragon, the authorities agreed to let the Karmapa meet the public, including foreigners, in strictly regulated group audiences. Initially, this involved almost comic security overkill. Passport numbers, names, arrival and departure dates, domiciles had to be laboriously recorded in a large register. This practice is common at immigration counters at airports, at the Foreigner's Regional Registration Offices, government office buildings, and areas considered high security zones. The bureaucratic legacy of the British Raj embellished by independent India has made paperwork both a means and an end. People queued up for hours waiting as the lengthy vetting process was accomplished.

Nothing, literally nothing, could be taken inside the monastery building. Although it was winter and freezing cold, everyone was made to strip down to the barest decent minimum—no coats, sweaters, shawls, not even socks to buffer the

235

numbing, icy marble floor of the Gyuto audience hall. Of the mix of Indian and Tibetan security, the Tibetans were, for some reason, the worst: officious, rudely pushing and ordering people about. When it came time to offer ritual prostrations after the lama entered the room, one Tibetan security guard shouted at people who began prostrations—*de rigueur* before such a high tulku—telling them stop it and sit down. After sentiments had been sufficiently bruised, people at last were allowed to see the Karmapa.

There was a stir at the side door. A group of monks dressed in neat maroon robes and bright yellow vests entered quietly. A tall young man detached himself from the group to take a seat front-and-center in an ordinary chair that had a piece of red and golden brocade thrown over it. He was cordoned off from the audience by yellow tape, as if he were a museum exhibit or a crime scene. This was the Seventeenth Karmapa Orgyen Trinley Dorje, who had, but a few weeks before, scrambled over the Himalayas to get to India. Despite the low-key entrance, his presence was potent. The room fell silent, expectant faces turned toward him. On the day I attended the audience, a few days after the routine had been established, the fourteen-year-old spoke in Tibetan, confidently and without hesitation. His penetrating eyes surveyed the audience seated on the floor in front of him as he thanked us all for coming, Asians and Westerners alike. "May you all have happiness, health, prosperity, and live in freedom," he said. He mentioned democracy, as he often does, although his speech is not political in tone. A flap was created among Tibetan and Chinese Karmapa watchers when his first official speech, at a cultural performance in Dharamsala, was mistranslated by a Tibetan government translator and given a political cast. The Karmapa chooses his words carefully, and Tibetans who heard him speak in the days after his escape comment on the remarkable sophistication of language in one so young.

Soon the Karmapa was occupied composing masterful poetry, an intricate art in Tibet and one of his favorite pastimes. His teachers agree that his ability is precocious. Musicians from the

Tibetan Institute of Performing Arts were called in for an elevated kind of jam session, collaborating with the Karmapa to set his poetry to music. Under the Karmapa's guidance and within months of his arrival, the musicians recorded his songs on cassette and CD. One of the first songs translated into English reflects the Karmapa's chief concerns, with verses about Tibet, the Dalai Lama, Tibetan culture, and world conditions. The following poem is "Aspiration for Culture and Knowledge":

> The most excellent virtue is the brilliant and calm flow of
> culture;
> Those with fine minds play in a clear lotus lake.
> Through this excellent path, a songline sweet like the
> pollen,
> May they sip the fragrant dew of glorious knowledge.[173]

In another song he makes interesting references to religion and politics, doubtless inspired by his own situation:[174]

> Always awake, the deer's eyes are wide open.[175]
> The two traditions of religion and politics are a golden
> necklace,
> Perfectly aligned and radiating their brilliance to everyone.

And then:

> Lineage holders with no bias are brilliant suns for sentient
> beings;
> Not veiled by the darkness of wrong conduct,
> They are present above our crown, seated on a swaying
> lotus.[176]

A later line notes that such individuals "risk even their body or life for the sake of honesty and truth." The poetry is full of rich imagery and Buddhist philosophy, and calls to conquer "the darkness of the shadow side." "Let us travel to the springtime of the glorious, young sun of freedom. The summer's pleasing thunder brings news to gladden the people of Tibet." More recently, *Sacred Buddha,* an album of Tibetan Buddhist chants put together by Iranian composer Sina Vodjani, features the Seventeenth Karmapa's actual voice. Recorded when the Karmapa was still at Tsurphu, it is the first recording of the Seventeenth Karmapa's voice to be brought out commercially.

The Karmapa wasted no time in applying himself to his studies. After a recuperative day or two, he began to ask for texts to study, even before his tutors had time to set his curriculum and daily discipline. Suddenly an abundant resource of texts was within reach, and he was eager to immerse himself in the books that were unavailable in Tibet. The Library of Tibetan Works and Archives in Dharamsala is at the center of Tibetan cultural preservation. One of the first things the Dalai Lama did was save precious Buddhist texts that had been carried out of Tibet. The Library is a humming hive of scholars, Tibetan and foreign. The Karmapa had some of these scholars running back and forth every few days bringing him famous commentaries and scholarly works. It was a suitable way to occupy himself, but then he hadn't many other options. He was, for all practical purposes, a prisoner of Gyuto Monastery. Gyuto was a calm, well-guarded epicenter of a political storm.

By the end of January the story of the Seventeenth Karmapa's escape had been on the front pages of newspapers and was featured on the covers of international editions of *Time, Newsweek,* and other popular weekly news magazines. It was an irresistible tale of adventure, intrigue, winning against the odds, with exotic and mysterious Tibet thrown in for good measure. And it had international ramifications. Within days of his escape, the Chinese government issued a press release stating that the Karmapa left a letter indicating he had gone to retrieve his Black Crown and musical instruments from India and would soon return. While the Karmapa did leave a letter, according to him it was an apology to his monks for leaving. In it, he explained why he had to leave: that under the circumstances he could not carry on his mission of Buddhist study, practice, and teaching, not as long as religion was oppressed in Tibet. In an interview in April

2000 the Karmapa told me,[177] "Everyone knows the situation now in Tibet. The possibilities of study and practice did not satisfy what I felt I needed. I must study the literature of Tibet and the philosophy of Buddhism, and to do that I had to come to India." He also said he wished to visit the sacred places in India, pointing out that Sikkim is one of these. It is considered sanctified by the ninth-century master Padmasambhava.

The Black Crown is an important piece of paraphernalia identified with the Karmapa for hundreds of years. "The Black Crown ceremony is a part of the Karmapa's activity and in that respect, to have the blessing of the crown and the holy objects is important, in order to continue that activity. But I did not come to India for my belongings," the fourteen-year-old Karmapa said. One year later, when asked about it at his first press conference, he was more assertive: "It is true that I left a letter behind me, but as I wrote the letter myself, I'm perfectly aware of what was in it and what wasn't. I said in the letter that I left because, although I had for a long time persistently and repeatedly requested permission to travel internationally, I had never received it, and so I had to leave. I did not, in the letter, mention the Black Crown. Why would I want to retrieve that from India and bring it back to China except to put it on Jiang Zemin's head?" This flash of ironic humor was doubtless in reaction to the Chinese government's spin on his escape, a remark unlikely to amuse Chinese officials.

The Karmapa said he regrets having to leave his monks at Tsurphu, putting some of their lives in jeopardy by his flight. But he added that he would still have contact with many Tibetans and other Buddhists from around the world because the Dalai Lama has a government-in-exile in India. People who were unable to meet him in Tibet can meet him in India. "Just because I came here doesn't mean I won't go back. I think that the time will come when the Dalai Lama, and everyone who wants to, will be able to freely go back to Tibet."[178] Assertions in this vein certainly encourage young Tibetans, who see the Karmapa as a dynamic future leader. This is one of the important aspects of his escape, in fact. Whether he wants to be or

The Karmapa and Sakya Trizin watch a cultural performance in Dharmsala. (Photo by Lynsey Addario)

not, he is seen as a possible political heir of the Dalai Lama. The Karmapa speaks even-handedly about China. "On the personal level the Chinese did not treat me badly. At certain times they tried to influence me to reject the views of the Dalai Lama. I was uncomfortable there only when they did this, and I tried to avoid these situations when they came up. But I do not blame the Chinese for bad treatment, because they did not treat me badly. Physically, they treated me very well." He believes, however, that change in the style of government in Tibet is inevitable. "There is impermanence in life. Things change and will continue to change."

The young Karmapa explained the seamy politics that have erupted in connection with his own recognition philosophically: "Because of this dark age,[179] because of that spirit, it looks like the true and pure aren't really very powerful. The bad and impure seem more powerful. But ultimately the true is more powerful and will prevail for the long term." Repeating himself for emphasis, he said, "Truth will prevail, but for the time being the negative influence appears stronger. Overall, the negative way will not succeed." He paused for a moment and then added, "I offer this prayer: May all untruth subside and be dispelled. May the power of truth prevail. And individuals who are accumulating bad karma, may all their activities be transformed into those of bodhisattvas." Listening to the teenager with a shy smile voice these mature thoughts was a little disconcerting, like hearing a wise old man speak from an incongruously young body.

240

The Karmapa was grateful to be accepted by India, but his incarceration in Gyuto Monastery was as surprising as it was difficult for him. An energetic youth, he naturally needed more scope for activity than a few turns on the monastery roof. Initially, followers expected that he would move to nearby Sherab Ling, Tai Situpa's monastery, until he was allowed to go to Rumtek in Sikkim. It is the appropriate thing to do, since Tai Situpa is one of the chief lamas of his own Karma Kagyu lineage and one of his teachers.

But years of concerted efforts to malign Tai Situpa had their effect. The Indian government bristled with suspicion about the Karmapa, his party, and those India-based lamas who are close to him. Although neither the Home nor External Affairs ministry produced any proof of "anti-national activities" against Tai Situpa, enough suspicions were kept alive to impede the Karmapa's freedom to visit, not to mention stay, at Sherab Ling. It is easy to awaken Indian government paranoia about Pakistan and China, neighbors with whom there is a history of hostility. Unsubstantiated stories that Tai Situpa was a Chinese agent, or that the Karmapa escaped with the help of the Chinese and the CIA, were just the sorts of conspiracy tales that had appeal in the corridors of bureaucratic power. It doesn't matter that the stories might be false, spread by "motivated" agents within the ministries to serve the agenda of those who want to cause trouble for the Seventeenth Karmapa. Stirring up doubt was the only tool people who wanted to supplant the Karmapa had, apart from filing endless court cases.

Now that the Karmapa's escape made him a geopolitical force, it was not difficult to fuel government skepticism. From the beginning officials treated the Karmapa like the political hot potato he certainly was. Slow to move under normal conditions, in a delicate situation that involves superpower China, Delhi became nearly paralyzed. Immediately after being informed about India's new, illustrious Tibetan guest, the Ministry of External Affairs sent Joint Secretary T.C.A. Rangachari to meet the Dalai Lama, but Rangachari refused to accept the Karmapa's letter requesting asylum. In it the Karmapa wrote:

"I was deeply distressed at being used as an instrument to further the campaign of Beijing to repress the freedom of our people and to undermine our genuine heritage and 'Dharma,' which is most dear to me, more than my own life. I found this unbearable, therefore I decided to flee from Tibet, knowing well that if I failed I would lose my life."[180] Eventually a letter from the Karmapa, stating his case to the prime minister of India and requesting asylum, was accepted by the prime minister's office several months after his escape. The Karmapa and his associates were extensively and repeatedly interrogated by Indian intelligence operatives from the Intelligence Bureau (IB) and Research and Analysis Wing (RAW). The government put off making any statements about granting full political asylum to avoid antagonizing China, but the Karmapa's presence was tacitly accepted. Popular support for granting the Karmapa asylum was reflected in the Indian media. It would have been unprecedented if India spurned him. So India appeared to operate on the principle that the passage of time might dissolve the embarrassing situation.

The Chinese, for their part, were restrained in spite of bringing up the Panchsheel Agreement between India and China that prohibits interference in each other's internal affairs. The press release about the letter left by the Karmapa was clearly damage control. The report by the official Chinese news agency *Xinhua,* dateline Beijing, January 7, 2000, that the Karmapa "left the Curbo [Tsurphu] monastery in Lhasa of Tibet not long ago together with a small number of people" was carefully worded. The Chinese language newspaper *Mingpao* (Hong Kong) reported at the same time: "[according to] information sources, the Beijing authorities have been furious after hearing the news. The Tibetan Public Safety Bureau is currently hastening to investigate the background and details of the Karmapa's departure. Belying the internal tension, Beijing is showing a relaxed face outwardly." The report stated that Beijing avoided using strong language against the Karmapa so as not to block his return and indicated they were secretly preparing "future attempts to lure him back."

Even after the Seventeenth Karmapa's first press conference at Gyuto Monastery in April 2001, where he made remarks that might well have affronted a sensitive Chinese government, the reaction was muted. A May 4, 2001, report by the Tibetan Information Network (TIN) notes: "China gave a measured response to the Seventeenth Karmapa's press statement, refraining from overt criticism but nevertheless cautioning him against attempts by 'anti-China forces to use him to split Tibet from the motherland.'" Chinese Foreign Ministry spokeswoman Zhang Qiyue said, "We are strongly opposed to anybody using Karmapa in conducting political activities aimed to split China, we hope Karmapa [will] not be fooled or taken advantage of by anybody," (April 29, PTI news agency). When asked to comment on the Karmapa's statement that he would return to Tibet only when the Dalai Lama also returned, Zhang simply said, "We have taken note of the remarks of the Karmapa." She declined to answer a question concerning the Karmapa describing Sikkim as an Indian state.

One unfortunate aspect of the Karmapa's escape is the disappearance of people suspected of helping him. At least one monk and a security guard were arrested and not much is known about their fate. The Karmapa's family, who were living in Lhasa, were moved back to their nomadic pastures in Lhatok, where they are kept under surveillance by the authorities. A visit by a maternal relative of the Karmapa, Namgyal Rongae, who claimed to represent the Chinese, painted a darker picture when he told the Karmapa's sister Ngodup Palzom in May 2000 that the authorities in Tibet would retaliate against the parents in an effort to get the Karmapa to return. The Karmapa refused to see him, and anyway security would not allow Rongae access. The Karmapa often expresses concern about his parents, saying that he greatly misses them.

Monks at Tsurphu were interrogated, security was tightened, and no new monks allowed to enter the monastery, according to reports by TIN. Those who are there were reportedly treated to "re-education" sessions and discouraged from studying and practicing their religion. The young Pawo Rinpoche, the first tulku recognized by the Karmapa and one of the most important Karma Kagyu tulkus, was taken from Nyenang Monastery and put in a Chinese school, apparently barred from receiving a traditional religious education.[181]

Radio Free Asia cited anonymous sources in Tibet and Dharamsala in a report that two of the Karmapa's personal attendants were apprehended in early 2002. The news prompted the Karmapa to publicly ask the Chinese to release them: "'I appeal to the Chinese government and the Tibetan Autonomous Region government that those arrested may be released quickly, and that they may be spared harsh treatment while in prison,' the Karmapa told RFA's Tibetan service. 'I am greatly disappointed and also worried,' he said. 'I escaped to pursue my religious studies and not to achieve political goals.'[182] Lama Tupten, the Karmapa's cook, was reportedly arrested while trying to escape to India, as was Lama Panam, a three-year retreat master, in Kham. Both monks upheld the ruse that allowed the Karmapa to escape in December 1999. Lama Nyima, the Karmapa's teacher, was also arrested in Kongpo. Lama Nyima had posed as the Karmapa and Lama Tupten cooked for him to buy time while the young lama made good his escape.

As months went by after the Karmapa's escape, his followers became restive over his continued detention at Gyuto. The stress of the sensitive situation with the Indian government heaped another burden on a group already troubled by nearly a decade of controversy. The Karmapa's escape seemed like a miracle, and the Karmapa's disciples felt that the power of his presence would eventually dissipate any obstacles. But this wasn't happening quickly enough. Meanwhile, Shamarpa gave interviews to the press and sent out PR people to promote his views with journalists and others. Shamarpa clung to his contention that Tai Situpa and other key Karmapa supporters were Chinese agents. He refers to Orgyen Trinley Dorje as the "Chinese Karmapa." When it became apparent that Orgyen Trinley Dorje was widely accepted as the Seventeenth Karmapa, he declared that he would accept two Karmapas, if his own candidate got Rumtek and Orgyen Trinley Dorje went back to Tsurphu. In interviews he has tried to imply that his nominee, Thaye Dorje, is not from Tibet, a fact that was documented even by the Shamarpa's own supporters when giving the boy's background.

In a *Hindustan Times* guest column written shortly after the Seventeenth Karmapa's escape, Shamarpa rejected the Dalai Lama's authority to confirm the Karmapa recognition and maintained that the Karmapa Trust "must hand over its assets to both the Indian and Chinese Karmapa when they are 21 years old. At that point the Karmapas themselves must decide who owns what property. Obviously, I added the caveat that the Chinese Karmapa must be an Indian to own property in India."[183] In the article he failed to mention his own ongoing efforts to gain legal control over the Karmapa Charitable Trust and thereby its assets.

Among some Karma Kagyupas there was suspicion that politicians within the government-in-exile were colluding with the Indian government to restrict the Karmapa's freedom. The Minister for Religious Affairs Tashi Wangdi was suspect, because he acted as the only liaison between the Tibetans and the Indian government on this issue. This arrangement was not his doing, however. The mechanism for dealing with the influx of Tibetan refugees through the Dalai Lama's government-in-exile was set up long ago. As an elected kalon, or minister, it was his job to act as liaison between the Tibetans in exile and the Indian government. Wangdi was stuck in the middle, having to respond to the demands of Indian bureaucrats while satisfying the needs of the refugees.

But there was the atavistic fear, rooted in ancient history and prejudices, that some people in the Dharamsala government did not want to see a rise of "Karma Kagyu power." At the same time the Karmapa and his supporters were very grateful for the Tibetan government's role as his protector and intercessor. They felt uncomfortable about the prolonged inconvenience to the Gyuto monks, who had their own monastery and monks' college to look after. However much some of his officials might be scrutinized, the Dalai Lama himself was a hero to all except the Shamarpa faction and the Chinese.

When interviewed, the Dalai Lama himself brought up "the gossip around town," as he put it. "One gossip is, 'Oh, Dalai Lama and Dharamsala administration, they want to control Karmapa and use for political matters.'" Another rumor was that the Sixteenth Karmapa and the Dalai Lama were on poor terms with each other, but this was not true, he said. "The late Gyalwa Rinpoche and I, personally, were always very friendly and trusted each other." But some people interpreted some of the Sixteenth Karmapa's decisions in a sectarian manner. The Dalai Lama said it is inaccurate to see it this way, noting that the Karmapa has his own Kagyu heritage and the obligation to preserve it. Referring to the ambitions and dissension of the Shamarpa he said, "The problems that we have with Karmapa Rinpoche are totally unrelated to any kind of sectarian problem." But troubling sectarianism is still an issue, decades after Tibetans fled Tibet.

When queried, Indian government officials indicated they have made no policy about where the Karmapa can stay, although they admitted that relocation of the Seventeenth Karmapa to Rumtek was sensitive and would have to wait for a while. The Karmapa himself has said he would like to go to Sherab Ling if he can't go to Rumtek, since it is the monastery of his teacher, Tai Situpa, from whom he must receive essential Karma Kagyu lineage transmissions. This option would afford him more breathing space while he awaits permission to go to Rumtek. The wooded hills above Bir, the spacious, secure rooms at the top of the monastery designed for his use, and the fact that it is a Karma Kagyupa monastery, would be much more pleasant for him. The Karmapa's chambers at Sherab Ling even feature a small Japanese-style garden. Certainly it would be more comfortable than the set of rooms that are allotted him at Gyuto, situated just off the main road. Visits from Sherab Ling to Dharamsala are easy enough when required. Gyuto monks would like to free up the space that has been occupied by the Karmapa and his entourage, as well. Nevertheless, even a short visit to Sherab Ling was denied him. The government has so far not budged on his confinement at

Gyuto. There has been discussion about moving him to another, government-approved location, but nothing has materialized as of this writing.

Whatever private agendas politicians may have for the Karmapa, his relationship with the Dalai Lama is one of warm affection and respect. They formed a very strong bond in a short time and appear to have a natural affinity. The Dalai Lama, in an interview in late 2000, expressed his sympathy for the Karmapa, a "young Tibetan boy who comes from a difficult situation" whom "we have a moral responsibility to look after." The Dalai Lama voiced concern about the attitude of the government of India. "Usually I describe it as overcautious." He said he feared that after coming out of Tibet "at great risk, with great expectation," that the implacability of the Indian government in allowing him normal freedoms will disillusion the Karmapa. "Theoretically speaking, this is a free country," the Dalai Lama went on, "He came to join with the rest of the Tibetan community here, to enjoy freedom completely." He addedthat he hoped it would not "demoralize and discourage." This is one reason for the special attention he has given the Karmapa from the beginning, he said. He wryly observed that in his experience, the Indian bureaucracy could be discouraging, everything goes so slowly. "Whatever we ask, that they will provide. But it takes time, so that when our request is fulfilled, then our enthusiasm is no longer there. That's the usual thing that happens," he said with a smile. The Karmapa's concern after escaping to India, only to be confined again, is understandable. The Dalai Lama added, "At some point even his human rights seem to be becoming an issue."

The Dalai Lama is cognizant of the Seventeenth Karmapa's potential as a Tibetan leader, at least in religious affairs. And this is one of the key issues that concerns Tibetans, too. "As far as I am concerned, my time—now noon is already past, isn't it? That is the reality. So we need some sort of preparation for what comes after me, at least in the field of spirituality," he said. He reiterated the importance of proper education for the Karmapa and a number of other young lamas who are his contemporaries and who will assume the responsibility of preserving Tibetan religious culture. Nothing must be left out of their education, which includes learning hundreds of texts, receiving the oral teaching, or transmission, of their lineages from elder masters, retreat, and meditation. "It takes time. So if he is fifteen years old, that means another twenty years."

Ideally, the Dalai Lama would like to see the political responsibilities of his own position handed over to a democratically elected Tibetan government, allowing lamas to focus on religion. "I think their main responsibility is to build a happy society, a peaceful society. They should not create more divisions," he laughs. This separation of church and state is a big departure from what Tibetans were used to in old Tibet. It has raised controversy among Tibetans in exile, too, some of whom oppose the Dalai Lama's progressive reforms. Other Tibetans fault the Dalai Lama for not being radical enough after he ceased demanding independence for Tibet in favor of genuine autonomy. Many young Tibetans look up to the Karmapa, are inspired by his courage, and see him as one who might carry on the standard of Tibet when the Dalai Lama is gone.

Questions about the Karmapa's authenticity are dismissed by the Dalai Lama. The Dalai Lama observed, "Officially right from the beginning we recognized Orgyen Trinley Dorje, and now he himself is showing some great potential." It is firmly believed by the Dalai Lama and others that the exceptional qualities of genuine tulkus will naturally manifest, regardless of the situation. As far as the Karmapa being a Chinese plant, the Dalai Lama reiterated, "One hundred percent I trust that Gyalwa Rinpoche (Karmapa) came as a genuine refugee, came with high spirits. Not that China allowed him to come. There is no basis to suspect these things. On Shamar Rinpoche's side, he creates that kind of impression, that he (Karmapa) is sent by China." He continued, "Truth is extremely precious. At the international gathering here of Karmapa followers, I told them my own experience of the strength of truth, the power of truth, over the last forty-one years. Some rumors, some accusations, some differences, some previous conflict, but if oneself is truthful, honest,

248

open, then these things will disappear." The Dalai Lama speaks warmly of the young Karmapa, and the two meet about once a week when the Dalai Lama is in Dharamsala.

After thirteen months of isolation at Gyuto Monastery, surrounded by security and repeatedly questioned by intelligence operatives, the Karmapa was at last officially given "refugee status" by the Indian Government.[184] The declaration was made shortly after the visit of China's premier Li Peng to India. Although there was speculation that the Karmapa issue would figure in conversations between the Li Peng and the Indian officials, nothing was made public. Not only was the Karmapa officially allowed to stay on as a refugee—terming it "political asylum" was studiously avoided by the government, but picked up by others—he was at last allowed to move about, albeit under restrictions. He has made several pilgrimages to Bodhgaya and got as close to Rumtek as Calcutta. All his trips must be sanctioned by a battery of bureaucrats.

The Seventeenth Karmapa's daily life is a quiet one. Gyuto Monastery is located off the main drag of Sidhabari, a village situated on the green, fertile agricultural land below the Dauladar Range. In winter the mountains behind the monastery are dusted with snow. The monastery is built on land that rises toward the mountains. The Karmapa stays on the upper floor of the pale yellow residential wing behind the main audience hall. Yellow is a color traditionally associated with Buddhist monks. He takes his exercise on the roof. His disciplined daily life is confined to about 1,200 square feet. He rises early to pray and eat breakfast before spending a few hours with his tutors. His first *puja* of the day is to Green Tara, the female bodhisattva who brings good fortune and fulfillment. At 11 A.M. the Karmapa usually devotes an hour to audiences with carefully screened visitors in his private sitting room. Some visitors are local disciples, some are from far away. Quite a few Sikkimese have made the long journey to see him, and they remain impatient for him to settle in Rumtek Monastery, where they believe he belongs. Tibetans newly arrived from Tibet visit the Karmapa. So do foreigners from other parts of Asia and the West. Many Indians

touring the Dharamsala area come to seek his blessing. Local
bureaucrats and politicians stop by. There are regular visits from
Indian intelligence agents, his watchers, some of whom stay at
the monastery. Three or four police are always present, some
armed with machine guns, and a guard paces around the circum-
ference of the building day and night. Interviews with the
Karmapa are usually brief and formal, likely to be interrupted.
Journalists who want to tape an interview must go to the local
police station to get permission to use a tape recorder or camera.
Most of his public conversations are monitored by police, who
stay in the room during interviews. At noon the Karmapa has
lunch followed by some rest time. Several times a week he gives
a mid-afternoon public audience in the main shrine hall, a routine that was established in the months after his escape. He deliv-
ers a short Buddhist teaching and prayer before he retires
upstairs to resume his study.

At sunset the Karmapa does Mahakala puja, sometimes with
his monks, sometimes alone. Mahakala, the great protector of
the Karma Kagyu, is a daunting manifestation of the bodhisattva Chenrezig, blue-black in color, who often appears with his
consort Palden Lhamo, arms flailing, implements of war in
hand, visage distorted in challenge, surrounded by a field of
bright red-orange fire. Evening Mahakala prayers are required of
the high lamas and anyone who is seriously leading the spiritual
life because Mahakala is deemed the most effective remedy
against the toughest obstacles to spiritual practice. Since he
began practicing debate, the Karmapa's early evenings are spent
defending philosophical arguments in the traditional stance,
mala swinging, hands clapping as he steps forward to make a
point. Otherwise his evenings are devoted to more study and
prayers.

Most of the Karmapa's companions are much older lamas, in
their thirties or older. Drupon Rinpoche, the eldest son of the
late chandzo, Damchoe Yongdu, stays with the Karmapa most
of the time. Tai Situpa, Gyaltsap Rinpoche, and Thrangu
Rinpoche also come to stay and teach him. The people who
came out of Tibet with him are there, as are his elder sister

Ngodup Palzom and his personal attendants. Some of these are old retainers from Rumtek Monastery. A number of his companions are well-educated and well-traveled monks.

One of them, Lama Tenam Shastri, translated for me during one of my interviews with the Karmapa for this book, shortly after the Karmapa's escape. Lama Tenam is an old friend, and between questions I made a joke in English at which the Karmapa laughed. He obviously understood it because he began to comment on what I said—in Tibetan. Lama Tenam said afterward that it seemed he did understand it. At the conclusion of his first press conference, he read a short statement in English, and he appears interested in learning the language. Perhaps the most striking thing about the Karmapa is what a well-integrated contradiction he is. He behaves and speaks like a sage when called upon, quite cognizant of situations, but then suddenly the teenager peeks out, interested in teenage things. He might shyly ask a question and smile. A favorite pastime is playing with his little dog Dekyi, a beige puff ball of mixed Shih Tzu and Apso ancestry. He also has a tame cockatoo who struts on a perch outside his door, a gift from Gongkar Rinpoche.[185]

Partly because the Karmapa is tall for his age and has that remarkable, penetrating gaze, and because he responds to questions so astutely, it is hard to view him as merely a boy. Even as a child of eight he had a powerful personality, which has only become more self-confident with age. His moods can be like thunder at times, and when he is angry, everyone—even the high lamas—tread lightly. After all, his strong will and tenacity got him out of Tibet. He is decisive and not one to vacillate. While maintaining the compassionate view, he is also realistic. His response to the Shamarpa is typical. The Karmapa told me that while he respects the Shamarpa as a lama of the Karma Kagyu lineage, "He has done some wrong things, and it is hoped he will one day have an awakening to what he has done." He added, "It is not just a question of saying he's sorry, but there must be sincere resolve in his heart."

Not long after the Indian government told the Karmapa he could stay in India, they gave the green light for him to go on a pilgrimage in March 2001. Coming down to Delhi for the first time since his harrowing escape, he was met by government officials, among them Chief Minister of Sikkim Pawan Chamling. It was commonly believed in Sikkim that Shamarpa had backed Chamling's election campaign so as to get even with Nur Bahadur Bhandari, the incumbent who supported the Karmapa's recognition. But politics are politics, and, as Chief Minister Chamling told me when I met him in Gangtok in April 2000, most of his Sikkimese constituents want the Seventeenth Karmapa Orgyen Trinley Dorje to be installed in Rumtek, and he wants that, too. "Whatever the Dalai Lama says, I respect."

He later approached Indian Prime Minister Vajpayee with a request to allow the Seventeenth Karmapa to settle at Rumtek. This irked the Shamarpa, who attacked Chamling in a letter, saying bitterly, "Now when I analyse the whole episode incorporating the incidents of the past, it makes me come to the conclusion that you are the one behind everything, just like you had done in the past. It was in fact you who sent out rumours hand in hand with the joint action committee. You chose to be behind the scene." He added, "I would like to refresh your memory on how you had mentioned that the monks ousted from the Rumtek monastery could go back when you formed the government in Sikkim. But contrary to what you said, when the monks tried to go in, the police on your orders lathi-charged186 on them." He further accuses Chamling, "Your trip to New Delhi in December and then your recent statement that Ugyen Thinle [Orgyen Trinley] should be installed in Rumtek—all these lead me to the conclusion that the trip to New Delhi was in fact to get a handsome amount of money since that is the only good reason I see why you made the statement."[187]

More recently Chamling has expressed fears that the protracted delay in allowing the Karmapa to come to Sikkim could cause escalation of agitation among his constituents who want Karmapa Orgyen Trinley Dorje to be installed at Rumtek. Bringing the Seventeenth Karmapa to Rumtek would also stem the tide of false claims to his spiritual throne. Besides the candidate set up by the Shamarpa, a Sikkimese man, born in 1977, four years before the previous Karmapa died, has repeatedly tried to get into Rumtek and sit on the Karmapa's throne. The man, Dawa Zangpo Sherpa, claims the late Jamgon Kongtrul recognized him.

In the Karmapa's first significant excursion outside Gyuto since his escape from Tibet, he spent less than a day in Delhi, but he made good use of the time. He met and was photographed on the Radisson Hotel balcony with Chief Minister Chamling. He also met former cabinet minister and members of parliament Ram Jethmalani and Buta Singh. Jethmalani is a well-known lawyer who championed the cause of Tai Situpa after the disinformation campaign began against him and opposed the ban order. He also supported the Karmapa's request for asylum. The Karmapa, at their meeting, was quoted as saying, "I have come to see my devotees and followers all across India. We want to especially meet the devotees in Sikkim, which is a state of India."[188] It was a fairly shrewd remark for a fifteen-year-old, perhaps calculated to put Indian government suspicions at rest. It certainly was at odds with the Chinese view of Sikkim.

Leaving the politicians behind, the Karmapa went to his chief tutor Thrangu Rinpoche's monastery in Saranath, near Varanasi, to spend Tibetan New Year. Tibetan New Year, or *Losar*, is a festive occasion that may last from three days to two weeks, depending on how much time people have on their hands. In the days preceding Losar, rituals are done to purify all the evils of the previous year. A twenty-four-hour Mahakala puja is done beginning the week before Losar. Lama dances are held at important Kagyu monasteries during which the most agile monks don colorful brocade costumes and masks, enacting the purification puja. The high points are when the tantric master, in his wide, tall hat and Mahakala apron, vanquishes all obstacles, and when the "deer" breaks into his exuberant dance. The impurities are symbolized by a black figure made from roasted barley flour, which is in pieces by the end of the ritual. On Losar, "new-moon day" itself, people from the local community travel to the monastery to meet the high lamas and then return home to party all day.

From Saranath the Karmapa progressed to Bodhgaya, to visit the site of Buddha's enlightenment. Bodhgaya has a certain magic, like a jewel in a cesspool. Bihar is one of the most backward states of India, with great poverty, crime, and intercaste violence. Gaya, the nearest city, is a dirty place where taxi drivers refuse to drive the twelve kilometers to Bodhgaya at night because of the bandits who rob and kill along the road. But Bodhgaya exists in a kind of bubble of sanctity and peace, full of devotees who are there to perform a religious duty. Many have come from across the world at great sacrifice to be there. There is a hush around the Mahabodhi Stupa as the devout circumambulate and pray before statues that are carved and mounted on the walls of the temple. Voices are raised in muted prayer, mantras are recited, prostrations are done as the devotees pay homage. Some of the statues are plastered with layers of gold leaf, frequently renewed by affluent Buddhists. The tangy, fresh scent of Tibetan incense floats in the air, mingled with the smell of thousands of butter lamps that burn in and around the temple. The holiest place is where the Buddha is believed to have sat and attained enlightenment under the Bodhi tree. A descendant of that original tree grows there still, dropping its leaves on the surrounding lawn. Many famous Buddhist teachers spent time here, including Atisha, who helped establish Buddhism in Tibet. Previous Karmapas visited Bodhgaya, too. Now it was the turn of the Seventeenth Karmapa, Orgyen Trinley Dorje, to be a pilgrim at this most sacred of Buddhist spots.

Upon the Karmapa's return to New Delhi he was welcomed at two official ceremonies, one a civic welcome and the second a "felicitation" sponsored by the Joint Action Committee of Sikkim. This group energetically supports the Karmapa's return to Rumtek, opposes the claims of Shamarpa and his followers, and lobbied against the order banning Tai Situpa's entry to India.[189] Committee members made the long trip from Sikkim in a mood of celebration, joined by several other Buddhist groups from Ladakh, Himachal Pradesh, and Delhi. They offered a statement of felicitation and appreciation to the Karmapa, along

The Karmapa
looking off
into distance
from the roof
of Gyuto.
(Photo by
Tenzin Dorjee)

with other eminent guests. The Karmapa responded with his
own carefully chosen words and gave a short initiation. The next
day, several thousand people attended an initiation the Karmapa
gave at the Buddha Jayanti Park.

After a few days in Delhi the Karmapa returned to Gyuto,
where he rested before setting out for the sacred lake Tso Pema
(Rewalsar), the place where legend says Guru Rinpoche and his
princess consort Mandarava meditated. On the way the
Karmapa stopped at the Tibetan school in Bir, which is near
Sherab Ling Monastery. The principal of the school pointed out
Sherab Ling in the distance. It was the closest the Indian government would allow the Karmapa to get to his teacher's
monastery.

By this time the Karmapa was a regular item in the press. Not
long after he completed his first pilgrimage, the Karmapa's name
inexplicably appeared on a hit list found on three alleged mili-
tants of the Pakistan-based Jaish-e-Mohammed group, gunned
down in Lucknow in April 2001. Other names on the list of
strange bedfellows were Priyanka Gandhi, the granddaughter of
Indira Gandhi, and Ashok Singhal, a Hindu extremist leader.[190]
Threats against the Karmapa are possible, although Pakistan is
not the expected source of them. Alleged Chinese spies are rou-

tinely apprehended in various parts of India. It is relatively easy for them to sneak in with Tibetan refugees.

Amid this tangle of intrigue, there is clearly a debate going on within the Indian establishment. Mavendra Singh, son of the former foreign minister Jaswant Singh, wrote an op-ed piece for *The Hindustan Times* with the kicker "Our intelligence agencies insist that the Karmapa is a Chinese agent. This is ludicrous."[191] Singh says, "It is not the job of the intelligence agencies to make policy, let alone try an influence it through clandestine techniques. This, unfortunately, is what some in the intelligence fraternity are trying to do vis-à-vis the Karmapa." Singh challenges their theory that the Chinese were complicit in his escape, declaring, "The intelligence agencies should let him be. It is not for them to decide who is right for the seat at Rumtek—only Tibetans will determine that."

The debate continues, and the Karmapa remains sequestered, only occasionally being let off his leash by the Indian government, and not to visit his preferred destinations. The Indian government allowed his pilgrimage in 2001, and a shorter trip to Calcutta in 2002, another pilgrimage to Bodhgaya in 2002, and one in early 2003 to attend the Dalai Lama's Kalachakra initiation, but by and large, the Karmapa is forbidden to travel. The usual reason is "security" or he must wait until "his papers" are issued, "which could take some time," in Indian bureaucrat-speak.

Hemmed in by ironies and tight security, the Seventeenth Karmapa is nonetheless growing into adulthood under the guidance of the teachers who are so essential for him to fulfill his life's work. Almost all high lamas of all four lineages are now outside Tibet. The Karmapa had to leave Tibet to receive the direct transmission from his own Karma Kagyu lamas. That is his primary task right now.

The Shamarpa and his group, including Ole Nydahl's followers, still promote the story that Tai Situpa colluded with the Chinese on the Karmapa's recognition. Shamarpa continues to air his accusation that Tai Situpa forged the recognition letter. The Shamarpa's vitriol against the Dalai Lama has steadily increased. He denies that the Dalai Lama has any role in recognition of tulkus outside his own Gelug lineage or, indeed, as political leader of Tibet. Members of the Shamarpa's group continue to file cases in any courts that will admit them, naming the Dalai Lama, along with Tai Situpa and Gyaltsap Rinpoche, as "anti-national" elements. Since the plaintiffs produce no evidence of crime, these cases are generally thrown out. In June 2000 the Shamarpa met the Dalai Lama in Washington, D.C. He handed the Dalai Lama a letter asking him to accept his candidate, Thaye Dorje, as a second Karmapa, "to see the wisdom of this compromise and accept it." But the Dalai Lama would not compromise the truth and rebuffed his request.[192] The Shamarpa faction formed the International Karma Kagyu Forum to continue the barbs against the Karmapa and the Dalai Lama, whose interference, they charged at a Kathmandu meeting in March 2001, was responsible for splitting the Karma Kagyu school. Tibetans do not seem to take these contentions seriously. They continue to hold the Dalai Lama in the highest regard and flock to the Karmapa's teachings and initiations wherever they are given. In any case, Tibetans are only too well aware of the politics of reincarnation. As learned Tibetan masters maintain, a genuine tulku will distinguish himself, or herself, regardless of letters, portents, politics, and opportunity. The Seventeenth Karmapa Orgyen Trinley Dorje gives indications of doing just that.

The link between the Karmapa and the Dalai Lama, and those others who are close to him, are relationships developed over time—since the young tulku was discovered in Tibet, or perhaps over centuries, depending on how you look at it. Tibetans see it as a long-term relationship spanning lifetimes. The young Karmapa pledges to support the Dalai Lama. "I regard it as my duty and responsibility to support the religion and culture of Tibet as much and as vigorously as I can," he says. This can only be dissonant music in China's ears. Both the Dalai Lama and Karmapa have speculated, with who knows what deep source of information, that circumstances may soon change in China. The Karmapa, demurring when asked if he would replace the Dalai Lama, merely asserts, "I do not plan to return to Tibet until the Dalai Lama returns. I will go back with him."

With the emergence of the Seventeenth Karmapa into the international spotlight, the culture and politics of Tibet have made an impact unimaginable a few decades ago. He is now on the verge of adulthood. And while he may be a religious figure with no real political aspirations, he might play a role similar to his predecessors, who often smoothed political tensions. In former times the parties to the conflicts mostly involved Tibetan clans and warlords, and occasionally a Chinese emperor. In today's world the stakeholders are bigger, more powerful: not only Tibet but China and its neighbors. Could this poised young man be an instrument toward future resolution of the problems between China and Tibet? And how will he integrate the growing exchange between East and West? It will certainly be interesting to watch.

Appendix 1

THE BLACK CROWN CEREMONY

THE RITUAL THAT HAS become the trademark of the Karmapas since the Fifth Karmapa, Dezhin Shekpa (1384–1415), is the Black Crown Ceremony, sometimes called the Vajra Crown Ceremony. It is believed that the First Karmapa Dusum Khyenpa (1110–93), after attaining realization of the "beyond meditation" level of mahamudra practice, was presented with a spiritual crown by dakinis. It was a black, indestructible *(vajra)* crown woven from the hair of these celestial beings and was an inner insignia of the Karmapa's accomplishment. This vajra crown was only visible to those whose insight was refined enough to perceive the supernatural. Karmapa Dezhin Shekpa's disciple, the emperor Yung Lo, was such a person. When he saw the mystical crown on his guru's head, he wanted others to share in the blessing, so he commissioned a material crown to be made in its likeness. Since that time the Karmapa has performed a ceremony during which he displays this Black Crown, or *usha,* in public.

The Black Crown Ceremony links the mystical and material world for believers. It may be performed in a shrine room or outside. The ritual itself is simple. The gyaling horns blow as the Karmapa enters and takes his seat on his high throne, followed by his attendant carrying the cylindrical, brocade-upholstered box that contains the crown. Some short, preparatory prayers are said by the monks. The attendant approaches with the crown, his mouth covered to prevent polluting breath from wafting over this sacred object. The parts of his hands in contact with the box are likewise covered so as not to touch it directly. He offers it to the Karmapa. The Karmapa takes off the gold brocade "Gampopa Hat" that he customarily wears to this ceremony and puts it aside. He removes the Black Crown from its box and unwraps the protective covering. As soon as he does this, the gyaling horns begin to blow. He then places the crown on top of his head, holding it with his right hand, while he tells the beads of a crystal mala in his left hand. He repeats the mantra of the bodhisattva Chenrezig, *Om mani peme hung,* and gazes straight ahead, serenely. He may sit, motionless except for the clicking beads, for ten minutes or more, as the gyalings continue uninterrupted. When he is finished, he rewraps the crown, replaces it in its box and the gyalings cease. The ceremony concludes with prayers to dedicate the merit for the benefit of all beings.

Pious Tibetan Buddhists believe that during this ceremony the Karmapa actually transforms himself into the bodhisattva of compassion, Chenrezig. Witnessing a Black Crown Ceremony is thought to bring tremendous merit to the devout, even severing links to lower rebirths and speeding progress toward enlightenment.

There were two crowns at Tsurphu when the Sixteenth Karmapa fled in 1959, the original dating from the fourteenth century and a copy made a hundred years or so ago. Only one crown was brought out of Tibet by the Karmapa and is now at Rumtek Monastery in Sikkim. The other is presumed to have been destroyed during the Cultural Revolution.

KARMAPA INCARNATIONS

Dusum Khyenpa (1110–93)
Karma Pakshi (1206–83)
Rangjung Dorje (1284–1339)
Rolpe Dorje (1340–83)
Dezhin Shekpa (1384–1415)
Tongwa Donden (1416–53)
Chodrak Gyatso (1454–1506)
Mikyo Dorje (1507–54)
Wangchuk Dorje (1556–1603)
Choying Dorje (1604–74)
Yeshe Dorje (1676–1702)
Jangchub Dorje (1703–32)
Dudul Dorje (1733–97)
Tekchok Dorje (1797–1869)
Khakyab Dorje (1871–1922)
Rangjung Rigpe Dorje (1924–81)
Orgyen Trinley Dorje (1985–)

Appendix 3

INCARNATIONS OF THE FOUR HEART SONS

SHAMARPA INCARNATIONS

1	Drakpa Senge (1283–1347)
2	Khacho Wangpo (1350–1405)
3	Chopal Yeshe (1406–52)
4	Chokyi Drakpa (1453–1524)
5	Konchok Yenlak (1525–83)
6	Chokyi Wangchuk (1584–1630)
7	Yeshe Nyingpo (1631–94)
8	Palchen Chokyi Dondrup (1695–1732)
9	Konchok Jungne (1733–40)
10	Mipam Chodrup Gyatso (1741–92)

Recognition banned by Tibetan government in 1792.
(Privately acknowledged:)

11	Jamyang Rinpoche (1892–1946)
12	Trinley Kunkhyab (1948–50)

(Recognition allowed, 1964:)

13   Chokyi Lodro (1952–)

TAI SITUPA INCARNATIONS

1   Chokyi Gyaltsen (1377–1449)
2   Tashi Namgyal (1450–97)
3   Tashi Paljor (1498–1541)
4   Chokyi Gocha (1542–85)
5   Chokyi Gyaltsen Palzang (1586–1657)
6   Mipam Chogyal Rabten (1658–82)
7   Nawe Nyima (1683–98)
8   Chokyi Jungne (1699–1774)
9   Pema Nyingje Wangpo (1775–1854)
10   Pema Kunzang Chogyal (1854–85)
11   Pema Wangchuk Gyalpo (1886–1953)
12   Pema Donyo Nyingje Wangpo (1954–)

JAMGON KONGTRUL INCARNATIONS

1   Lodro Taye (1813–1901)
2   Khyentse Ozer (1904–53)
3   Lodro Chokyi Senge (1954–92)
4   Lodro Chokyi Nyima (1995–)

GYALTSAPA INCARNATIONS (DATES APPROXIMATE)

1   Goshir Paljor Dondrup (1427–89)
2   Tashi Namgyal (1490–1518)
3   Drakpa Paljor (1519–49)
4   Drakpa Dondrup (1550–1617)
5   Drakpa Choyang (1618–58)
6   Norbu Zangpo (1659–98)
7   Konchok Ozer (1699–1765)
8   Chopal Zangpo (1766–1820)
9   Drakpa Yeshe (1821–76)
10   Tenpai Nyima (1877–1901)

11   Drakpa Gyatso (1902– 53)
12   Drakpa Tenpai Yaphel (1954–)

Kagyu tulkus whose associations with the Karmapas date back centuries include Pawo Tulku, Chogyam Trungpa, Sangye Nyenpa, Dzogchen Ponlop, Kalu Rinpoche, Akong Tulku, Traleg Rinpoche, Dabzang Rinpoche, Tenga Rinpoche, and Dzongsar Khyentse Wangpo. Dilgo Khyentse Rinpoche is of the Kagyu and Nyingma lineages and has been closely associated with the Karmapas in the past.

NOTE: Dates for Karmapas, Shamarpas, and Tai Situpas are from Hugh Richardson; Goshir Gyaltsap from E. Gene Smith; Kongtrul from Kongtrul Labrang.

Appendix 4

I am happy to set foot on the soil of India, a free country, the birthplace of many great world religions including mine, Buddhism. I am happy to breathe the air of freedom in the land of the Buddha, where freedom of religion is highly and truly cherished. India has been the refuge of H. H. the XIVth Dalai Lama since he fled Tibet to escape the persecution of the communist regime of China who took over Tibet, followed by tens of thousands of Tibetans including my predecessor, the XVIth Karmapa, Rangjung Rigpe Dorje.

India has given shelter and refuge to all of them with tremendous love and sacrifice. I am confident that the people of India and the Government of India will accord to me the same refuge with love and compassion. I fled from my motherland Tibet with a heavy heart. I have left behind hundreds of followers, devotees and friends including my very dear parents. I am not abandoning the people of Tibet and the people of China. I have sincere affection for all of them. I had to take this decisive action as part of my religious duty as the XVIIth Karmapa. The duty lies upon me as the "Karmapa," whose responsibility is to uphold the teachings and the unbroken linage of Lord Buddha in general and of the Kagyu school of Tibetan Buddhism in particular.

In Tibet I was placed under constant surveillance, which made it impossible for me to practice Dharma and perform my religious duties freely. In many situations and on many occasions I was used to distort and falsify historical truths about Tibet, my heritage, and my religion. I was forced to condemn H.H. the XIVth Dalai Lama and denounce the genuine causes for which many individuals have sacrificed their lives—"freedom" and a free Tibet where people can practice their religion and culture and continue the their heritage with human dignity.

I was deeply distressed at being used as an instrument to further the campaign of Beijing to repress the freedom of our people and to undermine our genuine heritage and Dharma, which is most dear to me, more than my own life. I found this unbearable, therefore I decided to flee from Tibet, knowing well that if I failed I would lose my life.

My companions, including my sister and myself, are fully responsible for our actions. No one should be held responsible for our undertaking except us.

In the past, Karmapas have never engaged in any political activity, therefore I sincerely follow in their footsteps. As far as the future of Tibet and the Tibetan people is concerned, I fully endorse and support everything that "Avalokiteshvara," H.H. the XIVth Dalai Lama, stands for, based on universal love and compassion, as the supreme leader of Tibet and the champion of world peace, human rights, and all the lineages of Buddhism.

[Translation by Tashi Tsering]

Glossary

Amitabha Buddha—The "Buddha of Limitless Light," who embodies the completely purified faculty of discrimination, and is the focal point of one of the five "buddha families." Each of these families personifies the purified state of one of the five "aggregates," or five senses, that must be transformed to achieve enlightenment.

Black Crown—A unique hat worn only by the Karmapa tulkus, it signifies advanced spiritual attainment. It is said to be a material copy of a spiritual crown woven from the hair of celestial beings called dakinis. A Black Crown Ceremony is performed by the Karmapa during which he displays this ancient crown on his head while reciting a mantra and, it is believed, transforming himself into the actual embodiment of the bodhisattva of compassion.

Bodhisattva—An individual highly advanced on the path of enlightenment who has dedicated his or her existence to liberate all sentient beings from suffering. There are at least ten grades of bodhisattvahood, all of which must be attained before buddhahood is realized.

Bon—The animistic religion that was practiced in Tibet at the time Buddhism was introduced and which is thought to have greatly influenced the evolution of Buddhism there. It still is practiced by a small number of Tibetans, who are called *Bonpos.*

Buddha—A Sanskrit term meaning "enlightened" or "awakened," it denotes one who has gone beyond the limitations of duality and illusions such as ignorance, attachment, aversion, pride, and so forth to realize the completely purified wisdom and compassion of "buddha mind." It also refers to the historical Buddha who lived circa 500 B.C. and whose philosophy is the basis of the Buddhist religion.

Buktam Rinpoche—The letter of approval issued by the Dalai Lama that confirms the recognition of a tulku, or incarnate lama.

Chandzo—Chief administrator of a Tibetan monastery, usually translated as "general secretary," it is the most powerful post in the monastery. The high lama or abbot is the only person with more power than the chandzo. The chandzo is essentially the treasurer, the most trusted person, who handles the money and ensures there is enough to support the monks and any projects undertaken by the high lama.

Chenrezig—The bodhisattva of compassion, perhaps the most popular entity invoked by Tibetan Buddhists, and the patron bodhisattva of Tibet. Buddhists meditate upon the attributes of Chenrezig. Recitation of the bodhisattva's mantra, *Om mani peme hung,* is universal among devout Tibetans. Both the Dalai Lama and the Karmapa are believed to be emanations of the consciousness of Chenrezig.

Chogyal—"Dharma king" in Tibetan, it is the title of the kings of Sikkim.

Cycle of Rebirth—*Samsara* in Sanskrit, it is the round of existence in which suffering is perpetuated for countless numbers of lifetime, due to habitual patterns and the consequences of past actions *(karma)*. The conditions that cause this bondage are meticulously detailed in Buddhist texts, as are the means of freeing oneself from it. The goal of Buddhism is to be liberated from endless rebirth and follow the Buddha's path to enlightenment.

Dakinis—Female celestial beings, analogous to angels, who assist other beings along the path to enlightenment by setting tests and giving guidance to the seeker.

Dharma—This Sanskrit term has a number of meanings, but it is commonly used in Tibetan Buddhism to signify the body of Buddhist teachings, which are considered pure and true guides to transformation. It is one of the three objects in which a Buddhist "takes refuge," a formal act and commitment that signifies faith in Buddhism.

Doha—An inspirational verse, originating spontaneously after realization of profound truths, recited by certain realized masters as a means of teaching or expressing devotion.

Dzogchen—Translated usually as "Great Perfection," it is the core teaching of the Nyingma school of Tibetan Buddhism and is considered by them as the highest path to enlightenment.

Garchen—A "great encampment"; the Karmay Garchen was the famous nomadic, tented monastery in which the Karmapas ceaselessly traveled around Tibet as they ministered to the faithful. The tradition ceased when the Sixteenth Karmapa fled Tibet in 1959.

Gelug—One of the four schools of Tibetan Buddhism, it is the most recent, founded by Tsongkhapa in 1409. It emphasizes scholarship and monasticism. Its name means "followers of virtue." Most Gelug lamas are monks. The Dalai Lamas have traditionally been associated most closely with the Gelug tradition.

Gyaling—A short Tibetan horn used for rituals, it is traditionally blown when the Karmapa enters his monastery or the shrine room to perform a ceremony. Gyalings are blown during the most sacred part of the Black Crown Ceremony performed by the Karmapa.

Gyalwa Rinpoche—Meaning "victorious precious gem," it is an honorific name used by many Tibetans to refer to the Karmapa. Only a very high lama may be called this. Another name used for the Karmapa by devotees is Yizhin Norbu, or "wish-fulfilling gem," an epithet for the bodhisattva Chenrezig.

Hinayana—One of the "three vehicles" of Tibetan Buddhism, it means "small vehicle," and emphasizes individual enlightenment, in contrast to the Mahayana, which emphasizes enlightenment for the benefit of all beings. Methods of attaining the end are similar, and it is the motivation that distinguishes the two paths of practice. The Vajrayana refers to the tantric path that emphasizes a swift path using specific yogic practices outlined in the tantras but with the same motivation as the Mahayana.

Kadampa—Once a distinct school of Tibetan Buddhism founded by the eleventh-century scholar Atisha, it focuses on applying ideals of compassion in daily life. Its tenets are incorporated into the four extant schools, but are given particular emphasis by the Gelug school. The Gelug sect was founded upon Kadampa principles.

Kagyu—One of the four main lineages of Tibetan Buddhism, it traces its origin to the Indian mahasiddhas Tilopa and Naropa. It was brought to Tibet by Marpa the translator. It utilizes methods from the sutras and tantras, and its core practice is mahamudra.

Kalon—A cabinet minister in the Tibetan government. The Tibetan government-in-exile preserves this post, although the Dalai Lama has striven to introduce democratic reforms, and the kalons are now elected rather than appointed. Ministers are also called *zhabpe*.

Kangyur—A collection of Buddhist sutras and tantras translated into Tibetan from Indian sources. With the Tengyur, it makes up the Tibetan Buddhist canon.

Karma—The doctrine of cause and effect: actions result in consequences that may manifest in a future life or over a number of lives during the cycle of rebirth. Negative actions create negative conditions in the life of the individual, and positive actions create fortunate circumstances. The impact of negative, "bad" karma may be lessened or dissolved through purification practices.

Karmapa—The incarnate lama who heads the Karma Kagyu lineage of Tibetan Buddhism. There have been seventeen incarnations of this lama, whose monastic seat is Tsurphu in central Tibet. His seat in exile is Rumtek, in Sikkim, India. Twenty-one Karmapa incarnations have been predicted.

Karma Kamtsang—The name by which the Karmapa's branch of the Kagyu lineage is commonly known.

Kashag—The governing council of ministers or cabinet of the Tibetan government.

Labrang—The administrative body that manages the monastery. It can also refer to the "household" of a high lama. The labrang is usually headed by the chandzo, or "general secretary."

Mahamudra—A Sanskrit term meaning "great seal," it is the core practice of the Kagyu lineage. The term refers to the attitude that all phenomena have relative and ultimate natures, and deepening realization of the ultimate nature of all things leads to liberation. It is done through systematic practices that establish a ground of understanding, a path of action or practice, and the fruition or result. It is also practiced in the Gelug lineage.

Mahapandita—A Sanskrit term meaning "great scholar," such as those who greatly distinguished themselves at the Buddhist universities of India. Some of these sages, e.g., Shantarakshita, Atisha, and Kamalashila, traveled to Tibet and were instrumental in establishing Buddhism there.

Mahasiddha—A Sanskrit term meaning one who has great spiritual accomplishment, usually for those who have achieved such high levels of realization that they can perform miracles.

Mahayana—The "great vehicle," one of the three vehicles of Tibetan Buddhism, distinguished by its emphasis on generating compassion for others and aspiring to enlightenment for the benefit of all sentient beings as well as oneself. The attitude differs from the Hinayana focus on enlightenment for oneself alone.

Maitreya—A bodhisattva who is the embodiment of loving kindness, and who is said to be the coming buddha, i.e., the next buddha who will manifest on earth. So far four buddhas of the predicted thousand buddhas have entered this world. Maitreya Bodhisattva will be the fifth.

Mandala—Literally, it means a wheel and is depicted as such in Tibetan and Indian art. Mandalas may be either conceptually understood or symbolically portrayed on tangkas, sand paintings, or three-dimensional structures made from various materials. They are linked to specific aspects of enlightened mind as embodied in particular buddhas or bodhisattvas. Mandalas representing the entire cosmos are traditionally offered at the beginning of teachings, tantric practices, and pujas, and the practice of offering 100,000 mandalas is also one of the preliminaries to extended tantric retreats.

Mantra—Sacred syllables that are uttered to protect or focus the mind. A mantra is thought to be purified speech of enlightened beings, and each bodhisattva has a particular mantra; e.g., *Om mani peme hung* is the mantra for Chenrezig. Usually mantras are short, although special practices sometimes employ long mantras, such as the hundred-syllable mantra of Vajrasattva, the buddha of purification.

Mara—A Sanskrit term for negative influences, sometimes personified as a devil of sorts.

Mudra—A Sanskrit term for "gesture," usually referring to ritualized hand postures.

Nyingma—The oldest school of Tibetan Buddhism—its name literally means "old" in Tibetan. It was founded by Padmasambhava and follows the tantric tradition brought to Tibet by masters in the earliest days of Tibetan Buddhism.

PLA—People's Liberation Army of China

Pundit—Native Indians employed by the British as explorers and spies in remote areas on the periphery of India such as Afghanistan, Turkistan, and Tibet during the years of the Great Game, in the late nineteenth century. They often posed as Buddhist pilgrims, using rosaries and prayer wheels to camouflage their surveying equipment.

Refuge—The first step in becoming a Buddhist is "taking refuge" in what are considered the only three reliable objects of refuge, the Buddha, the Dharma, and the Sangha, i.e., the enlightened masters, the teachings, and the teachers and companions on the spiritual path.

Regent—In the Tibetan monastic system, a lama who is responsible for the property and other assets of an incarnate lama in between incarnations or during the lama's childhood.

Rimé—A renaissance period in nineteenth century during which eminent scholars, led by Jamgon Kongtrul Lodro Taye, Jamyang Khyentse Wangpo, and Chogyur Lingpa, worked to preserve and integrate the sacred teachings of all schools of Tibetan Buddhism. Palpung Monastery in Derge, Kham, was the epicenter of the activity. Rimé is characterized by its non-sectarian approach.

Rinpoche—This is a Tibetan honorific meaning "precious" and is used for high lamas, somewhat in the way "reverend" might be used in English for a clergyman. "Rinpoche" is usually reserved for incarnate lamas or lamas who distinguish themselves as spiritual masters.

Sakya—One of the four schools of Tibetan Buddhism. It grew out of Sakya Monastery founded in the eleventh century by Khon Konchok Gyalpo. Sakya means "grey earth," descriptive of the terrain surrounding the monastery, and leadership of the lineage is passed along through members of the Khon family. Sakya Monastery had the most renowned library in Tibet, and it historically produced many great scholars.

Samaya—It is the Sanskrit term for a solemn vow or sacred oath, and it refers to the relationship between a guru and disciple. Breaking it is a serious matter that can cause a setback on the path toward enlightenment.

Tangka—A Tibetan scroll painting, usually depicting religious themes or figures such as buddhas, bodhisattvas, and saints.

Tantra—Tantra is often misunderstood in the West because of the symbolic sexual imagery that is associated with it in Tibetan art. In Tibetan Buddhism tantra has two meanings: the texts that describe the practices for purifying body, speech, and mind leading to enlightenment and the actual utilization of these methods in a continual application in practical life. Ordinary body, speech, and mind with attendant conflicting emotions are utilized as tools of transformation into ultimate mind, realization of enlightenment.

Tashi Lama—Another name for the Panchen Lama, historically the most powerful Gelug lama after the Dalai Lama. His monastic seat is Tashilhunpo Monastery in Shigatse.

Tengyur—The part of the Buddhist canon that comprises the commentaries by early Indian masters on aspects and practices of Buddhism. The Kangyur, which contains what are believed to be the actual teachings of the Buddha recorded after his death, and the Tengyur together consist of hundreds of volumes and represent the scripture that was translated into Tibetan from Indian texts.

Terma—A "hidden treasure"—a teaching or revelation believed to have been hidden by the tantric master Padmasambhava or his disciples, meant to be discovered at the appropriate moment in the future. These may be actual objects or texts, or they may be in the form of visions or inspirations that will benefit others.

Terton—Typically an incarnate lama in the Nyingma tradition who is a "treasure finder," believed to have been a disciple of Padmasambhava, and who returns to discover hidden texts or objects deemed helpful for spiritual progress. Tertons sometimes occur in other lineages, but the Nyingmapa are most noted for termas and tertons.

Tisri—A vice-regent appointed by the Mongol Khans between 1247 and 1358 through which the Khans attempted to extend their influence into Tibet. The first tisri was Sakya Pandita, and thereafter heads of Sakya succeeded to the title, until it became defunct. The Mongol hegemony as represented by the tisri was not universally accepted in Tibet.

Tukdam—The state of meditation into which an accomplished yogi enters at death. Traditionally it lasts for three days or more, during which time the body may remain seated in a meditation posture, with perceptible warmth around the heart and a lifelike look to the skin, even though vital signs are absent.

Tulku—The Tibetan term for incarnate lama, literally translated as "emanation body" (Skt. *nirmanakaya*). The first recognized tulku was the Second Karmapa, Karma Pakshi. It is believed that the consciousness of the same spiritually advanced being repeatedly incarnates to perform good deeds for the benefit of all sentient beings. Tulkus are recognized in a number of ways, most of these mystical: predictions left by the former incarnation, as is usual with the Karmapas, visions and dreams or meditational experiences of high lama associates, certain forms of divination, including oracles, and testing the candidates themselves. Besides the Karmapa, the Dalai Lama and Panchen Lama are other well-known tulkus. There are hundreds of tulkus among the various schools of Tibetan Buddhism.

Usha—The Karmapa's Black Crown.

Vajradhatu—The name of the main hub of the Buddhist centers founded by Chogyam Trungpa Rinpoche in the United States. Satellite centers are called Dharmadhatu centers.

Vajrayana—The "diamond" or "adamantine vehicle," it relies on special yogic practices outlined in the tantras to attain spiritual realization. Techniques of mahamudra, which focuses on purifying the ground, the path, and the fruition, are Vajrayana methods. It is regarded as the fastest and most difficult path to enlightenment.

Vinaya—The rules of behavior and discipline for monks and nuns as set down in Buddhist scripture.

Wheel of Life—A graphic depiction of the cycle of existence *(samsara)* incorporating all the elements of illusion that perpetuate suffering and impede progress toward liberation. These include delusion, attachment, and aversion represented by a pig, a bird, and a snake in the center; the "twelve links of dependent origination," which entice sentient beings into the bonds of karma; the "six realms of existence," including the hot and cold hells, hungry ghost *(preta)* realm, animal realm, human realm, god realm, and warlike demigod *(asura)* realm that are portrayed in a wheel held in the jaws of Yama, the lord of death. The wheel of life is customarily painted near the entrance of monastery shrine rooms as a reminder of the condition of suffering sentient beings.

Notes

1. *Yabse,* or heart son, is a term used to refer to a Tibetan lama's closest disciples. The Sixteenth Karmapa is said to have had six heart sons, four of whom play major roles in the story told in this book: Shamarpa, Tai Situpa, Jamgon Kongtrul, Gyaltsapa, Pawo Rinpoche, and Treho Rinpoche.

2. "It is proper that you have doubt, that you have perplexity, for a doubt has arisen in a matter which is doubtful. Now, look you Kalamas, do not be led by reports, or tradition, or hearsay. Be not led by the authority of religious texts, nor by mere logic or inference, nor by considering appearances, nor by the delight in speculative opinions, nor by seeming possibilities, nor by the idea; 'this is our teacher.' But, O Kalamas, when you know for yourselves that certain things are unwholesome and wrong and bad, then give them up...And when you know for yourselves that certain things are wholesome and good, then accept them and follow them." From the *Kalama Sutra,* translated in Walpola Rahula, *What the Buddha Taught* (New York: Grove, 1974).

3   *Prisoners of Shangri-la* by Donald S. Lopez, Jr. (Chicago: University of Chicago Press, 1999) chapter 3.

4   For more on the history of Westerners' perceptions of Tibet, including Donald Lopez's account of T. Lobsang Rampa, see *Imagining Tibet: Perceptions, Projections, and Fantasies*, ed. Dodin and Räther (Boston: Wisdom Publications, 2001).

5   *Awakening the Sleeping Buddha* (Boston: Shambhala, 1996); *Relative World, Ultimate Mind* (Boston: Shambhala, 1992).

6   Interview with Lea Terhune, Dharamsala, April 2000.

7   Interview with Lea Terhune, Dharamsala, July 7, 1993.

8   *Newsweek* noted the incident in "China's Balkan Crisis," by Melinda Liu, April 19, 1999: "The sense of conspiracy and intrigue in China's Tibetan communities grew last summer when three intruders, allegedly Chinese, reportedly tried but failed to assassinate the 14-year-old Karmapa."

9   Details of the escape are based largely on interviews with Nenang Lama done by Lea Terhune in February 2000.

10   Some Tibetan lamas dislike the term "sect" because of its cultish connotations in English. They frequently point out that, as far as Buddhist teachings are concerned, there is virtually no difference between the lineages.

11   The suffix "-pa" is added to Tibetan words to indicate a person. Thus, a person from Kham is called a Khampa, and an adherent of the Nyingma school is called a Nyingmapa.

12   Richardson, Hugh E., *Tibet and Its History* (London: Oxford, 1962) chapter 2.

13   Goldstein, Melvyn C., *A History of Modern Tibet, 1913–1951* (Berkeley: University of California, 1989) introduction.

14   *Ibid.,* p. 21.

15   *Ibid.,* p. 34.

16   *Dalai* means ocean in Mongolian, a reference to "ocean of wisdom," a common designation for enlightened beings.

17   *An Account of Tibet: The Travels of Ippolito Desideri 1712–1727*, ed. Fillipo de Fillipi (London: Routledge & Sons; reprinted Delhi: AES, 1995) p. 171.

18   *Ibid.,* p. 157.

19   Richardson, p. 90.

20 Equivalent to ambassador.

21 Goldstein, p. 36.

22 Shakya, Tsering, *The Dragon in the Land of Snows* (New York: Columbia, 1999) p. 5.

23 Goldstein, p. xxii.

24 Shakya, chapter 7.

25 *Ibid.*

26 *Jataka Tales,* ed. Francis & Thomas (Bombay: Jaico, 1987) p. 77.

27 Choephel, Gendun, *The White Annals,* trans. Samten Norboo (Dharamsala: Library of Tibetan Works and Archives, 1987) p. 20.

28 Büton Rinpoche, cited by Charles Bell in *The Religion of Tibet* (Oxford: Clarendon, 1931) p. 41.

29 *The Life of Marpa the Translator: Seeing Accomplishes All,* by Tsang Nyon Heruka, trans. Nalanda Translation Committee (Boulder: Prajna, 1982) p. 10.

30 The teachings given to Naropa by Tilopa are enshrined in Tibetan Buddhism as the "Six Yogas of Naropa." They are the core teachings of the Karma Kagyu. Another branch, the Shangpa Kagyu, preserves the "Six Yogas of Niguma," named for Naropa's consort. She became his peer in realization after receiving the transmission of Tilopa's teaching.

31 *The Life of Marpa,* p. 18.

32 *The Teachings of Don Juan: A Yaqui Way of Knowledge,* by Carlos Castaneda, published in 1968, was the first in series of books that describe an apprenticeship to the sorcerer Don Juan that included tests, tricks, and object lessons. Castaneda was an anthropologist at UCLA who said he met Don Juan while researching his doctoral thesis on Mexican medicinal herbs.

33 *The Life of Marpa,* p. 37.

34 *The Life of Milarepa,* trans. Lobsang P. Lhalungpa (London: Granada, 1979) p. 41.

35 *The Hundred Thousand Songs of Milarepa, Vols. I and II,* trans. Garma C.C. Chang (Boulder & London: Shambhala, 1977).

36 *The Life of Milarepa,* p. 43.

37 *The Rain of Wisdom,* trans. Nalanda (Boston: Shambhala, 1980) pp. 241–42.

38 *Garuda VI,* ed. Chogyam Trungpa Rinpoche (Berkeley: Shambhala, 1976).

39 Other accounts credit the Second Karmapa, Karma Pakshi, with beginning the tradition, and the Drikung Kagyupas claim that the recognition of tulkus began with their branch of the Kagyu.

40 Namkhai Norbu is a Nyingma tulku who was born in 1938 in Derge, Kham, and has lived and taught for many years in the West. Since 1964 he has been a professor of Oriental Studies at the University of Naples, Italy. He is an author and travels widely to lecture. He knew both the previous Tai Situpa and the previous Karmapa. He related this anecdote in an interview given to Lea Terhune, January 13, 1993, in New Delhi, India.

41 The Eleventh Situ, Pema Wangchuk Gyalpo (1886–1952).

42 There were two main lines of the Kagyu school, the Shangpa and Marpa. Both lines came from Naropa, but the Shangpa came via Naropa's consort Niguma. In recent years, the Marpa Kagyu is sometimes referred to as Dagpo (Takla Gampo) Kagyu after Gampopa, who was known as "the man from Dagpo," the place where he meditated and first attracted attention as a teacher. It is this lineage that branches into "four great and eight lesser" schools. The four were the Karma Kagyu—also called the Karma Kamtsang—the Pagdru, the Tsal, and the Baram Kagyu. The eight lesser schools all derived from the Pagdru Kagyu.

43 *Awakening the Sleeping Buddha,* by the Twelfth Tai Situpa, ed. Lea Terhune (Boston: Shambhala, 1996) p. 155.

44 The usual practice in the Kagyu tradition starts with calming the mind through simple techniques, such as watching the breath, and progressing to insight meditation, which stimulates deeper levels of realization. Then follows contemplation on the chief factors that turn the mind from harmful toward positive thoughts and actions: the preciousness of human life; impermanence and death; action and result; and so on. All these derive from Hinayana practices. After calm and insight have been stabilized, there follows the meditation of "sending and receiving" in which generation of compassion

for others is the goal, a mainstay of Mahayana practice. After this, the Vajrayana practices to purify and transform the body, speech, and mind, called the "four foundations," may be undertaken. These must be completed before any deeper levels of Vajrayana mind training and meditation may be attempted.

45 The chief sources of information in this chapter are *The History of the Sixteen Karmapas of Tibet* by Karma Thinley (Boulder: Prajna, 1980) and the writings of Hugh Richardson.

46 Thinley, p. 43.

47 Thinley, p. 45.

48 This capital, where Kublai Khan built his palace Khan-Balik and the first Forbidden City as a sanctuary of Mongol culture in China, is now greatly transformed and subsumed into modern Beijing. The third Ming emperor Yung Lo, who figures later in the Karmapa story, destroyed Kublai Khan's complex and relocated the Forbidden City to where it now stands.

49 Polo, Marco, *The Travels* (London: Penguin, 1958) pp. 110–12, 173–74, 182–83. Healing oracles are men and women who are believed to have the gift of contacting the spirit world and the ability to channel that power to heal, to predict the future, or to answer questions while in a trance. Such oracles may still be found in places like Ladakh. The Dalai Lama has his own State Oracle who is consulted on important matters, including the recognition of tulkus.

50 This relationship between Sakyapas and the Mongol Khans was important in the evolution of theocratic political power in Tibet. According to Tibetan accounts, Godan Khan, grandson of Chengis Khan—he was son of Chengis' third son Ogodoi—appointed Sakya Pandita viceroy, or *tisri,* of Tibet. A few years later, around 1251, both Godan Khan and Sakya Pandita died. Power moved from Godan Khan's branch of the family to the sons of his brother Tolui when Mongke Khan was chosen Great Khan. Sakya Pandita's nephew Pakpa, who first came to Mongolia as a child with his uncle, was astute enough to shift loyalties to the new ruling branch

by attaching himself to Kublai Khan, Mongke's younger brother. He thereby safeguarded the Sakyapa's position beside the Khans. A forceful teacher, Pakpa became spiritual advisor to Kublai Khan. And like his uncle, Pakpa was appointed tisri, with viceregal authority over the whole of Tibet. Upon Pakpa's death, the title devolved upon another head of Sakya. Kublai Khan went on to become emperor of China, founding the Yuan dynasty. The Mongols used the Sakyapa tisri as a political pipeline to Tibet for nearly a hundred years. It was a convenient means for the Mongols to exercise overlordship of Tibet. As years went on the Sakyapa hegemony was increasingly resented by the lay nobility and was ultimately deposed.

51 Richardson, Hugh E., "The Karma-pa Sect: A Historical Note," *Journal of the Royal Asiatic Society* (October 1958), 139–64; (April 1959), 1–18.

52 Douglas, Nik, & White, Meryl, *Karmapa The Black Hat Lama of Tibet* (London: Luzac, 1976).

53 Richardson, "The Karma-pa Sect: A Historical Note."

54 "Karmay" is the possessive form of Karma: "Karmay Garchen" means "the Karmapa's great encampment."

55 Thinley, p. 66.

56 Richardson, "The Karma-pa Sect: A Historical Note." Richardson wrote about them at some length and later obtained a copy of the Tibetan text from the Sixteenth Karmapa. As Richardson comments, "Although De-bzhin gshegs-pa's [Dezhin Shekpa's] visit and its extraordinary occurrences are well documented in Tibetan and Chinese sources, the imperial confirmation of a series of miracles warrants quotation in full." Richardson did so, and provides the translation in an appendix to his essay.

57 Thinley, p. 75.

58 Richardson, Hugh E., *High Peaks, Pure Earth,* ed. Michael Aris (London: Serindia, 1998) p. 351.

59 Shakabpa, Tsepon W. D., *Tibet: A Political History* (New York: Potala, 1984).

60 Thinley, p. 129.

61 The five precepts of lay ordination are not to kill, lie, steal, use intoxicants, or indulge in sexual misconduct. Children are often given these vows in the monastery but must repeat them as adults if they choose to continue the monastic life.

62 Tsering, Tashi, "A Biographical Sketch of the Sixteenth Karmapa," *Tibetan Review*, August 1992, pp. 14–17.

63 Interview with Dalai Lama given to Lea Terhune, Dharamsala, July 7, 1993.

64 Dukhen Sungjonma temple at Pangpug Monastery, Litang.

65 Wangmo, Dorji, *Of Rainbows and Clouds: The Memoirs of Yab Ugyen Dorji* (Thimphu: Ashi Dorji Wangmo Wangchuk, 1997).

66 Tsering, "A Biographical Sketch."

67 *Ibid.*

68 *Freedom in Exile: The Autobiography of the Dalai Lama* (New York: HarperCollins, 1990).

69 Namkhai Norbu interview, *ibid.*

70 Interview with H. H. Dalai Lama, given to Lea Terhune in Dharamsala, July 7, 1993.

71 *Om mani peme hung.*

72 Thinley, p. 135.

73 Copy of text and translation courtesy of Department of Religion and Culture, Central Tibetan Administration of H.H. Dalai Lama.

74 Kornman, Robin, "The Visit of His Holiness the Gyalwa Karmapa to the United States," *Garuda IV*, ed. Chogyam Trungpa Rinpoche (Berkeley: Shambhala, 1976).

75 For more on Smith's legacy and work, see E. Gene Smith, *Among Tibetan Texts: History and Literature of the Himalayan Plateau,* (Boston: Wisdom Publications, 2001).

76 Interview with Clemens Kuby in *Living Buddha,* Condor Films, 1993.

77 Although sometimes six *yabse,* or heart sons, are spoken of, four played prominent roles in the events surrounding the recognition of the Seventeenth Karmapa. Other important Karma Kagyu tulkus are Pawo Tulku, Sangye Nyenpa, Karma Thinley, Chogyam Trungpa, Khenchen Thrangu Rinpoche, Dabsang Rinpoche, Traleg Rinpoche, and Jamyang

Khyentse Wangpo. Dzogchen Ponlop Rinpoche is a Nyingma tulku but has had a close relationship with the Karmapas.

78 Birth in a pious family, with access to a genuine spiritual guide, being neither too rich nor too poor, and having the means to perform good deeds are all features of a precious human birth.

79 *Awakening the Sleeping Buddha,* by the Twelfth Tai Situpa, (Boston: Shambhala, 1996) p. 79.

80 Nydahl, Ole, *Riding the Tiger* (Nevada City, CA: Blue Dolphin, 1992) chapter 11.

81 It is a custom that is thought to have developed as a result of the disinclination of those who knew the Karmapa to be responsible for any violence done to him, even his dead body.

82 *Nectar of Dharma,* Kagyu International Newsletter, vol. I, no. IV (1981–82)

83 Conversation with Dzogchen Ponlop Rinpoche at his house at Rumtek, February 1993.

84 Ashi Chokyi was the daughter of King Jigme Wangchuk, the second king of Bhutan, by his second wife. She is an aunt of the current and fourth king, Jigme Singye Wangchuk.

85 Sources within the Karmapa's labrang who were there at the time maintain that the Karmapa appointed him reluctantly, and only after assiduous pressure from Topga Yugyal, who wished to upgrade his social status. Although Topga was married to a princess he had no rank of his own, so could not be called by the honorific *dasho,* the title of Bhutanese noblemen, nor could he wear a distinctive *kamne,* or scarf, as part of his Bhutanese national dress.

86 The late chandzo offered me that hospitality when I arrived in October 1982. Before coming I had volunteered to do some write-ups to help with fundraising for the Delhi project during my stay. I met him during the few days I spent at Rumtek in November, when the Sixteenth Karmapa's shrine room was dedicated, but there was very little time to discuss brochures. He said I should familiarize myself with the Delhi project and he would be more specific about what he wanted when he came to Delhi in December. I was awaiting his return to Delhi when the news came of his death.

87 The seven original trustees of the Karmapa Charitable Trust were Rai Bahadur Tshi Dadul Sensapa, Ashok Chand Burman, Gyan Jyoti, Sherab Gyaltsen, Thuncheo Yangdu, Jewon Takpoo Yondu, and Gonpo Namgyal.

88 In 1983, following the death of the Karmapa and Chandzo Damchoe Yongdu, a document was filed updating the trust to include new trustees (Athing Rai Bahadur Densapa, Topga Rinpoche, Yangthang Kazi Sonam Wangchuk, Passang Tsering, Dechhang Lodey Dawa, Dungchhe Tenzing, and Dr. Urgyen Jigmee) and a "council of seat holders" consisting of the four heart sons, who would administer the Karmapa's monasteries "until a new incarnation is consecrated and until He attains the age of 18 years."

89 *The Lama Knows: A Tibetan Legend is Born,* R. B. Ekvall, (Novato, CA: Chandler & Sharp Publishers, 1981) introduction.

90 *Tibet: In Search of a Miracle* (New York: Nyack College, 1985).

91 The male pronoun here reflects the historical reality that tulkus have been overwhelmingly male.

92 There is an exhaustive and interesting study of these protectors, *Oracles and Demons of Tibet,* by R. de Nebesky-Wojkowitz (Mouton: 's-Gravenhage, 1956). The author himself came to an unfortunate end, in an accident, and there are those who say that his detailed exposure of the previously secret hierarchies of protector spirits may have contributed to his early demise. Such spirits are believed to have powers that can work both ways, for well or for ill, and for that reason they are not to be tampered with—or even named, in some cases.

93 Batchelor, Stephen, "Letting Daylight into Magic: The Life and Times of Dorje Shugden," *Tricycle,* Spring 1998. The article is part of an extensive examination of "Tibet's 'Unmentionable' Feud" in the cited issue, which includes "Two Sides of the Same God," by Donald S. Lopez, Jr., and interviews by Lopez of Geshe Kelsang Gyatso, the UK-based teacher who spearheads the pro-protector movement, and of Thubten Jigme Norbu, elder brother of the Dalai Lama.

94 There is often confusion about red-, yellow-, and even white-hatted sects. Here the "zhanagpa," black hat lama, and

"zhamarpa," red hat lama, refer to two specific tulkus and lines of tulkus.

95 Sources for this chapter include Richardson, Thinley, Shakabpa, Nik Douglas, and other histories cited elsewhere in the text.

96 Markham, Clements R., *Narratives of the Mission of George Bogle to Tibet and the Journey of Thomas Manning to Lhasa* (Delhi: AES, 1999).

97 Shakabpa, Tsepon W. D., *Tibet: A Political History* (New York: Potala, 1984) chapter 10.

98 *Ibid.,* chapter 10.

99 Shakabpa; Richardson.

100 The current Shamarpa, previously known as the thirteenth, has in recent years called himself "His Holiness the Fourteenth Shamarpa" on his letterhead and his Web site. Strictly speaking, he is the eleventh Shamarpa to be officially enthroned. Any other incarnations who may have been born between 1792 and 1964, when the Dalai Lama lifted the ban, were not recognized except informally and confidentially.

101 Based on notes from conversations with the Shamarpa between 1980 and 1984.

102 The Derge king, for reasons inexplicable to many Khampas, ceded Derge to the Lhasa government. Subsequently governors were installed there by the Central Tibetan government.

103 Shakya, Tsering, *Dragon in the Land of Snow,* chapter 6.

104 The Tibetan name for Padmasambhava is *Pema Jungne.*

105 In the introduction by E. Gene Smith to *The Autobiography and Diaries of Si-tu Pan-chen* (New Delhi: International Academy of Indian Culture, 1968).

106 This story is told by some of Tai Situpa's elderly attendants, who were young men when the previous Tai Situpa was alive.

107 Bon was never eradicated in Tibet, and it survives alongside Buddhism today. There are even some Bon monasteries in exile: in Dolanji near Solon in Himachal Pradesh and in Kathmandu. Its practices are reminiscent of Nyingma Dzogchen, though the names of the pantheon of deities and

color scheme differ. Bonpos are partial to blue, where red and yellow are the colors preferred by Buddhists.

[108] Pandit, Tooshar, "Gold-Running: The Royal Way," *Sunday Magazine*, July 11–17, 1982.

[109] Although some monks lived there, the property was actually more of a palace than a monastery.

[110] I observed some of this, because Topga Yugyal's Calcutta lawyer, Samir Roy Chaudhury, when he was in Delhi, showed the document he had written to Karma Damdul and I. Both Karma and I remarked on the fact that the other regents names were not mentioned as signatories, as might be expected. We assumed that the other rinpoches knew about it, but when it was mentioned to Jamgon Kongtrul, he told me they had not been aware of it. Letters were exchanged, and the four rinpoches had a meeting in Darjeeling—where most of them had gathered to take the Rinchen Terdzo initiations from Kalu Rinpoche—to hash it out. Shamarpa denied he was trying put the property in his name, and Chaudhury wrote a letter indicating it was a misunderstanding. Nevertheless, Shamarpa was very angry, and when he returned to Delhi he kept asking us who told the other rinpoches about it. I didn't volunteer anything, and Jamgon Rinpoche refused to tell him how he found out about it. We had no idea it would precipitate such recriminations among the four tulkus.

[111] From conversation with Tai Situpa at Sherab Ling, 2001.

[112] These are an equivalent to a master's and doctorate of divinity in a Western context. The program linking the shedra to Sanskrit University foundered while Shamarpa presided over the shedra but was later reestablished.

[113] Translation from the Tibetan as reproduced in the booklet *Karmapa Khenno: A Sikkimese Point of View*, by Ani Dechen Zangmo, 1994.

[114] Letter dated September 1, 1991, signed by officers of the Tibetan Religion and Cultural Protection and Development Association, The Derge Friendship Society.

[115] Interview with Goshir Gyaltsapa, Rumtek, May 27, 2000.

[116] *Sikkim Observer*, "Void in Rumtek," May 23, 1992.

[117] From a transcript of a talk given by Tai Situpa and Goshir Gyaltsapa, May 1992.

[118] the expanse of all phenomena

[119] "The land of snow" is how Tibetans sometimes refer to central Tibet.

[120] Lhatok, the Seventeenth Karmapa's birthplace means "divine thunder" or, in the poetic language of the text, "sky iron" *(namchak)*.

[121] Bakor, the actual site of the birthplace, means "cow place."

[122] Method is symbolic for father and wisdom for mother.

[123] Refers to the Wood Ox year.

[124] Refers to the sacred conch shell, which is blown as a horn.

[125] The name of the current Tai Situpa is Pema Donyo Nyingje Wangpo.

[126] Translated by Michele Martin.

[127] Interview with Ngodup Palzom by Lea Terhune, Gyuto Monastery, April 27 and 30, 2001.

[128] Michele Martin's notes.

[129] Interview with Clemens Kuby, Dharamsala, October 13, 1992.

[130] Reuters, June 28, 1992.

[131] Transcript of a tape of the English speech given by Shamarpa at Rumtek on June 9, 1992. I heard the speech at Rumtek when it was given and witnessed the events recounted.

[132] *The Living Buddha,* a film by Clemens Kuby.

[133] *Karmapa Khenno: A Sikkimese Point of View.* Atuk reiterated this account to me in 1993.

[134] *Sikkim Observer,* "Army entry in Rumtek Monastery provokes violence," by Jigme N. Kazi, June 20, 1992.

[135] The order in which security forces are deployed in India is very explicit. First the state armed police intervene during civil unrest. If they cannot contain it, the Central Reserve Police Force are called in. Next in line is the Border Security Force. Only after that would the army be deployed. Such military intervention is reserved for serious civil unrest such as the militancy in Kashmir or the northeast states, election violence in Bihar, or relief operations after massive earthquakes, but hardly for squabbles between lamas in a monastery.

136 In an interview of Chief Minister Nur Bahadur Bhandari by Lea Terhune at Mintokgar, the chief minister's residence, Gangtok, February 22, 1993, he said, "When I was in distress, because of the Sikkim merger (with India), I was the saddest man. So I used to go to Rumtek to call on His Holiness Karmapa, and he always made the worries in my mind subside." Visibly moved, he added, "I was dependent on him because of his wide thinking. That was why I started helping his establishment after the formation of my government."

137 Signatories included Tai Situpa, Goshir Gyaltsapa, Urgyen Tulku Rinpoche, Beru Khyentse Rinpoche, Thrangu Rinpoche, Bokar Rinpoche, Dzogchen Ponlop Rinpoche, Sangye Nyenpa Rinpoche, Surmang Garwang Rinpoche, Chokyi Nyima Rinpoche, Lopon Tsechu, Dzogdzi Jetrung, Tutop Tulku, Nendo Tulku, Drupoeng Rinpoche, Dilyak Drupon Rinpoche, and lay representatives. Some of these lamas later became ambivalent about their support of the recognition or outright backers of the Shamarpa. Among the strong pro-Shamarpa lamas are Lopon Tsechu from Nepal, Nendo Tulku, and Beru Khyentse.

138 Letter from Shamarpa, May 1992.

139 Interview with Lea Terhune, Dharamsala, July 7, 1993.

140 Nydahl, Ole, *Entering the Diamond Way: My Path Among the Lamas* (Nevada City, CA: Blue Dolphin, 1985); *Riding the Tiger* (Nevada City, CA: Blue Dolphin, 1992).

141 *Riding the Tiger,* p. 134.

142 A qualified lama is one who successfully completes the three-year, three-month, and three-day meditation retreat, and who passes the tests of his or her expertise in the practices at the end. It is a title that is earned by hard work, or by being born a tulku—or both. Even tulkus are expected to complete their course of studies before they are fully launched as teachers.

143 This term was later translated by Hannah as "Buddhist Master," which is misleading. The term is applied to discussion group leaders who are like teaching assistants to the teaching lama. The Tibetan *(skyor dpon)* literally means "leader of repeating."

144 *Riding the Tiger,* p. 111.

145 *Ibid.,* p. 239

146 *Ibid.,* p. 163

147 Kalu Rinpoche gave the *Rinchen Terdzo,* which lasted nearly six months. It is a once-in-a-lifetime occasion, and was attended by all the major Karma Kagyu tulkus with the exception of the Shamarpa, who left a few days after it began.

148 Eighth in Tibetan reckoning.

149 For ordination to take place there must be a fully qualified *gelong* preceptor, i.e., one who has taken the full number of greater and lesser vows of monkhood. There must also be a specified number of other fully ordained monks present. There are three levels of vows: *genyen,* which involves taking the basic lay precepts of not to kill, steal, lie, indulge in sexual misconduct, or take intoxicants; *getsul,* which is the partial ordination taken by young monks; and *gelong* ordination, a serious commitment taken usually after a monk achieves majority, and requires the taking of 253 precepts, including those of genyen and getsul.

150 TIN News Update, June 27, 1992.

151 *China's Tibet,* Spring 1993.

152 Translated by Kalon Tashi Wangdi.

153 Oracles are believed to access information by allowing familiar spirits to possess them. In the Tibetan tradition oracles are most often consulted for healing, and many are believed to have healing powers when in the grip of a trance. They may speak in strange languages. Here the oracle refers to Palden Lhamo, the great protectress, and Zugme is the spirit speaking through him.

154 The Palpung Monastery abbot, Khenpo Juno Dawa, gave an exposition of the Buddha's teaching on the Perfection of Wisdom. Adi Rinpoche, of the Drukpa Kagyu monastery Tsechu and traditional spiritual advisor of the Nangchen king, gave a short teaching on body, speech, mind, knowledge, and activity. Khenpo Lodro from Bokar Gonpa and Sonada spoke on the prayer to Manjushri, the bodhisattva of wisdom.

155 The important Gelug monasteries, Ganden, Sera, and Drepung, the Jokhang, the Potala, and Tashilhunpo; offerings were made by Sakya and Ngor monasteries, Talung Kagyu, Drukpa Kagyu, and Drikung Kagyu; Nyingma monasteries like Dorje Dra Mindroling made offerings, followed by Bon monasteries such as Menji Gonpa. The Karma Kamtsang monasteries of Tsurphu, Palpung, Kamchin Gonpa, and Karma Gon concluded the offerings from monasteries within Tibet. More came from outside of Tibet, from Pullahari, Thrangu Gonpa, and Swayambhu in Nepal and Sonada in India.

156 The publisher of *The Karmapa Papers,* when queried about the identity of the authors, replied in a letter: "The people who did the work on the Karmapa Papers do not prefer to be publicly known probably due to the controversy that has been involved." Translator Kiki Eskelius' name appears in the book as a contributor.

157 *The Return of the Karmapa: Two American Buddhists examine the recently published compilation called "The Karmapa Papers,"* by Karma Tendzin Namgyal and Karma Dondrup Chogyal (New York: Green Horse Press, 1993).

158 *Karmapa: The Sacred Prophecy* (Wappinger's Falls, NY: Kagyu Thubten Choling Publications Committee, 1999).

159 *Samaya* is the sacred vow binding guru and disciple that is a Vajrayana commitment. It is believed that to break this commitment by doubting or doing anything detrimental to the lama, or the lama to the disciple, results in severe karmic consequences.

160 *Nata* has several meanings: relation, protector, and nephew among them.

161 Translated by Michele Martin, 1992.

162 Interview, 1993.

163 "Taiwan PM's mystery Sikkim visit rings alarm bells," by K. Govindan Kutty, *Indian Express,* January 8, 1994, run at the top of the front page, was the first of a series of articles based on the erroneous claim in the headline. In fact, a cabinet minister and Karmapa devotee, Li-An Chen, had made a

private visit. This was fashioned into a tale of political intrigue. The article provoked a letter to the *Indian Express* from Li-An Chen's lawyer David J. W. Liu of Tsar & Tsar Law Firm, Taipei, Taiwan, objecting to "the inaccuracies and unfounded speculations provided in the article." Liu clarified that the visit was private and corrected other errors. But articles continued to run: "A red-faced Govt lies low on Chen Li affair," January 30, 1994, and "And now, a French connection thickens Sikkim plot," January 28, 1994, or "Taiwan minister's foray into Sikkim takes queer turn," February 28, 1994. All the articles present a murky political nexus between then Sikkim chief minister Bhandari, the Chinese, and the lamas who recognized the Seventeenth Karmapa, chiefly Tai Situpa. The contention was made on the basis of few facts and many innaccuracies.

[164] Sikkim is a relatively minor state of India. Its significance where New Delhi is concerned comes from the short stretch of border it shares with China. India has long been concerned about Sikkim as a sensitive border area. Since the McMahon line was drawn in 1916 the India-China relationship has been an uneasy one. After India's independence, China failed to respond to Nehru's idealistic policy of a new, united Asia. India allied with the Soviet Union and China sided with Pakistan during the Bangladesh war. There were Indo-Chinese border skirmishes and, in 1962, a war. The sore points were bits of territory along the mountainous borders of Ladakh and Arunachal Pradesh, remote places with names like Aksai Chin—places of little practical use to India. Exchanges of fire have occurred at Natu-la, the pass that separates Sikkim from Tibet, most memorably for six days in September 1967 and on October 1st of the same year at Chola. These border skirmishes are known in India as the 1967 Indo-Chinese War.

After 1947, Sikkim became a protectorate of India, a role inherited from Britain, which never acknowledged Sikkim as an independent kingdom as it did Nepal and Bhutan. The relationship dated back to a treaty signed between the British and Sikkim in 1817, after the conclusion of a war with Nepal.

The treaty returned territories to Sikkim that had been confis-cated by the Nepalese, but it also gave Britain extensive pow-ers over Sikkim. This suited the British, who saw Sikkim as an excellent sentinel post from which to observe and, they hoped, develop relations with Tibet. The Great Game was starting up. British presence did not suit all of the Chogyals, however. When the British failed to honor a lease agreement for the "gift" of Darjeeling, the Sikkimese imprisoned two Britons, an official and a botanist. They were later released, but this gave the British the excuse they needed to confiscate Darjeeling and cease making payments to the Sikkimese king. There were bad feelings all around, and when a new Chogyal reigned, the British resumed paying the subsidy for Darjeeling to regain favor with him. Sikkim was too important for estab-lishing coveted trade links to Tibet. A British political officer was installed in 1889, and Sikkim remained a protectorate of Britain until Independence.

The 1947 treaty between independent India and Sikkim put foreign affairs and defense in the hands of the larger country, while the Chogyal remained monarch. There were also some provisions for greater popular participation in gov-ernment. Sikkim was subsequently made an "associate state." But in 1973 India dispensed with formalities when civil distur-bances caused the king to ask for the Indian army to preserve law and order. "The policy makers in Delhi were now seri-ously concerned with the political instability in Sikkim. The Chinese were mounting pressure all along the Sikkim-Tibet border and internally the area had become vulnerable to inter-national intrigues," writes G. S. Bajpai in *China's Shadow over Sikkim* (chapter 7). India annexed Sikkim, and that was the end of its history as a kingdom. This unneighborly act is still cited in the region as an example of "Indian imperialism" by those who resent or fear India's power. From the Indian point of view, Sikkim was politically in the same category as the for-mer princely states that the government had derecognized a few years prior to Sikkim's annexation, or "integration," as retired Indian diplomats like to call it in their memoirs.

Sikkim eventually became India's twenty-second state. China has not acknowledged the Indian Government's takeover of the Sikkimese kingdom. Sunanda K. Datta-Roy, an eminent journalist, is intimately acquainted with Sikkim and its politics, maintains, "The artful mix of force majeure and political legerdemain used to annex tiny Sikkim, which Delhi was treaty-bound to protect, earned India a reputation for bullying duplicity that persists to this day in many parts of Asia, without bringing any tactical or political advantage."

The 1962 war with China and the border incidents in 1967 caused India to take security issues in Sikkim seriously. Until the early 1990s, non-Indians required special "inner line" permits to visit Sikkim. These involved a lot of red tape and were strictly limited to a stay of a few days. Only high-level officials begrudgingly granted extensions. Today troops are still stationed on both sides of the border, although tourists may now go as far as Natu-la, which was restricted for decades. Since the dissolution of the Soviet Union, relations between China and India have warmed to the point of discussing the opening of the Natu-la pass for trade between the two countries. In 2003, after high-level talks, China tacitly recognized India's claim to Sikkim so that cross-border trade could be developed. The Indian tourism industry has a stake in this, too, since opening the Natu-la would be a boon for tourism. Tour operators, like the British centuries earlier, see the strategic advantage of the land route to Tibet through enchanting Sikkim.

[165] *Rogues in Robes,* p. 226.

[165] Tibetan Information Network, 1993.

[167] Although both sides suspect the other of taking things from the relic room, the court-ordered inventory showed the collection to be mostly intact.

[168] Interview, 1993.

[169] *Ema Ho! The Reincarnation of the Third Jamgon Kongtrul* (Kathmandu: Jamgon Kongtrul Labrang, 1998).

[170] A writ petition filed with the High Court of Sikkim by Shamarpa's allies Dugo Bhutia and Karma Gompu in 1993

continues to come up in the court. Other cases continue to be filed by other Shamarpa allies. Deepak Kumar Thakur, a lawyer who has represented the late Jamgon Kongtrul and now is one of the Seventeenth Karmapa's lawyers, detailed some of these cases in a document he drafted in late 1999, and I quote the following with his permission:

a. Dugo Bhutia and another v. Union of India and others, CWP No. 16/1993, in the High Court of Sikkim. The main contention here was the challenge to the recognition of Urgyen Trinley Dorje as H. H. Gyalwa Karmapa XVII by H. H. Dalai Lama XVI. This was dismissed as withdrawn on August 19, 1994.

b. Ngedon Tenzing v. The State of Sikkim and others, CWP No. 139/1996 under Article 32 of the Constitution, in the Supreme Court of India. This was dismissed as withdrawn in limine on February 8, 1996.

c. Dr. Ambedkar Bodhi Kunj Foundation v. Union of India and others, CWJC No. 2378/1997, in the High Court of Patna. Serious allegations were made about H. H. Dalai Lama XIV and others by the petitioners. This was dismissed on March 31, 1997.

d. Shree Narayan Singh and another v. Tenzing Gyatsho, Dalai Lama and others, Title Suit No. 576/1997, in the Court of the Munsiff II, Munger, Bihar. This is based on the same pleas and grounds as the above CWJC No. 2378/1997, and is pending. Written statements have been filed in this suit.

e. Karmapa Charitable Trust and others v. The State of Sikkim and other, Civil Suit No. 40.1998, pending in the Court of the District Judge, North and East, Gangtok, Sikkim. Shamar Rinpoche is arrayed as plaintiff No. 3 in the said suit. This is an attempt to cease control of the assets and properties of H. H. Gyalwa Karmapa, both moveable and immovable.

f. Dugo Bhutia v. Union of India and others, CW No. 4205/1998, in the High Court of Delhi. This writ petition was dismissed in limine by an order dated August 26, 1998.

g. Dugo Bhutia v. Union of India and others, SLP © No. 14421/1998 filed in the Supreme Court of India against the above order dated August 26, 1998, passed by the High Court of Delhi in CW No.

4205/1998. The special leave petition was also dismissed by the Supreme Court by an order dated November 16, 1998.

h. Shri Narayan Singh v. Tai Situpa Rinpoche and others, Criminal Complaint No. 41/I/1998 filed in the Court of the Chief Metropolitan Magistrate, Delhi, alleging sedition against H. H. Dalai Lama XIV and other senior Tibetan Buddhist Lamas. The Central Bureau of Investigation filed a couple of reports in this complaint. The chief Metropolitan Magistrate, Delhi, dismissed this complaint by an order dated January 13, 1999.

Thakur goes on to say that through these cases Shamar Rinpoche "accuses people who support the Tibetan cause and H.H. Dalai Lama XIV as being anti Indian, Chinese spies and so on." Many more similar cases have been filed and dismissed in the interim between 1999 and the publication of this book.

Thakur points out that Shamarpa "is known to be in close association with people whom the Government of India has asked to leave India under section 3(2) of the Foreigners Act 1946, including Kathog Shingchong Tulku, formerly of Dehradun, who returned to China after being asked to leave India and now lives in Chengdu, Szechwan; Se Lingtsang, who also returned to Chengdu; and Barchung Pon, who lives in Nepal."

[171] NDTV, 1994.

[172] By 2003, eighteen such cases had been filed and thrown out of various courts.

[173] From "Sweet Melody for the Fortunate Ones," translated by Michele Martin, 2000.

[174] From "A Song of Blossoming Goodness to Celebrate Youth's Golden Age," translated by Michele Martin, 2000.

[175] Two deer flanking a wheel of Dharma appear on the seal of the Karmapa and other high lamas; the deer are symbolic of the Buddha's first teaching at the deer park in Saranath and are often rendered in gold and placed atop the roof of the monastery shrine hall.

[176] This line refers to the exalted position of the enlightened

guru as an inspiration and guide, who is always visualized above the crown of one's head.

[177] Interview with Lea Terhune, at Gyuto Monastery, Sidhabari, April 2000.

[178] Interview, April 2000.

[179] Buddhists as well as Hindus believe in a dark age called the *Kaliyuga,* where negativity is in the ascendancy. The most beneficent of the four epochs is the *Satyuga,* in which truth prevails. At the end of the Kaliyuga, Tibetans believe, there will be a period of good and peaceful rule of he kingdom of Shambhala for about one thousand years before the worst part of the Kaliyuga resumes.

[180] See appendix 4 for complete text of translated letter.

[181] "Tsurphu remains tense," *Tibetan Bulletin,* Jan.–Feb. 2001.

[182] Radio Free Asia, August 20, 2002.

[183] *The Hindustan Times,* January 23, 2000.

[184] Technically India doesn't grant refugee status since it refuses to sign the United Nations agreement on refugees.

[185] Gongkar Rinpoche lives at Sherab Ling Monastery and is the reincarnation of the same Gongkar Rinpoche who was the great Karma Kagyu scholar of the last century, teacher of the Sixteenth Karmapa and who figured in the anecdote by Namkhai Norbu Rinpoche in chapter 5.

[186] A lathi is a bamboo truncheon used by Indian police.

[187] *Asian Age,* March 12, 2001.

[188] *Indian Express,* Feb. 21, 2001.

[189] The Shamarpa has his own groups, such as the International Kagyu Forum, to promote his views.

[190] *Asian Age,* April 21, 2001.

[191] *The Hindustan Times,* March 21, 2001.

[192] This was conveyed to the Shamarpa in a letter drafted by the Dalai Lama's personal secretary, Tenzin Geyche Tethong.

Index

Karmapa

Karmapa

Acknowledgments

THERE ISN'T SPACE to acknowledge the many, many people who have contributed to this book. More than anyone I must thank the Seventeenth Karmapa, Orgyen Trinley Dorje himself, who from the outset cooperated with its writing and, indeed, gave his blessing, and according to Buddhist practice, dedicated the merit, saying, "Because you are writing this book with sincerity, I dedicate the merit of the book that all beings may be transformed to bodhisattvas. I welcome it and support your efforts." Following his example, I can only likewise humbly dedicate this book for the benefit of others.

It could not have been written without the ever-generous cooperation, inspiration, and encouragement of the Twelfth Tai Situpa, who has been my teacher and a dear friend for more than two decades. Many photographs that appear on the pages of this book are from his personal collection. The Dalai Lama has been consistently gracious and his office tremendously helpful in accommodating my requests for interviews. Posthumous thanks

307

are due to the late Jamgon Kongtrul, who told me many things I later relied upon in the writing. I am equally grateful to Goshir Gyaltsap Rinpoche for his willingness to answer my many questions. I thank Chandzo Tenzin Namgyal and the Rumtek labrang for their assistance. Akong Tulku, Bardor Tulku, Namkhai Norbu Rinpoche, and others who submitted to my interviews, monks and nuns who gave generously of their time, thank you. I thank Lama Tenam, Tai Situpa's private secretary and now one of the Karmapa's helpmates, for his friendship and advice. Tashi Tsering, one of the most significant Tibetan scholars of his generation, has kindly given me his opinion and shared his vast knowledge whenever asked, in spite of the many demands upon his time. I thank Michele Martin for her generosity in sharing notes and going over the text; Robbie Barnett for being an objective sounding board for the geopolitical angles; Burmiak Rinpoche (Tashi Densapa), the Martam family, the Atuk family, and others in Sikkim who shared their views, especially the late Ani Dechen Zangmo.

Friends who urged me to write this book and who read and commented on the final manuscript deserve special thanks: the late Rick Fields for his encouragement; Daniel Lak, whose perceptive comments helped immeasurably; Jan and Tim McGirk; Tiziano Terzani, who came up with the title one evening in 1996, as we sat discussing the book in front of his Ming Dynasty Buddha in his New Delhi flat; Ramesh Sharma; and many other friends who put up with me during the long time it took to complete this book.

The encouragement and suggestions of Tibetologist *nonpariel* E. Gene Smith were invaluable. Those who offered photos deserve special thanks, particularly Dieter Ludwig, Lynsey Addario, Tenzin Dorjee, Angus MacDonald, Bryan Miller, and Ward Holmes. The insightful suggestions of editor Leonora Olivia helped me through some difficult territory. And I thank publisher Tim McNeill, editor David Kittelstrom, and others at Wisdom Publications who patiently put up with extended deadlines in the interest of getting the most complete and accurate story.

About Wisdom

WISDOM PUBLICATIONS is a nonprofit publisher of books on Buddhism, Tibet, and related East-West themes. Our titles are published in appreciation of Buddhism as a living philosophy and with the special commitment to preserve and transmit important works from all the major Buddhist traditions.

If you would like more information, or a copy of our mail order catalogue, and to keep informed about our future publications, please write or call us.

Wisdom Publications
199 Elm Street
Somerville MA 02144 USA
Telephone: (617) 776–7416 Fax: (617) 776–7841
Email: info@wisdompubs.org
www.wisdompubs.org